MW00562259

HIKING WITH KIDS
COLORADO

HELP US KEEP THIS GUIDE UP TO DATE

Every effort has been made by the author and editors to make this guide as accurate and useful as possible. However, many things can change after a guide is published—trails are rerouted, regulations change, techniques evolve, facilities come under new management, etc.

We appreciate hearing from you concerning your experiences with this guide and how you feel it could be improved and kept up to date. While we may not be able to respond to all comments and suggestions, we'll take them to heart and we'll also make certain to share them with the author. Please send your comments and suggestions to the following address:

Globe Pequot Press
Reader Response/Editorial Department
246 Goose Lane, Suite 200
Guilford, CT 06437

Thanks for your input, and happy trails!

HIKING WITH KIDS
COLORADO

52 GREAT HIKES FOR FAMILIES

Jamie Siebrase

FALCONGUIDES

GUILFORD, CONNECTICUT

For you, Dad

FALCONGUIDES®

An imprint of The Rowman & Littlefield Publishing Group, Inc.
4501 Forbes Blvd., Ste. 200
Lanham, MD 20706
www.rowman.com

Falcon and FalconGuides are registered trademarks and Make Adventure Your Story is a trademark of The Rowman & Littlefield Publishing Group, Inc.

Distributed by NATIONAL BOOK NETWORK

Copyright © 2021 The Rowman & Littlefield Publishing Group, Inc.

Photos © Ben Siebrase unless otherwise noted
Maps by The Rowman & Littlefield Publishing Group, Inc.

All rights reserved. No part of this book may be reproduced in any form or by any electronic or mechanical means, including information storage and retrieval systems, without written permission from the publisher, except by a reviewer who may quote passages in a review.

British Library Cataloguing in Publication Information available

Library of Congress Cataloging-in-Publication Data

Names: Siebrase, Jamie, author.

Title: Hiking with kids Colorado : 52 great hikes for families / Jamie Siebrase.

Description: Lanham, MD : FalconGuides, an imprint of the Rowman & Littlefield Publishing Group, Inc., [2021] | Includes index. | Summary: "A parent's guide to 52 of the best hikes to take with kids in the state, walkable for all—toddlers to teens"— Provided by publisher.

Identifiers: LCCN 2020045846 (print) | LCCN 2020045847 (ebook) | ISBN 9781493047550 (paperback) | ISBN 9781493047567 (epub)

Subjects: LCSH: Hiking for children—Colorado—Guidebooks. | Family recreation—Colorado—Guidebooks. | Colorado—Guidebooks.

Classification: LCC GV199.42.C6 S43 2021 (print) | LCC GV199.42.C6 (ebook) | DDC 796.5109788—dc23

LC record available at https://lccn.loc.gov/2020045846
LC ebook record available at https://lccn.loc.gov/2020045847

∞™ The paper used in this publication meets the minimum requirements of American National Standard for Information Sciences—Permanence of Paper for Printed Library Materials, ANSI/NISO Z39.48-1992.

The author and The Rowman & Littlefield Publishing Group, Inc. assume no liability for accidents happening to, or injuries sustained by, readers who engage in the activities described in this book.

CONTENTS

THE HIKES

Spring

Summer

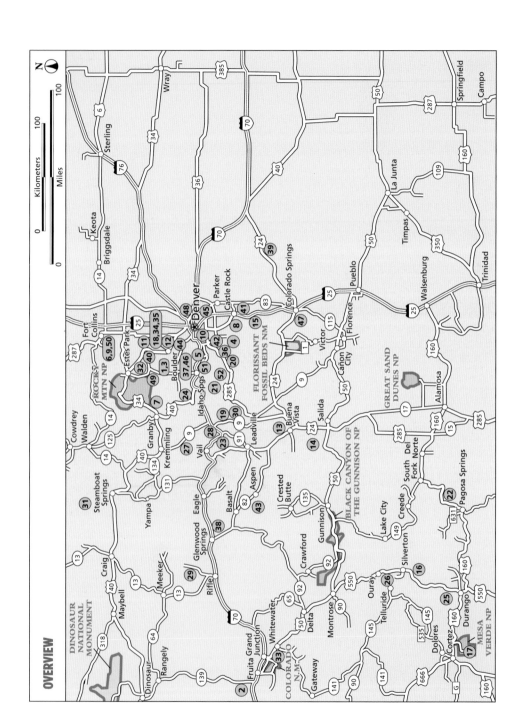

OVERVIEW

N

0 Kilometers 100
0 Miles 100

DINOSAUR
NATIONAL
MONUMENT

ROCKY
MTN NP

FLORISSANT
FOSSIL BEDS NM

GREAT SAND
DUNES NP

BLACK CANYON OF
THE GUNNISON NP

COLORADO
N.M.

MESA
VERDE NP

Rangely
Dinosaur
Maybell
Craig
Meeker
Rifle
Glenwood
Springs
Eagle
Basalt
Aspen
Fruita
Grand
Junction
Whitewater
Gateway
Delta
Montrose
Crawford
Gunnison
Crested
Butte
Lake City
Creede
Silverton
Ouray
Telluride
Dolores
Cortez
Durango
Pagosa Springs
South
Fork
Del
Norte
Alamosa

Cowdrey
Walden
Steamboat
Springs
Yampa
Kremmling
Granby
Vail
Leadville
Buena
Vista
Salida
Cañon
City
Florence
Victor
Pueblo
Walsenburg
Trinidad

Fort
Collins
Estes Park
Boulder
Idaho Spgs
Denver
Parker
Castle Rock
Colorado Springs

Sterling
Keota
Briggsdale
Wray
Springfield
Campo
La Junta
Timpas

318
64
13
40
139
70
141
90
550
145
145
535
666
G
160
550
160
631
149
92
65
92
50
50
550
90
141
134
131
40
14
125
14
34
40
9
82
135
50
15
285
160
17
17
50
24
9
91
24
285
285
24
83
115
25
25
160
350
287
109
160
287
50
385
6
34
36
76
70
70
70
24
39
40
41
47
1

6,9,50
11
18,34,35
12
44
32
40
1,3
49
7
24
37,46
5
51
21
52
19
30
28
23
27
38
31
29
33
2
8
10
42
36
20
4
15
13
14
22
16
26
25
17
48
45
9

ACKNOWLEDGMENTS

Thanks to my son Brian for having the fantastic idea to write a hiking book for kids. Brian is the reason this book exists.

I couldn't have finished writing *Hiking with Kids Colorado* without ongoing support from my family. I had a little over a year to write about Colorado's most kid-friendly trails. To meet my deadline, I dragged my three children along on a whole lot of hikes. Sometimes we completed multiple hikes in a single day. Louise was a newborn baby, so she was carried the whole time. My sons had to walk, and I'd like to thank Jon and Brian for being willing, and sometimes unwilling, participants in this project. Even when you were tired, thank you both for always tagging along on "just one more hike . . . PLEASE, YOU GUYS!"

Thank you to my husband, Ben, for putting up with me while I wrote this book, for waking up to feed the baby at 4 a.m. so I could work, and for making me laugh when I was tired. Thanks, too, for making my words beautiful with your photography.

Thank you to my dad, Brian Berglund, for being my weekday hiking partner, first reader, and advisor in writing and life. Thank you for encouraging me to find a job I love. You were right that work is much more fun when you enjoy what you do. Thank you to my mom, Sally Berglund, for knowing all about Colorado flora, and for meeting me for lunch when I needed a break. My mom was one of those bold 1980s career women. She showed me that moms are the strongest, most capable people in the world. For that I am also grateful.

Thanks to all of the friends who kept me sane during that crazy year when I wrote a book and had a baby. A special thanks to Lisa and Erin: The lunches, surprise baked goods, and walks kept me going. Thank you to Sophia Jung for always being there to chat after school, and for picking up my kids whenever I was running late. To the Dorsts, Lickos, Jungs, Reists, Joseph Graves, and Tara Wilson, thank you for letting me drag your children along on a few of our adventures. Kyle Velte and Jana Hunter, thanks for sharing photos of your sweet kids. And thank you to Audrey Siebrase for always being there with a funny message when I need it.

I owe many thanks to Barb Smith, who routinely overlooked my chronic tardiness to after-school pickup. Coach Weiss and Coach Skuce, thank you for letting Jon and Brian come to school early to help you set up for PE while I worked on *Hiking with Kids Colorado*.

I really appreciate my FalconGuides editor, Katie O'Dell, and all the park rangers and communications gurus who helped me plan and fact-check these fifty-two hikes. Finally, thank you to the staff and volunteers who manage and protect Colorado's beautiful parks, open spaces, and forests.

MEET YOUR GUIDE

Jamie Siebrase grew up in the city, on asphalt tennis courts and groomed soccer fields. Her first camping trip was a three-day, hike-in excursion with AmeriCorps St. Louis—and after that, she was hooked. Since moving to Colorado in 2007, Jamie has hiked all over the state with her husband and their three children. When she isn't on an adventure, Jamie is writing about the outdoors and parenting for a variety of magazines and newspapers.

INTRODUCTION

While writing this book, there were plenty of times I wished I'd pitched a series on hiking alone with a six-pack of Raspberry Sours from Avery Brewing Company. Just like yours, my kids have to be reminded that hiking is fun. Sometimes I remind them with doughnuts; other times it's a visit to a playground or nature center. It's not bribery if you call it something else, and as far as I'm concerned, it doesn't matter how you get your kids on the trail—just that you get them there in the first place.

YOUR KIDS ARE GOING TO COMPLAIN ABOUT HIKING SOMETIMES! I'm sorry I had to yell, but this is a fact I needed to drive home. Kids complain, whine, and cry. They do it mid-hike, on the drive to the trailhead, and at the bench near the outhouse. If you jump ship at every gripe, you're not going to do very much hiking with your children.

Besides, run-of-the-mill, ordinary experiences rarely create lasting memories. Some of my family's all-time favorite outings have been the ones where everything went completely wrong. So don't think of hiking with your kids as a mini-vacation from life. It's an adventure, and the best adventures are going to be a little bumpy.

Here in Colorado, families have access to thousands of miles of stunning trails spanning forty-two state parks, two national grasslands, four national parks, eight national monuments, eleven national forests, and 14ers galore. The state's diverse terrain is flush with Instagram-worthy wildflowers, vivid fall foliage, and ample wildlife, not to mention spectacular views of river canyons and the snowcapped Rockies.

Better still, Colorado's backcountry was made for youth. From dinosaur-themed day hikes and cliff dwellings to elk crossings, beaver dams, and secret waterfalls, the state's expansive trail network is an open-air classroom just waiting to be discovered.

I've written widely on the topic of nature deficit disorder, which is the notion that modern-day people, especially kids, experience a range of behavioral problems when they're cooped up indoors. Studies show that being in nature reduces the risk for ADHD (attention deficit hyperactivity disorder), stress, anxiety, depression, type 2 diabetes, high blood pressure, and much more. If that doesn't do it for you, consider this: Getting sunshine during the day will help everyone in your family sleep better at night.

Yet a growing body of research indicates that families today are spending way more time indoors on screens than outside in the wild. Kids went on 15 percent fewer outdoor outings in 2018 than they did in 2012, according to the "2019 Outdoor Participation Report," a comprehensive annual research paper produced by the Outdoor Foundation.

Families of color are excluded from the outdoors at far higher rates than white families. In 2018, about three-quarters of outdoors participants were listed as "Caucasian." Data from the USDA Forest Service shows extreme inequality in the ethnic and racial mix of visitors to public lands. Black recreationists, for example, make up only 1.2 percent of all national forest visitors. Hispanic and Latinx groups participated slightly more, at a rate of

5.7 percent, despite the fact that they make up an estimated 18.3 percent of the national population. Indigenous people also lack access to many of these outdoor activities. As we explore Colorado trails, we have the opportunity to deepen our knowledge of the area and to respectfully acknowledge that this book covers the traditional land of Native peoples.

The outdoors is for everyone, and several Colorado-based organizations—ELK (Environmental Learning for Kids), Big City Mountaineers, and Blackpackers, for starters—are working to provide marginalized groups with easy access to authentic nature experiences. There's also My Outdoor Colorado, a city-led network of nonprofits providing resources for low-income youth and families living in Denver's urban core.

If a lack of knowledge and/or experience keeps you from exploring the outdoors, then this book is a great place to start. There's no better way for new participants to get acquainted with Colorado's wilderness than on one of the family-friendly hiking trails listed in this guide. A lot of outdoor activities are complicated and costly, requiring special knowledge, skills, and equipment. That's not the case with hiking, which has a very low barrier to entry.

Aside from a pair of sturdy shoes and this guide, you really don't need anything special to get started. Anyone can hike at any age, and there are several routes in this guide for all abilities too, including trails with guidelines and wheelchair access points. If your child has mobility differences, be sure to check out Staunton State Park's innovative new Action Trackchair program (see hike 52).

Hiking with Kids Colorado is designed to introduce families to hiking on some of Colorado's most kid-compatible trails. If you're a seasoned mountaineer looking for remote backcountry experiences and full-day expeditions, this is not the right book for you. A few hikes into my research, I realized that my kids bore quickly. While a challenging ascent is usually doable for a 5-year-old, excessive mileage can be a deal breaker. So I traded lengthier routes for shorter treks packing plenty of pint-size fun, including giant troll sculptures, scavenger hunts, and unique wildlife viewing opportunities. Hikes covered are suitable for all ages—walkable for kids from toddlers to teens. A couple of the hikes in this guide might not seem like "real hikes," but I promise, if you're on a trail with your children, surrounded by nature, and everyone is moving their feet . . . you are hiking!

Parents looking for a rigorous workout should hit the gym before hiking with their kids. In my experience, hiking with children isn't a major athletic feat. Rather, it's an opportunity to slow down between busy days and experience the world through your child's curious, brilliant eyes.

Kids love to explore. They love to point out bugs, turn over rocks, throw sticks, and splash around in puddles and streams. Buy your child a pair of designated hiking shoes, and let her get really dirty if that's what she wants to do.

Keep children engaged with games. Have a contest to see who can spot the most blazes on trees. Race twigs in the creek. Use binoculars to look for birds. When you run out of things to do, sing silly songs with made-up verses. Geocaching is another option, or go low-tech by incorporating a scavenger hunt into your hike. If your children are old enough, let them carry a daypack filled with snacks and water. To make sure you're moving at your child's pace, ask the youngest hikers in the group to lead the way. Bring along a friend. My kids always have more fun hiking when there are friends involved.

Hikers are responsible for protecting the environment, for the sake of the wildlife inhabiting it and for future human generations who wish to experience it. The following section will help you better understand what you can do to preserve delicate ecosystems while still making the most of your hiking excursion. Anyone can take a hike, but hiking well is an art.

TRAIL ETIQUETTE

Zero impact: Always leave an area exactly as you found it—if not better than you found it. Pack out all trash and extra food. No exceptions, no excuses. This is the Golden Rule of hiking.

If your child needs to pee during a hike, walk at least 200 feet away from the trail and any water sources. If your daughter is shy about squatting, hold up a jacket for privacy. On a slope, always pee facing downhill so the urine flows away from you.

Stuff happens, especially when you're hiking with kids. Never leave human waste or toilet paper on the ground. It might not seem like a big deal "just this one time," but imagine what Colorado's beautiful trails would look like if everyone thought that way. The easiest option for feces is to bring along a dog bag, and pack out your child's excrement. If this is too gross, carry a small shovel. Generally, human waste should be buried at least 100 feet from water sources under 6 to 8 inches of topsoil. Families who don't camp should go online to learn about the proper technique for burying feces.

Stay on the trail: There's nothing an inquisitive child loves more than wandering off a trail. Teach your child that paths serve an important purpose by limiting impact on natural areas. Straying from a designated trail might seem innocent, but it can cause damage to sensitive areas that may take years to recover, if they can recover at all. Even simple shortcuts can be destructive.

Leave no weeds: Noxious weeds tend to overtake other plants, which in turn affects animals and birds that depend on them for food. To minimize the spread of noxious weeds, hikers should regularly clean their shoes and hiking poles of mud and seeds. Brush your dog to remove any weed seeds before heading into a new area.

Keep your dog under control: If a four-legged family member is tagging along, always obey leash laws, and be sure to pack your dog's waste out in sealable plastic bags.

Respect other trail users: With the rise in popularity of multiuse trails, you'll often encounter mountain bikers and equestrians using the same trail. A little common sense and courtesy goes a long way. If you hear activity ahead, step off the trail, just to be safe. You're not likely to hear a mountain biker coming, so be prepared and know ahead of time whether you share the trail with them. Cyclists should always yield to hikers, but smart hikers are aware of their surroundings. When approaching horses or pack animals on the trail, step quietly off the trail, preferably on the downhill side, and let them pass. If you're wearing a large backpack, it's a good idea to sit down. To some animals, a hiker wearing a large backpack might appear threatening.

GETTING INTO SHAPE

Hiking is walking, but in a prettier setting. With their vast supplies of energy, kids are built to be active, and most children won't need to do anything special to prepare for the routes in this book. Adults who are out of shape can get ready for these hikes by beginning a walking program, preferably eight weeks in advance. Start with a 15-minute power walk during your lunch break, and gradually increase your walking time to an hour. Walking briskly up hills strengthens leg muscles and gets your heart rate up. If you work in a high-rise building, take the stairs instead of the elevator.

PREPAREDNESS

Even on a short hike, parents should be prepared by having the following bases covered.

Water: Invest in stainless-steel bottles; brands such as EcoVessel and Klean Kanteen make excellent insulated products. Colorado's dry climate causes sweat to evaporate quickly, so you may not realize how much water your body is losing on a hot summer day. Even on a cold day, water is critical. As a general rule, pack 2 cups of water—per person—for every hour you'll be on the trail. Then pack extra water, just to be safe. Don't expect to find water in the woods; and unless you know exactly how to treat it, do not rely on natural water sources.

Food: Try to avoid foods that are high in empty calories. Instead of candy bars and potato chips, pack healthy snacks, including gorp trail mix, dehydrated fruit, applesauce squeeze packs, and energy bars (try Kate's Real Food bars and bites). When it's cold, carry high-energy snacks that won't freeze, such as nuts, chocolate, and cheese.

First aid: It's always a good idea to carry a first-aid kit. Many companies make lightweight and compact options, and big box stores like Target carry inexpensive, prepackaged kits containing some of the following recommended items:

- adhesive bandages
- moleskin or duct tape
- various sizes of sterile gauze and dressings
- white surgical tape
- an Ace bandage
- an antihistamine
- aspirin
- Betadine solution
- tweezers
- antibacterial wipes
- triple-antibiotic ointment
- sterile cotton tip applicators

The wilderness can seem like a scary place if you don't know how to prevent and treat potential ailments. Here's a quick rundown. Yes, there's a lot that could go wrong. But most of the time, it won't. So don't get panicky on me. Instead, let the knowledge you're about to gain empower you to hike confidently with your kids.

Sunburn: At higher elevations, the sun's radiation is intense. Use sunblock, sun-protective clothing, and sunglasses. A wide-brimmed hat is a good idea. If somebody gets burned, treat the area with aloe vera gel and protect it from further exposure.

Blisters: These hike-spoilers can be quickly treated mid-trail with moleskin (a lightly padded adhesive), gauze and tape, or bandages. An effective way to apply moleskin is to cut out a circle of moleskin, remove the center like a doughnut, and place it over the blistered area.

Insect bites and stings: Treat most insect bites and stings by applying hydrocortisone 1 percent cream topically and administering a pain medication such as acetaminophen or ibuprofen (ibuprofen also helps to reduce swelling). If you forgot to pack these items, a cold compress or a paste of mud and ashes can sometimes relieve the itching and discomfort. Remove any stingers by using tweezers or scraping the area with your fingernail. Don't pinch the area, which will spread the venom.

Poison ivy, oak, and sumac: These skin irritants grow across Colorado and come in the form of a bush or a vine, having leaflets in groups of three, five, seven, or nine. The oil they secrete can cause an allergic reaction (usually blisters) about 12 hours after exposure. Prevent contact with poisonous plants by wearing clothing that covers the arms, legs, and torso. If you think you or your children were exposed, take a hot shower with soap when you're back home. This will help remove any lingering oil. If a rash appears, use an antihistamine to reduce itching.

Dehydration: Symptoms of dehydration include fatigue, headache, and decreased coordination and judgment. When you're hiking, your body's rate of fluid loss depends on the outside temperature, humidity, altitude, and your activity level. It's important to always carry plenty of water and to stop often and drink fluids regularly, even if you aren't thirsty. If keeping your children hydrated is a struggle, try adding electrolyte-rich Nuun tablets to their water bottles. On cold days, fill steel canteens with warm herbal tea from Celestial Seasonings, made locally in Boulder.

Heat exhaustion: Drinking plenty of electrolyte-rich fluids can prevent heat exhaustion. Avoid hiking during the hottest parts of the day, between 10 a.m. and 2 p.m., and wear breathable clothing. Common symptoms of heat exhaustion include cramping, exhaustion, fatigue, lightheadedness, and nausea. You can treat heat exhaustion by getting out of the sun and drinking an electrolyte solution made with 1 teaspoon of salt and 1 tablespoon of sugar dissolved in 1 liter of water.

Hypothermia: This may sound strange, but hypothermia is one of the biggest dangers for day hikers in the summer. You start a hike in the mountains on a sunny morning in shorts and a T-shirt. It starts to rain, the wind picks up, and before you know it you're wet and shivering—the perfect recipe for hypothermia. More advanced signs include decreased coordination, slurred speech, and blurred vision. Avoid hypothermia by packing a windproof/rainproof shell and a fleece jacket.

Frostbite: Prevention is your best defense. Your face, hands, and feet are most prone to frostbite, so protect these areas with wool or synthetic fiber hats, gloves, and socks. If your child's feet or hands start to feel cold or numb, warm them right away. Place cold hands under your armpits; place your warm hands over your child's face, or use a balaclava head stocking. But don't try to thaw a frostbitten area unless you can maintain the warmth. This does more harm than good. Get off the trail as quickly as possible, and seek medical help.

Altitude sickness / acute mountain sickness (AMS): Altitude sickness is your body's reaction to insufficient oxygen in the blood due to decreased barometric pressure. While some hikers may feel lightheaded, nauseous, and experience shortness of breath at 7,000 feet, others may not experience these symptoms until they reach 10,000 feet or higher. Slow your ascent to give your body a chance to acclimatize. If you live at sea level and are planning a weeklong hiking trip to Colorado, start by staying below 7,000 feet for one night, and avoid strenuous exertion. It's also important to eat light food and drink plenty of water. The treatment for AMS is simple: Stop heading uphill. Descend to a lower elevation, and you'll feel better.

NATURAL HAZARDS

Besides tripping over a rock or tree root, there are some legit hazards to be aware of.

Lightning: Thunderstorms build over the mountains almost every day during the summer, and lightning can strike without warning, even several miles from the nearest overhead cloud. Lightning takes the path of least resistance. If you're the high point, it might choose you! Leave exposed peaks, ridges, and canyon rims by noon, at the latest, and always keep an eye on cloud formation. If you're caught in a thunderstorm, don't duck under a rock overhang. Dash below tree line, if possible, and avoid standing under the only tree or the tallest tree. If you're caught above tree line, stay away from anything metal. Move down off the ridge to a low, treeless point, and squat until the storm passes. Avoid having both your hands and feet touching the ground at once, and never lie flat. If you hear a buzzing sound or feel your hair standing on end, move quickly: An electrical charge is building up.

Flash floods: The spooky thing about flash floods, especially in western canyons, is that they can appear out of nowhere from a storm many miles away. While hiking or driving in canyons, keep an eye on the weather. Always climb to safety if danger threatens. Flash floods usually subside quickly, so be patient, and don't try to cross a swollen stream.

Bears: Colorado does not have a grizzly bear population, although rumors exist of sightings where there should be none. Black bears, however, are plentiful. There are several things you and your family can do to avoid startling a black bear.

Watch for bear tracks (five toes) and droppings (sizable, with leaves, partly digested berries, seeds, and/or animal fur). Talk or sing, and be especially careful in spring to avoid getting between a mother and her cubs. If you do encounter a bear, move away slowly while facing the bear, talk softly, and don't make eye contact. Give the bear room to escape. Since bears are curious, it might stand upright to get a better whiff. Stay calm. If a black bear attacks, fight back.

Mountain lions: Attacks are rare, but encounters are possible in both day-use areas and the backcountry. The best thing is to avoid mountain lions altogether by taking a few precautions. Don't hike at dawn or dusk. Stay on established trails. As you walk, make noise and look for signs of mountain lions, including scat, claw marks, and scratch piles. If you see a cougar and it doesn't see you, alter your route. If there's a confrontation, remain calm. Give the lion a chance to escape. Back away slowly while facing it, and talk firmly. If you run, you'll look like prey, which—duh!—is bad. Instead, make yourself appear large and formidable by opening a jacket or waving hiking poles. Without turning away from the lion, pick up small children. If the lion behaves aggressively, throw stones, sticks, a water bottle, or whatever you can. If a lion attacks, always fight back.

Moose: Because they have very few natural predators, moose don't fear humans like other animals do. You might find moose in sagebrush and wetter areas of willow, aspen, and pine, or in beaver habitats. Mothers with calves, as well as bulls during mating season, can be particularly aggressive. If a moose threatens you, back away slowly while talking calmly to it.

Other considerations: Hunting is a popular sport in Colorado, especially during rifle season in October and November. Learn when the different hunting seasons start and end in the area in which you'll be hiking. During this time frame, be sure to wear at least a blaze-orange hat, and possibly put an orange vest over your pack. If you would feel more comfortable without hunters around, hike in national parks and monuments, or state and local parks where hunting is prohibited.

GEAR

The outdoor market is flooded with products, but the truth is, you won't need much gear to enjoy the day hikes listed in this guide. Keep it simple. When you're trying to get out the door with children, the last thing you want is a bunch of stuff weighing you down. Sturdy athletic shoes and water are the two most important things. Here are a few more items to keep you and your family safe and comfortable.

Whistle: Kids should carry safety whistles. If your child isn't old enough to keep a whistle around her neck, buy a small backpack with a whistle built into a strap buckle. Teach children to use the whistle to call for help if they get lost.

Clothes: Since a good hiker is prepared for anything, get into the habit of packing rain protection and an extra layer. Eddie Bauer's kids Rainfoil jacket is a great item to stash in a backpack, since it can be used as a raincoat or windbreaker. Shop the company's website in off-seasons for steep discounts.

Summer: Carry sunscreen, wide-brimmed hats, and sunglasses. Ro-sham-bo makes flexible, durable shades for kids. Brands such as Eddie Bauer, Land's End, and Coolibar sell sun-protective clothing for kids. If your children are sensitive to the sensation of grass on their legs, check out Eddie Bauer's quick-dry convertible pants, which transform into shorts by zipping off the legs.

Winter: It's all about layering. Start with a wicking layer, preferably long underwear made from synthetic fibers. Reima's bamboo viscose base layer is sized for toddlers, kids, and adolescents. Build on your wicking layer by adding a breathable insulating

layer (fleece), followed by a waterproof/windproof shell with a hood that fits over a hat. Repeat after me: Cotton kills! Avoid this fabric entirely. Don't forget to protect your hands and face. In chilly, windy, or rainy weather, wear or pack hats made of wool or fleece, plus insulated, waterproof gloves.

Opt for affordable clothing. Some Gore-Tex jackets cost as much as $500, but there are less-expensive fabrics that work just as well. Keep an eye out for sales at REI. Sierra Trading Post carries off-price merchandise for outdoor recreation, and local shops such as the Wilderness Exchange and Feral sell used and discounted gear. If you're visiting one of Colorado's mountain towns in the summer, keep in mind that High Country shops often sell last season's gear at steep discounts.

Footwear: Children don't need hiking boots. An athletic sneaker should do the trick for everyone in your group. If you want to shell out the money for something fancier, go with lightweight boots or a trail running shoe. Brands such as Keen and Merrell make excellent waterproof shoes with traction. Wear quick-drying synthetic or natural-fiber socks from brands such as Smartwool and Swiftwick.

Traction: Between November and April, stash spikes or micro-spikes in the trunk of your car so you'll be prepared for snowy/icy trail conditions. Yaktrax are a lightweight and affordable traction device for older kids, and brands such as Milaloko and Freahap make traction cleats specifically for young children. Employees at REI can help you find the right sizes for your kids.

Hiking poles: Similar to technical footwear, poles are a discretionary item. They can be useful for balance on steep, rugged trails, and for us parents, poles take pressure off the knees. If you meet a mountain lion or unfriendly dog, poles can make you look a whole lot bigger. But before you buy them, think about your child's age and disposition. Will you be carrying several sets of poles by the end of the hike? If so, don't bother.

Backpacks: No matter what type of hiking you do, you'll need a pack to carry basic trail essentials. Buy a good quality backpack, and set it aside as your family's designated hiking pack. Fill your pack with first-aid supplies, several medium-size plastic bags, extra Smartwool socks (hello, puddles!), stuffable rain gear, and a few spare diapers, if applicable. Toss in healthy granola bars, an unopened bag of dried fruit, and other shelf-stable snacks. Store the backpack in a safe place, and replenish supplies as needed. There! Now you can head out the door with minimal fuss.

There are a variety of backpacks on the market. For the hikes in this guide, you'll need a daypack with external pockets to carry water and other items such as keys, a knife, and a wallet. Brands such as Topo Designs, Mountainsmith, and Osprey make excellent day-packs for hikers. Backpacks can be a big-ticket item; remember to shop clearance sales online and at local retailers.

For very short hikes, some parents like to use a fanny pack to store food, a compass, a map, and other small essentials. Many fanny packs have pockets for two water bottles. Since kids love having their own gear, one option is to outfit an adult with the family's main pack and allow children to carry extra items in a fanny pack.

HOW TO USE THIS GUIDE

Aside from a pair of sturdy shoes—and this book—you really don't need any special skills or equipment to hike with your kids. There are a few things, though, that are useful to know before hitting the trail.

Even in snowy Colorado, hiking is a year-round activity. The hikes in this book are sorted by season so that your family can hike whenever the mood strikes.

Every section begins with a brief introduction. Then I describe specific hikes that work well during a given season. With the right equipment, and the exception of Mount Bierstadt, most of the hikes in this guide can be safely completed anytime.

The hikes in this book begin with a quick summary followed by nitty-gritty details, which include trailhead location, hiking distance and time, difficulty, elevation gain, land status, nearest town(s), and other trail users your family might encounter. I added a few categories that pertain exclusively to families: age range, stroller compatibility, potential child hazards, and information about the availability, if any, of water, toilets, and benches for nursing moms. Most of these categories are self-explanatory, but here are a few that might need clarification.

Distance: The distance specified for loops and out-and-back routes is always a round-trip distance; e.g., "2.0 miles out and back" means the trail is 1 mile long in each direction.

Difficulty: Assessing a hike's difficulty is subjective. Verified facts such as absolute elevation, elevation change, distance, and trail condition play a role, as do uncontrolled variables, including weather and a hiker's fitness level. In addition to considering the facts, I consulted with my sons to determine if a hike was easy, moderate, or difficult. In general, if a hike gained 250 feet or more per mile, my kids ranked it as moderate or difficult. Long hikes were more difficult with children, because kids get bored. Other factors contributing to difficulty included heat and high elevations with thin air.

Potential child hazards: Please don't be nervous when you read this section. It's provided to make parents aware of risks, not scare you off. All the hikes in this guide are family-friendly and extremely safe. But it would be tough to explore the wilderness without running into a few potential hazards.

Miles and Directions: To help you stay on course, a detailed route finder specifies the distance between significant landmarks along the trail. Use common sense whenever you hike. There is no obligation to complete the route. You are out hiking to enjoy time in nature with your family, not prove anything.

Map Legend

Symbol	Description	Symbol	Description
70	Interstate Highway	Bench
160	US Highway	Bridge
46	State Highway	Building/Point of Interest
304	County Road	Campground
	Local Road	Cemetery
	Unpaved Road	City/Town
	Railroad	Dam
	County Line	Gate
	Featured Trail	Mountain/Peak
	Trail	Parking
	Paved Trail	Pass
	Small River/Creek	Picnic Area
	Intermittent Stream	Scenic View/Viewpoint
	Body of Water	Trailhead
	Glacier	Visitor/Information Center
	National/State Forest	Water
	State/County Park	Waterfall
	Natural Area/Open Space/Preserve/Refuge	

SPRING

Spring weather is unpredictable in Colorado, to say the least. Don't let that keep you and your family indoors. Your shoes might get muddy, but it'll be worth it to see meadows and hillsides awaken as wildflowers blossom and animals emerge from hibernation. Unless you're planning to snowshoe, it's best to hike at lower elevations in March and April, when high-country trails may be covered in snow. On the other hand, some foothills trails in Boulder and Jefferson County are notoriously soggy during "mud season": late April and May. Always check online for trail closures before heading out. Many parks and open spaces maintain a Twitter feed that describes real-time trail conditions. All-Trails is another reliable resource, since other hikers can leave reviews with information about the terrain on the day they hiked.

1 LAKES LOOP SNOWSHOE TRAIL

Most Boulderites are familiar with Eldora Mountain Resort and its 680 acres of unpretentious alpine terrain. The lodges serving the site's downhill skiers are usually bustling on powder days. And yet a few hundred yards east, at the Eldora Nordic Center, hikers find serenity while exploring a real-life winter wonderland spanning old-growth forests and alpine meadows. The hilly Lakes Loop Snowshoe Trail keeps kids engaged with a series of historical markers and wild-life viewing opportunities.

Start: Eldora Nordic Center
Distance: 2.2-mile lollipop
Hiking time: 1.5–3 hours
Difficulty: Moderate to difficult
Elevation gain: 286 feet
Trail surface: Snow
Hours: Open daily, 9 a.m. to 4 p.m.
Best seasons: Early Nov or Dec through Mar. Some years the trails stay open until mid-Apr. Hikers cannot use Nordic Center trails off-season.
Water: Inside the Nordic Center
Toilets: Inside the Nordic Center
Nursing benches: None. If you'll need to stop to nurse, bring a tarp to sit on.
Stroller-friendly: No
Potential child hazards: Frozen lakes, windchill

Other trail users: None
Dogs: Not allowed
Land status: Eldora Mountain Resort
Nearest town: Nederland
Fees and permits: Fee for trail passes
Maps: Eldora Mountain Resort Nordic Trail Map
Trail contact: Eldora Mountain Resort, 2861 Eldora Ski Rd., #140, Nederland 80466; (303) 440-8700, ext. 68510; www.eldora.com/things-to-do/nordic-center/nordic-center-at-eldora
Gear suggestions: Snowshoes (available to rent on-site), waterproof snow pants, ski jackets, waterproof gloves, wool or fleece hats, balaclavas, high-energy snacks that won't freeze, warm herbal tea

FINDING THE TRAILHEAD

From Boulder, take Boulder Canyon Drive (CO 119) west to the town of Neder-land. From Denver, you can come up through Golden, taking Coal Creek Canyon Road toward Nederland via 6th Avenue West. When Coal Creek Canyon Road dead-ends, make a sharp right onto CO 119. From CO 119, go to Eldorado Avenue and head north. In 1.5 miles, veer left (east) onto Shelf Road. Shelf Road ends at Eldora Mountain Resort. Following the flow of traffic to the north parking lot, but don't park here. Instead, loop around the alpine ski area and drive across the lower parking lot to reach the Eldora Nordic Center.

THE HIKE

First stop: the Eldora Nordic Center, a cute warming hut where hikers can purchase trail passes and snacks, re-up on water, and rent snowshoes. After checking in, walk out the back door of the Nordic Center, and put your snowshoes on outside. Be sure to strap children into their devices first, since it'll be harder to maneuver once your shoes are on.

Everyone in your group will need a valid trail pass to access the trailhead via the entry gate behind the Nordic Center. After walking through the gate, make a quick left onto

Lakes Loop. If your kids complain about the wind during the initial segment of this trail, reassure them that relief is coming in a few hundred yards, as soon as you've ducked into the trees.

Lakes Loop Snowshoe Trail is marked with orange blazes (those plastic diamonds nailed onto the trees). Red markers denote Eldora's other snowshoe trails, and cross-country ski trails are gray. Thanks to an abundance of blazes, it's pretty much impossible to get lost, even if you're making first tracks through powder.

Starting at 0.2 mile, there are several instances when snowshoers must cross groomed ski trails, or even hike alongside a cross-country trail. Go slow, and watch out for skiers, who might have a harder time stopping.

As the trail winds through the woods, ask children to look for squirrel, coyote, and moose tracks. It's highly unlikely, but if you see a moose, keep your distance. Because they have very few natural predators, moose don't fear humans the way other animals do.

The first historical marker appears as Peterson Lake comes into sight through the trees. In the early 1900s, the area was a tourist destination owned by Eldora Resort and Power Company.

An Eldora Resort brochure falsely advertised Peterson Lake as an extinct volcanic crater. Hovering at 9,255 feet, the alpine lake is still impressive. In fact, Eldora has the best snowmaking system in Colorado thanks, in part, to Peterson Lake's plentiful water supply, which is fed entirely by natural springs.

Can you see the green cabin across Peterson Lake? The Rocky Mountain Climbers Club owns the building, and has used its lakefront property to promote outdoor activities and conversation since 1935.

Further down the trail, discover the remains of Pine Log Inn, an early twentieth century lodge built by the Eldora Resort and Power Company. The inn was part of a last-ditch effort to keep a narrow-gauge railroad line in business after the gold boom abruptly ended.

Past the cabin, after a bend in the trail, the fourth historical marker comes into view, describing Beaver Lake, to your right. Heed the "Private Property" signs as you continue hiking through a chilly clearing before reaching the next historical marker, with information about the country's oldest continually operated performing arts camp.

Lake Eldora is the last frozen lake to appear, to the left. Be sure to watch children closely around both frozen and partially frozen bodies of water.

FUN FACTOR

EXPLORE ELDORA'S SECRET TRAIL.

Return to Eldora another time to check out the Jenny Creek Snowshoe Trail, a 10-mile out-and-back route blazed with blue diamonds. (You don't have to do the whole route.)

This USDA Forest Service trail is the only no-fee snowshoe trail departing from the Eldora Nordic Center. But you'll still need to check in at the Nordic Center and grab a (free) trail pass to get through the entry gate, located to the left of Tenderfoot, the bunny slope for alpine skiers.

Begin climbing straight uphill. After passing the lift behind the bunny slope, turn right and walk as close to the trees as possible. Turn left at the sign for Jenny Creek Trail, and follow the path through a serene pine forest. It'll be only a few moments before the alpine ski bustle disappears.

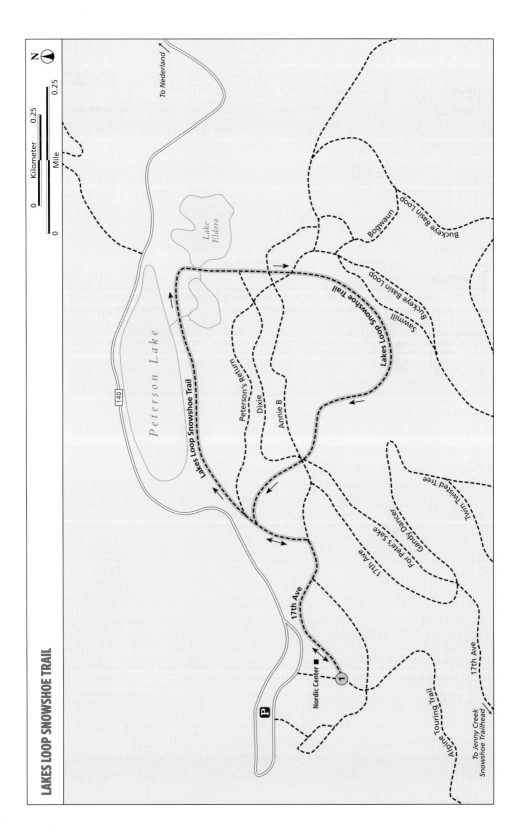

LAKES LOOP SNOWSHOE TRAIL

N

Kilometer
0   0.25   0.25

Mile
0   0.25

To Nederland

Lake Eldora

Peterson Lake

140

Lakes Loop Snowshoe Trail

Lakes Loop Snowshoe Trail

Peterson's Return

Dixie

Annie B

Bogwaum

Sawmill

Buckeye Basin Loop

Buckeye Basin Loop

Twin Twisted Tree

17th Ave

For Pete's Sake

Gandy Dancer

Nordic Center

17th Ave

1

P

Alpine Touring Trail

17th Ave

To Jenny Creek
Snowshoe Trailhead

When the Lakes Loop Snowshoe Trail intersects a cross-country ski trail at 0.97 mile, you can shorten the total route to 1.5 miles by turning right onto Low Down Snowshoe Trail. You'll see the signs.

If you stick to the directions below, the next section of Lakes Loop is a steep climb. Stay straight at the five-way trail intersection, and follow the Lakes Loop signs and blazes across the ski run. When a fork appears in the trail, bear right to continue on Lakes Loop.

At 1.15 miles the final historical marker presents a welcome opportunity to take a quick breather while reading about the area's logging history. In light snow years, families can see the remains of one sawmill, as well as an old woodcutter's cabin, alongside the ski trail below.

Take a break at the top of the hill, then enjoy flat, scenic terrain. You'll see the first "Return to Nordic Center" sign at the fork at 1.4 miles. Don't be surprised if the last leg of your journey—a steady, wooded descent—is a little tricky in snowshoes. Go slow, and watch for icy patches. Follow the orange blazes and signs back to the Nordic Center. The best way to end this hike is with a cup of hot chocolate at one of the coffee shops in the quirky town of Nederland.

MILES AND DIRECTIONS

0.0 Use your trail pass to get through the gate leading to the trailhead. Turn left immediately onto Lakes Loop Snowshoe Trail. Elevation: 9,370 feet.

0.2 Hike straight through a trail intersection, following the Lakes Loop signs and blazes.

0.3 The snowshoe trail merges with a cross-country ski trail. Stay to the far left side of the run.

0.33 Bear right at the "Snowshoe Trail" sign.

0.5 Reach Peterson Lake.

0.8 Arrive at an old cabin.

0.97 Arrive at a five-way trail intersection. Turn left, cross the groomed ski trail, and begin a challenging climb. If you're confused about where to go, follow the orange blazes.

1.07 Bear right at the trail fork.

1.2 Reach the highest point of the route.

1.4 Come to a fork in the trail. Go right to return to the Nordic Center.

1.6 Cross a groomed ski run and follow the "Return to Nordic Center" sign.

1.67 The Lakes Loop and Low Down trails intersect. Stay straight, following a "Return to Nordic Center" sign.

1.75 Cross another ski trail. Bear left at the fork in the trail.

1.95 Cross one more ski run.

2.2 Arrive back at the Nordic Center.

2 TRAIL THROUGH TIME

With its rich dinosaur history, and relatively temperate climate, Grand Junction is a four-season oasis of family-friendly hiking. An abundance of options could make it tricky to settle on the right trail. So ask yourself: What's more fun than viewing 140-million-year-old dinosaur bones while exploring a working fossil quarry? Located in the Rabbit Valley paleontological corridor, a stone's throw from the Colorado-Utah border, the Trail through Time is a self-guided interpretive loop that'll keep children engaged from start to finish.

Start: Trail Through Time Trailhead
Distance: 1.6-mile lollipop
Hiking time: 1–2 hours
Difficulty: Easy
Elevation gain: 134 feet
Trail surface: Dirt and gravel
Hours: Open 24 hours a day, 7 days a week
Best seasons: Spring and fall. Summer temperatures can exceed 100°F; trail conditions can be hazardous in winter.
Water: None
Toilets: Drop toilets approximately 500 feet past the trailhead
Nursing benches: Several along this short trail
Stroller-friendly: No
Potential child hazards: Heat, sun exposure

Other trail users: None
Dogs: Must be leashed or under voice command
Land status: Bureau of Land Management
Nearest town: Fruita
Fees and permits: None
Maps: BLM National Operations Center; Colorado Canyons Association MCNCA Travel Map
Trail contact: Bureau of Land Management, McInnis Canyons National Conservation Area, 2815 H Rd., Grand Junction 81506; (970) 244-3000; www.blm.gov/visit/rabbit-valley-trail-through-time
Gear suggestions: Trail running shoes or hiking boots, sunscreen, sun-protective clothing, brimmed hats, sunglasses

FINDING THE TRAILHEAD

From Grand Junction, drive 30 miles west on I-70 to the Rabbit Valley exit (exit 2). At the top of the off-ramp, turn right onto Rabbit Valley Road. Drive north for about 100 yards into a large parking area. The trailhead is on the north side of the parking lot.

THE HIKE

It's not the most scenic hike in this guidebook, but the Trail Through Time is a fascinating route nonetheless, given its paleontological significance. Beginning at the Rabbit Valley Natural Research Area, the trail travels about 100 yards along a graveled pathway toward the Mygatt-Moore Quarry, an active fossil quarry. The Museum of Western Colorado's Paleontology Division maintains the dig site, which has yielded more than 4,000 dinosaur bones from several genera, including *Allosaurus, Apatosaurus, Diplodocus,* and *Brachiosaurus.* The quarry is also the discovery site of *Mymoorapelta,* a small plant-eating dinosaur from the Jurassic period.

Through the museum's popular Dinosaur Digs program, families can enter the quarry and help paleontologists prospect, excavate, and prep fossil specimens. But formal digs

aren't the only way to enjoy this site. The Trail Through Time is a free, self-guided tour with twenty-one interpretive signs detailing local geology and past dinosaur excavations.

A welcome kiosk in front of the Mygatt-Moore Quarry gives families a broad overview of the area's Jurassic landscape and Colorado's incredible fossil legacy. The trail tracks right at the kiosk, and then the self-guided tour is officially under way. Follow the arrow on the big metal sign to begin climbing the side of a rocky hill.

This ascent is the only taxing portion of the route, and there's no need to worry about children getting tired—there are plenty of opportunities to rest while reading illustrated signs and viewing an abundance of dinosaur bones poking out along the trail.

The first bones appear at 0.25 mile, directly in front of an interpretive sign about the Camarasaurus skeleton. From there, switchbacks take families further up the hill. After passing through a cattle gate, visit the Rabbit Valley Overlook, where you'll get good views across I-70 of the Grand Mesa and La Sal Range, the latter located about 50 miles away in Utah.

Halfway up the hill, the Trail Through Time levels out as it crosses a broad ledge. The path is well maintained, but due to the nature of the area's arid landscape, you'll want to pay close attention to the trail to avoid wandering off course.

After making a wide U-turn, a gentle descent takes hikers into the valley below. Watch for rocks, and continue stopping at the interpretive signs. At 0.85 mile, a diplodocus skeleton preserved flawlessly in sandstone is a major highlight.

The final segment of the Trail Through Time is a flat, easy stroll through a barren valley. Portions of the trail are washed out; use the arrows on metal trail posts for guidance and reassurance. Don't miss the final interpretive signs about plant fossils and a dinosaur pelvis.

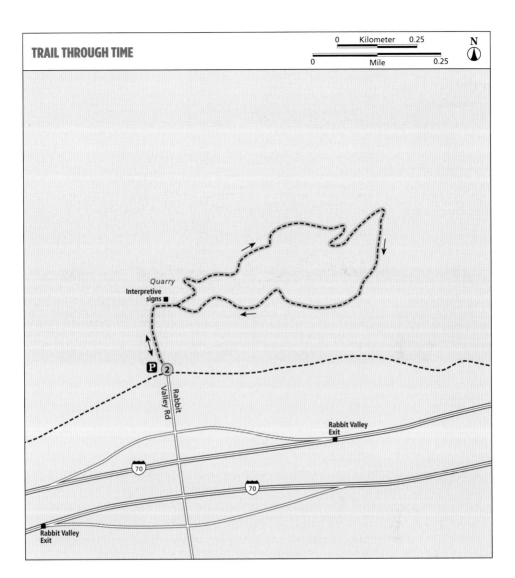

MILES AND DIRECTIONS

0.0 Start from the interpretive sign at the Trail Through Time Trailhead, hop onto the wide gravel path, and walk toward the hill. Elevation: 4,700 feet.

0.1 Pass an outhouse, and arrive at a welcome kiosk.

0.2 Bear left at a fork in the trail.

0.35 Walk through a cattle gate. Don't forget to close and latch it behind you.

0.43 Arrive at the Rabbit Valley Overlook.

0.60 Follow the trail as it makes a wide U-turn before descending into the valley.

0.85 Don't miss a diplodocus skeleton preserved in sandstone.

1.0 Come to a fork in the trail. Bear right to continue hiking alongside the hill.

1.2   The trail passes through wire fencing; the parking lot is visible ahead.

1.4   Turn left at the fork in the trail to return to your car.

1.6   Arrive back at the trailhead.

FUN FACTOR

KEEP ON TREKKING!

You're not going to drive all the way to the Utah border for one short hike! Create a dino-themed day trip by tacking on another quick hiking route, the Dinosaur Hill Interpretive Trail. Located in Fruita, overlooking a picturesque segment of the Colorado River, Dinosaur Hill was the site of several major dinosaur discoveries. The site's mile-long interpretive trail is a guided loop passing ten points of geological and paleontological interest, including an *Apatosaurus* site excavated in 1901 by Elmer Riggs. To reach it from the Trail Through Time, take I-70 to the Fruita exit, and drive south on Broadway (CO 340), following signs for Colorado National Monument (see hike 33). In 1.5 miles turn left (east) at the Dinosaur Hill sign, and follow the dirt road to a parking lot.

If you can handle yet another hike, the biggest dinosaur ever discovered was found at Riggs Hill, just 9.4 miles southeast of the Dinosaur Hill Interpretive Trail. Or skip Riggs Hill, and cruise on over to Dinosaur Journey, a regional museum with hands-on exhibits, real fossils, cast skeletons, and robotic reconstructions of dinosaurs.

3 CANYON LOOP TRAIL

Established around a stagecoach line from the 1800s, Betasso Pre-serve is a quintessential Boulder foothills hike. A few steps into the route, rocky dirt singletrack opens to sweeping views of the golden plains rising to meet the mountains. While parents will remember the picturesque landscape sprawled across miles of meandering trail, children will relish all the on-site activities, including wildlife viewing, visiting a historic homestead, and the chance to become a nature detective.

Start: Betasso Preserve Trailhead
Distance: 3.3-mile loop
Hiking time: 2–4 hours
Difficulty: Easy to moderate
Elevation gain: 439 feet
Trail surface: Dirt and gravel
Hours: Open daily, sunrise to sunset
Best seasons: Year-round
Water: None
Toilets: An outhouse near the trailhead
Nursing benches: In addition to shaded picnic benches at the trailhead, look for benches at 0.7, 2.6, and 2.8 miles.
Stroller-friendly: No
Potential child hazards: A sheer drop. During the final climb, instruct young children to hike on your right side, away from the ledge.

Other trail users: Equestrians and mountain bikers
Dogs: Allowed on leash
Land status: Boulder County Parks & Open Space
Nearest town: Boulder
Fees and permits: None
Maps: USGS Boulder
Trail contact: Boulder County Parks & Open Space, 5201 St. Vrain Rd., Longmont 80503; (303) 678-6200; www.bouldercounty.org/open-space/parks-and-trails/betasso-preserve
Gear suggestions: Spikes or micro-spikes (for early spring), closed-toed athletic shoes, high-energy snacks, extra water

FINDING THE TRAILHEAD

From downtown Boulder, take Boulder Canyon Drive (CO 119) 5.2 miles west to Sugarloaf Road. There is no discernable street sign at the onset of Sugar-loaf Road. Look for a sign for a three-way intersection preceding a hairpin turn in the road. Sugarloaf Road is the first street on the right immediately after the curve. Turn right onto Sugarloaf Road, and drive north for 1 mile before turning right onto Betasso Road. To access the site's main parking lot, go left onto Broken Fence Road at the large Betasso Preserve sign. Park in the first lot to the left, labeled "Trailhead and Group Shelter Parking." If this lot is full, follow the signs to the east lot, offering overflow parking down the road.

THE HIKE

It's all views during the first segment of the Canyon Loop Trail. The site was once a working ranch. During your adventure, ask children to keep an eye out for any farming remnants.

When you reach Mile Marker 0, stay straight to hike the Canyon Loop in a clockwise direction. This way you'll always be facing oncoming pedal traffic, since mountain bikers are required to ride the trail counterclockwise.

Betasso is a popular destination for bikers, but don't let that deter your family from enjoying the gorgeous 1,151-acre site. For a bike-free experience, visit on a Wednesday or Saturday. Other days of the week, parents can seize the opportunity to teach children about trail etiquette.

Good hikers are always aware of their surroundings. Polite bikers will call out as they come down slopes or blind switch-backs, and most will also let you know if there are others behind them. Mountain bikers are expected to yield to hikers, but there's no rule against being courteous. A thoughtful hiker recognizes that some-times it's easier for pedestrians to yield right-of-way, especially when a biker is grinding up a steep incline.

With pedestrian traffic, even some experienced hikers forget that those traveling uphill have the right-of-way. Don't be surprised, though, if an uphill hiker waves you and your family through. They might be ready for a breather. If you need to pass another hiker from behind, a friendly "Hello" is the best way to announce your presence. Always do your best to reduce erosion by staying on-trail when passing others.

FUN FACTOR

DON'T MISS BUMMER'S ROCK.

After completing the main hike, walk or drive to the Bummer's Rock trailhead—you'll see the signs—for a short but moderately steep out-and-back climb to the top of Bummer's Rock. This 0.5-mile round-trip trek is a great route for budding geologists and anyone who appreciates a good summit view. Betasso Preserve is underlain by 1.7-billion-year-old Boulder Creek grano-diorite, one of the oldest types of rock in the county. When you reach Bummer's Rock, help children look for visible crystals in the rock, as well as pink and white feldspar minerals, clear quartz, and dark mica minerals.

If Betasso's homesteading history piqued your child's interest, swing by the University of Colorado Museum of Natural History, a free museum located on the University of Colorado Boulder campus, just off Broadway Street in the Henderson Building. With five permanent exhibition galleries, including a hands-on Discovery Corner, this museum is ideal for families.

By 0.3 mile, the Canyon Loop cuts into a sparse forest of ponderosa pines and Douglas fir. In addition to locating yucca and Rocky Mountain juniper, task children with finding mouse-ear chickweed, purple-hued wild geranium, and the yellow blooms of western wallflower, all of which are visible during wildflower season, beginning as early as April some years.

The trees thicken at 0.5 mile, just in time for a shady, lulling descent to the Canyon Loop's lowest point. If your kids get antsy, start looking for wildlife: mule deer, wild turkey, and the peculiar Abert's squirrel, with its dark gray back and big tufted ears. Abert's squirrels love ponderosa pinecones and eat them like an ear of corn, rotating the pinecone while nibbling away.

If your child is interested in orienteering, point out the blue diamond blazes nailed to trees throughout this route, making it possible for winter hikers to use the trail when it's covered in powder. In addition to blazes, wooden mile markers appear every 0.5 mile.

The trail narrows before winding around a gully. Be mindful of the ledge, especially with young children. Shortly after passing the Canyon Loop and Loop Link intersection, you'll bottom out before starting a mile-long climb with plenty of shade.

Families hiking with toddlers and preschoolers can skip the Canyon Loop altogether. Have breakfast or lunch at one of the sheltered picnic tables near the trailhead, then take the super-short Blanchard Trail (composed of 177 steps) to the Blanchard cabin, a restored cabin and barn, circa 1912, when the Blanchard family homesteaded 160 acres in the area.

Grade-school children will be more engaged during a hike if they have specific tasks to complete. Enter Boulder County's fantastic Nature Detectives Club, created specifically for young hikers ages 5 to 12. Participants will need a pen or pencil and a "Mystery Guide," found in the Nature Detectives Club mailbox adjacent to the trail kiosk near the trailhead. In addition to a kid-friendly trail map, mystery guides contain several activities for children to tackle while hiking in Betasso. Afterward, return completed guides to the Nature Detectives Club mailbox. Leave your mailing address, and a ranger will send your child a prize.

MILES AND DIRECTIONS

0.0   Start from the large trail kiosk and walk downhill (and slightly right) toward the Canyon Loop Trail, which takes off from a mile marker located near the outhouse. Don't forget to grab a "Mystery Guide" at the Nature Detectives Club box. Elevation: 6,580 feet.

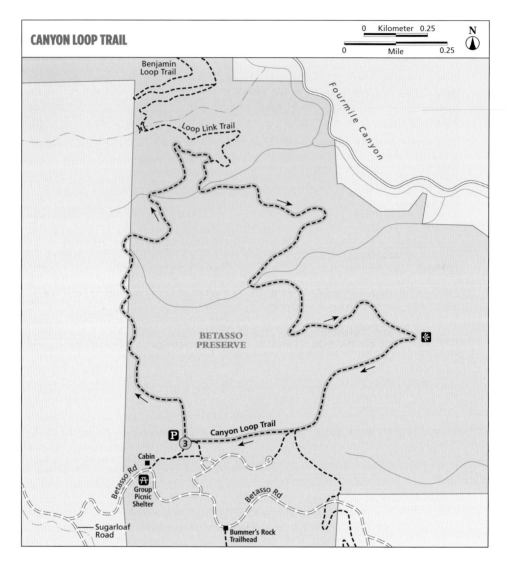

CANYON LOOP TRAIL

Benjamin Loop Trail

Loop Link Trail

Fourmile Canyon

BETASSO PRESERVE

Canyon Loop Trail

Cabin

Group Picnic Shelter

Betasso Rd

Betasso Rd

Sugarloaf Road

Bummer's Rock Trailhead

0.05 Arrive at mile marker 0. Stay straight on the Canyon Loop Trail.

0.7 Curve right with the trail, following the arrows on the barricade. A few feet later, arrive at a bench and scenic overlook.

1.2 After a U-turn, come to a three-way intersection for the Canyon Loop and Loop Link Trails. Turn right at the sign to stay on the Canyon Loop.

2.6 Reach a metal trail post. Turn left to visit a scenic overlook before continuing uphill on the Canyon Loop.

2.8 Pass a bench and scenic overlook.

3.0 Reach a four-way trail intersection. Turn right to complete the Canyon Loop. (A left puts you on the 1.3-mile-long Betasso Link Trail, dropping to Boulder Canyon Drive.)

3.3 Back at the onset of the Canyon Loop, turn left and hike another 200 feet to arrive back at the kiosk where you started.

4 FOUNTAIN VALLEY TRAIL

Roxborough State Park is frequently likened to the Garden of the Gods (see hike 47). But really, Roxy is beyond compare! As a Natural National Landmark, the diverse park claims 4,000 acres of biologically, ecologically, and geologically significant land featuring eight secluded hiking trails. By May, wildflowers dominate the jagged landscape.

Start: Visitor center
Distance: 2.6-mile lollipop
Hiking time: 1.5–3 hours
Difficulty: Easy to moderate
Elevation gain: 271 feet
Trail surface: Dirt, gravel, and rock
Hours: Vary by season and are posted on the park's website. Generally, trails are open 8 a.m. to 5 p.m. in winter, 7 a.m. to 9 p.m. in summer.
Best seasons: Year-round; snowshoeing on designated trails only
Water: Inside the visitor center
Toilets: Inside the visitor center
Nursing benches: Outside the visitor center and at both scenic overlooks
Stroller-friendly: The main loop is doable with a good jogging stroller; the overlooks are not.

Potential child hazards: Sheer drops at Lyons Overlook
Other trail users: None
Dogs: Not permitted
Land status: Colorado Parks & Wildlife
Nearest town: Littleton
Fees and permits: Per-vehicle day-use fee or Colorado Parks & Wildlife Pass
Maps: Colorado Parks & Wildlife Roxborough State Park
Trail contact: Colorado Parks & Wildlife, Roxborough State Park, 4751 East Roxborough Dr., Roxborough; (303) 973-3959; cpw.state.co.us/placestogo/parks/Roxborough/Pages/Trails.aspx
Gear suggestions: Micro-spikes (for early spring), sturdy waterproof shoes, windbreakers, sunscreen, hats or visors, sunglasses

FINDING THE TRAILHEAD

From Denver, take Santa Fe Drive south past CO 470 to West Titan Road. Turn right (southeast) onto West Titan Parkway and follow it for 2.9 miles. At the bend, West Titan becomes North Rampart Range Road. Continue south for 4 miles, until North Rampart Range Road ends at Roxborough State Park. After entering the park, continue down Roxborough Drive. Park in the third parking lot on the right; follow the paved pathway and signs to the visitor center.

THE HIKE

Start this adventure at the visitor center, where you'll find several interactive exhibits and a short historical film. Don't be shy about chatting up the rangers at the front desk. If your children are 10 and under, borrow an activity backpack, stuffed with trail essentials, and a Fountain Valley Trail guide. Nineteen interpretive signs are posted along Fountain Valley Trail—each corresponding to a page in the laminated guide.

Exit the visitor center through its front doors, and look right. Two trails depart from Roxy's main trailhead; we're taking the wide dirt path that tracks north. (To the left/south, Willow Creek is an easy 1.45-mile loop granting access to the park's remaining six trails.)

Right away you'll come to the first interpretive sign. Fountain Valley is named for a large formation of red rocks jutting out of a meadow. Known as the Fountain Formation, the tilted sandstone formed more than 300 million years ago. For a bird's-eye view, take a detour to Fountain Valley Overlook and look past the thickets of a round-crowned tree called Gambel oak, aka "shrub oak," one of the most common plants inside Roxy.

Back on Fountain Valley Trail, bear right at the fork at 0.3 mile to visit the interpretive signs in numerical order. Continuing up a gradual hill, the trail passes through a grassland community claiming nearly fifty species of grasses, ranging from narrow-leaved yucca to mountain mahogany.

Keep an eye out for pocket gophers: These critters tunnel along the park's trails. Black-tailed prairie dogs, mule deer, cottontail rabbits, and red foxes also call Roxy home.

If you enjoyed the Fountain Valley Overlook, you'll love Lyons Overlook, accessible via a narrow dirt trail shooting off to the left at 0.54 mile.

In the spring, expect a muddy ascent. After a sharp left at the "Leave No Trace" sign, the trail ends at a large scenic overlook surrounded by unique rocks and trees that might have you feeling like you've walked into a Dr. Seuss book. There's no better place for a stellar family photo, but don't let your kids lean over the ledge: It's a sheer drop to the valley below.

Return to Fountain Valley Trail, and go left to continue the loop. The next big stop is Persse Place, the former summer homestead of Henry S. Persse. Built in 1903 with locally quarried stone and red mud mortar, Persse's stone house (to the right) quickly became a guesthouse. Persse envisioned a bustling resort, but then-mayor Robert W. Speer felt the

FUN FACTOR

TIME YOUR HIKE RIGHT.

Roxy's robust educational programming is a huge point of distinction. From guided bird walks and photography classes to a kid-approved puppet theater, there's a lot going on at this state park. For a full list of seasonal offerings, check out the park's quarterly publication, *Roxborough Rambles*, available online.

The Junior Naturalist Program is a big hit with children ages 7 to 12. Games, activities, and guided hikes are keyed to various themes, such as wildlife, nature-based art, and preparedness. Participants can earn a Junior Ranger badge or continue on for their official Junior Naturalist patch. The programming is free, but advanced registration is required (call 303-973-3959). A similar Junior Ranger Program is available for younger kids, ages 3 to 6.

Roxy's naturalist-led activities are funded by The Friends of Roxborough, a nonprofit founded in 1993 to help the park acquire land and enhance its mission of bringing environmental education to the public. In the summer months, the organization raises funds through its concert series, as well as a very popular moonlight hike. Moonlight hike ticket donations go to the park's general education fund; concert donations bolster the shaded pavilion building fund.

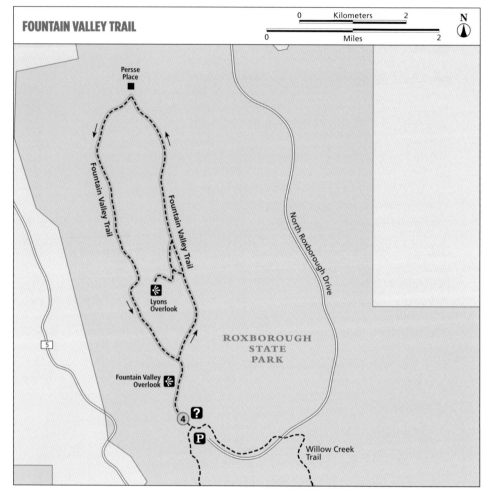

Persse
Place

Fountain Valley Trail

Fountain Valley Trail

North Roxborough Drive

Lyons
Overlook

ROXBOROUGH
STATE
PARK

Fountain Valley
Overlook

Willow Creek
Trail

place was too scenic for private ownership. Instead he nudged it into Denver's growing parks system.

Past Persse Place, the trail rounds a bend and winds through an unforgettable meadow. Here, families get a closer look at the Fountain Formation's red spires and awe-inspiring monoliths. If you're following along in the laminated activity guide, everyone in your group can enjoy finding shapes in the red rocks—George Washington's profile, for example, and a wolf howling at the sun.

Wildflowers thrive in Roxy's varied environment, but the sedge meadow community preceding the Fountain Formation gets mucky in the spring. Sometimes it even floods into a makeshift lake welcoming ducks, herons, and western chorus frogs. Ask children to listen for the frog's breeding call, resembling the sound of a finger strumming the tooth of a comb.

Spring is a good time to look for the park's fifty-plus species of butterflies, moths, and skippers. To return to the trailhead, walk past the nineteenth interpretive sign, which describes the dinosaur freeway, and turn right at the fork in the trail.

In addition to being a Natural National Landmark, Roxborough State Park is also a National Archaeological Register District. Since the 1970s, archaeologists have discovered more than 200 artifacts inside the park, mostly of the Archaic and Woodland cultures. New discoveries are possible. If you or your child uncovers an old-looking man-made object while hiking, leave it where it is, and report the finding to a ranger.

MILES AND DIRECTIONS

0.0 Start at the visitor center and look for the wide dirt trail. This is the Fountain Valley Trail. Elevation: 6,200 feet.

0.12 Note a sign for the Fountain Valley Overlook at the top of a hill. Turn left onto a narrow trail to visit the overlook, then return to the main trail.

0.2 Turn left onto the Fountain Valley Trail.

0.3 Bear right at a fork in the trail. This is the beginning of the loop.

0.54 Turn left onto the narrow dirt path, and climb a series of switchbacks to check out Lyons Overlook.

0.7 After a sharp bend at the "Leave No Trace" sign, the trail ends at Lyons Overlook. After enjoying spectacular views, backtrack to the main trail.

0.86 Turn left onto the Fountain Valley Trail.

0.98 Pass another offshoot leading to the Lyons Overlook. Do not turn left here.

1.44 Arrive at Persse Place. Stop to explore the historic homestead.

2.34 Reach the last interpretive sign, about the dinosaur freeway.

2.36 A fork in the trail signifies the end of the loop. Turn right to hike back to the visitor center.

2.6 Arrive back at the visitor center.

5 BRAILLE TRAIL LOOP

Nestled inside Denver's largest mountain park, the Braille Trail is one of my favorite hiking destinations for families. At 1.65 miles, the prescribed route is perfect for young hikers, with plenty of shady places to rest along the way. For older adolescents and teens, Genesee Mountain Park's extensive trail network presents opportunities to extend the hike—and even dip into the backcountry via the historic Beaver Brook Trail. The 2,413-acre site is home to the first buffalo and elk herds reestablished in Colorado, in 1914. Be sure to check out the bison viewing station preceding the parking lot and trailhead.

Start: Beaver Brook Trailhead
Distance: 1.65-mile lollipop connecting the Beaver Brook and Braille Trails
Hiking time: 1–2 hours
Difficulty: Easy
Elevation gain: 306 feet
Trail surface: Dirt and rock
Hours: 1 hour before sunrise to 1 hour after sunset
Best seasons: Spring through fall
Water: None
Toilets: Drop toilets at the trailhead
Nursing benches: Several creek-side benches along the Braille Trail
Stroller-friendly: No
Potential child hazards: None
Other trail users: None
Dogs: Must be leashed and under physical control

Land status: Denver Parks and Recreation
Nearest towns: Golden and Evergreen
Fees and permits: None
Maps: Denver Mountain Parks Genesee Park
Trail contact: Denver Parks and Recreation, 201 West Colfax Ave., Dept. 601, Denver 80202; (720) 913-1311; www.denvergov.org/content/denvergov/en/denver-parks-and-recreation/parks/mountain-parks/genesee-mountain-park.html
Gear suggestions: Micro-spikes (for early spring), sturdy waterproof shoes, layers if the temperature is below 45°F, windbreakers, extra water

FINDING THE TRAILHEAD

I-70 bisects Genesee Mountain Park. The Beaver Brook Trailhead is north of the highway. To reach it from I-70, take exit 253—bypassing the Genesee Park exit (254) if you're coming from Denver—and drive north to Stapleton and Moss Rock Roads. Turn right onto Stapleton Road. Follow it for about 0.5 mile to a parking lot, on the left. If this lot is full, overflow parking is permitted along Stapleton Road.

THE HIKE

There's a lot to love about Genesee Mountain Park. South of I-70, from the Patrick House Trailhead (exit 253) and Bison Meadows Trailhead (exit 254), families can view an 1860 toll station and climb Genesee Mountain's 8,284-foot summit, where the Daughters of the American Revolution have celebrated an annual commemorative flag raising on Flag Day since 1911. Those are hikes for another book.

The mellow haul to the Braille Trail Loop begins on the north side of I-70. Kick things off at the Bison Overlook. In 1914, when bison and elk neared extinction, Denver acquired herds at Yellowstone Park to introduce into the city's very first mountain park.

Read about the bison herd—and learn the distinction between buffalo and bison—while perusing interpretive panels at the overlook. If you're lucky, you'll see Denver's herd roaming along I-70. It's currently managed at about twenty-four adult animals. Looking north, you can see Bald Mountain, the 7,988-foot peak covered in hike 40.

Across the parking lot, the hike begins at the Beaver Brook Trailhead. We'll reach the Braille Trail via the historic 8.65-mile Beaver Brook Trail, which straddles the Clear Creek Land Conservancy, ending at the Windy Saddle Park Trailhead (see hike 37).

Bordered by wild lupine, columbine, and Queen Anne's lace, the first section of the Beaver Brook Trail is well marked and heavily trafficked. In 0.25 mile the dirt path breaks from Stapleton Drive and dips into strands of ponderosa pine.

Before the land was set aside for public use, private companies planned to log areas inside Genesee Mountain Park. Luckily, activists acquired the land, and Genesee became the first park in Denver's impressive 14,000-acre Mountain Park System.

Make a sharp right turn at the intersection at 0.4 mile, and descend to a service road. Soon after crossing the road, you'll come to a Braille Trail sign and guideline. The Braille Trail is an accessible route designed for hikers with vision impairments. In addition to the waist-high guideline, the trail's interpretive signs are written in Braille.

While the guideline comes in handy for balance on rocky terrain, it also presents a fantastic opportunity to help your children develop compassion. Ask children to grab the line and close their eyes. Hiking without vision can be a groundbreaking experience for those who typically rely on their sense of sight.

When you reach the wooden bench at 0.56 mile, break for a snack and conversation. Ask your kids if they heard, smelled, or felt anything they hadn't noticed before closing their eyes.

FUN FACTOR

DO YOU TRUST YOUR FAMILY? FIND OUT AT THE GENESEE CHALLENGE COURSE!

What family couldn't benefit from a little extra bonding? Set in a ponderosa pine forest 0.5 mile down a service road, the Genesee Experiential Center is a ropes and challenge course where family members can step out of their comfort zones together.

With roughly sixty low and high elements overlooking the Continental Divide, the center was designed to deliver a highly customizable experience to a range of ages and ability levels. In addition to school groups and Scouts, guides at the Genesee Experiential Center work with a variety of private parties, including families. Children must be at least 6 years old to tackle the challenge course.

To book a private group, you'll need at least eight participants. Grab another family for an unforgettable half- or full-day adventure that'll challenge your stamina and mental fortitude. The challenge course is open seasonally, April through October, by reservation only. For more information call (720) 865-0680 or e-mail outdoor.recreation@denvergov.org.

BRAILLE TRAIL LOOP

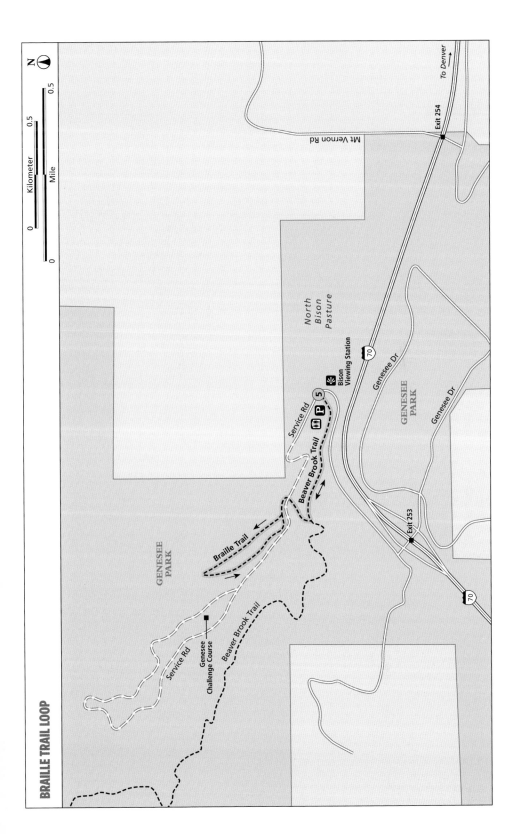

The Braille Trail continues sloping downhill alongside a babbling creek. Be mindful of rocks and roots during the descent. After passing several barricades and following stairs to the creek bed, you'll reach a cute wooden bridge and a fork. Families with older children can bear right onto Chavez Trail, which continues another 1.3 miles before reconnecting with the Beaver Brook Trail.

For this hike we'll go left at the fork to complete the Braille Trail Loop. On a beautiful spring day, take things slowly and savor the ascent. Back at the beginning of the Braille Trail Loop, turn right, cross the service road, and retrace your steps to the Beaver Brook Trailhead, remembering to bear left at the trail intersection at 1.28 miles.

MILES AND DIRECTIONS

0.0 Start from the Beaver Brook Trailhead, and begin hiking along the well-marked dirt trail. Elevation: 7,648 feet.

0.4 Arrive at a sign for the Chavez and Beaver Brook Trails. Make a sharp right, and follow the stairs down to the Chavez Trail.

0.5 After crossing a service road, you'll reach another trail sign. Continue hiking a few more yards to arrive at the Braille Trail, which is clearly marked. Bear right to begin the loop.

0.56 Pass a wooden bench.

0.75 Follow the staircase downhill.

0.83 Cross a wooden bridge. Turn left to complete the Braille Trail loop.

0.9 Pass a secluded bench.

1.01 The trail tracks right as you pass a wooden bench on a platform.

1.15 Back at the start of the Braille Trail Loop, make a sharp right. Hike uphill, cross the service road, and continue on the Beaver Brook Trail.

1.28 Turn left at the sign for the Beaver Brook Trail.

1.65 Arrive back at the trailhead.

6 COYOTE RIDGE TRAIL

Don't let its proximity to I-25 fool you. On a clear spring day, Coyote Ridge Natural Area is just plain pretty! If you're used to hiking in Boulder or Summit County, it might feel like you're in another state while gazing over the Eastern Plains. Coyote Ridge Trail is the only route into the 839-acre site, and it's filled with kid-friendly features: unusual topography, a beautiful cabin, and a special Hidden Clues Trail for youth.

Start: Coyote Ridge Trailhead
Distance: 2.4-mile lollipop
Hiking time: 1–2 hours
Difficulty: Easy
Elevation gain: 260 feet
Trail surface: Natural surface
Hours: Open daily, 5 a.m. to 11 p.m.
Best seasons: Year-round
Water: None
Toilets: An outhouse near the cabin
Nursing benches: Several along the trail and on the cabin's deck
Stroller-friendly: Yes, with a good jogging stroller
Potential child hazards: Sun exposure, rattlesnakes
Other trail users: Equestrians, mountain bikers

Dogs: One of the few Fort Collins natural areas where dogs are not allowed
Land status: City of Fort Collins
Nearest towns: Loveland and Fort Collins
Fees and permits: None
Maps: City of Fort Collins Natural Areas Program Coyote Ridge Natural Area
Trail contact: The City of Fort Collins Natural Areas Department, 1745 Hoffman Mill Rd., Fort Collins 80524; (970) 416-2815; www.fcgov.com/naturalareas/finder/coyote
Gear suggestions: Sunscreen, sun-protective clothing, brimmed hats, sunglasses, Nuun tablets, snacks or a picnic

FINDING THE TRAILHEAD

From I-25, take exit 257 for Loveland. Drive west on US 34, continuing past the intersection with US 287. In 6 miles you'll come to North Wilson Avenue. Turn right (north), and follow this road for 5.1 miles. North Wilson Avenue becomes Taft Hill Road. The Coyote Ridge Natural Area parking lot is on the west side of Taft Hill Road. With a big welcome sign, it's hard to miss. (If you get to Harmony Road, you've gone too far.) The parking lot is large, but Coyote Ridge is a popular destination. Do not park in the horse trailer spots, undesignated parking areas, or along Taft Hill Road. Have an alternative destination in mind in case you can't find a space (see hike 50).

THE HIKE

From the Coyote Ridge Trailhead and welcome sign, it's a straight shot into the natural area down a wide dirt and gravel path. The natural area's sole trail passes through a broad meadow and montane shrubland of rabbitbrush, mountain mahogany, and three-leaf sumac.

From this vantage, you really can't miss the site's thriving prairie dog colony. The rodents make their tunnels within an arm's length of the Coyote Ridge Trail, all the while providing a habitat for burrowing owls—tiny, spindly–legged birds that nest in abandoned prairie dog tunnels.

With their mottled brown feathers, burrowing owls are camouflaged in the prairie. Dawn is the best time to look for them, but even then they can be tough to spot—from afar, they look like just another prairie dog. Having trouble seeing burrowing owls? Ask children to listen for the animal's soft *coo-coo* and cackling calls.

After an easy start, the Coyote Ridge Trail rises up a hogback to an interpretive sign about snakes and local wildlife. Read the sign, and remember to be rattlesnake aware, especially on a sunny trail like this one. Snakes—they're just like us! On warm days, they come out to sunbathe. Always look before sitting down or putting your hands underneath something. Coyote Ridge is an important wildlife corridor, and there's a good chance you'll get up close with a mule deer during your hike. Visitors might also spy coyotes, lizards, rabbits, deer mice, and foxes.

FUN FACTOR

EXPERIENCE A NATURAL AREA AFTER DARK.

Incredibly, the City of Fort Collins Natural Areas Program manages more than fifty natural areas encompassing more than 36,000 acres and 100 miles of trails. June through October, Fort Collins hosts a series of free educational activities and events. If you loved this hike, plan to return in the summer or early fall.

Campfires at Coyote Ridge is a particularly popular offering for families of all ages. Bring a flashlight, and wear warm clothing: The evening includes a 30-minute hike along an unpaved trail, as well as campfire stories and s'mores. Families with teenagers age 16 and up can try a Full Moon Walk at Coyote Ridge. Offered near the full moon, when the site is bright with natural light, these guided tours consist of a 1- to 2-mile walk over unpaved trail.

If you're digging the after-hours programming, check out Astronomy at Bobcat Ridge, just west of Coyote Ridge, and Stargazing at Fossil Creek Reservoir to the east. The quirky Fort Collins Museum of Discovery houses the Natural Areas Visitor Center in its lobby. The visitor center is free and contains an interactive map and a live black-footed ferret exhibit.

The view from the first ridge is fantastic, and you'll learn more about why that is when you come to the next interpretive sign at 0.65 mile, providing information on the area's prehistoric significance.

Originally, this whole area was submerged in water. The hogbacks were created from ocean deposits raised from sea level during the uplift of the Rocky Mountains about 65 million years ago. Some of the site's rocks still have fossils in them, and budding paleontologists can look for organic remains during their water breaks.

After a respectable climb, the trail flattens out before descending just past a barricade at 0.8 mile. If your children need it, there's an outhouse a mile into the route. There's a water pump too, but the water is not potable. Do not let children drink from it.

Look north: The cabin is visible from the outhouse. Hike to the cabin, and enjoy a picnic on the shaded deck. When you're ready, simply follow the deck to the opposite side of the building, where preschoolers and elementary school children can test their observation skills on the Hidden Clues Trail, a 0.25-mile loop off the north side of the cabin.

Five interactive panels encourage children to sharpen their senses by detecting objects, sights, and smells they'd otherwise miss. The reward for parents is a few peaceful moments; don't feel guilty about taking in the picturesque landscape while your kids work on the clues.

When your child is finished exploring the Hidden Clues Trail, hike back across the cabin's deck toward the outhouse. Families with young children should turn left at the outhouse and follow the Coyote Ridge Trail straight back to the parking lot. With older kids, go right to ascend a second hogback, the Coyote Ridge, for sweeping views and a total elevation gain of 600 feet.

The additional climb produces great views of the Front Range and Eastern Plains. While the Coyote Ridge Trail itself isn't particularly long, it connects to the Rimrock and Blue Sky Trails, granting access to two more open spaces (Rimrock and Devil's Backbone) and making Coyote Ridge Natural Area a popular starting point for hikers looking for long-distance experiences. The Coyote Ridge Trail is fully exposed. Avoid hiking during the heat of the day, and bring plenty of water and sun protection.

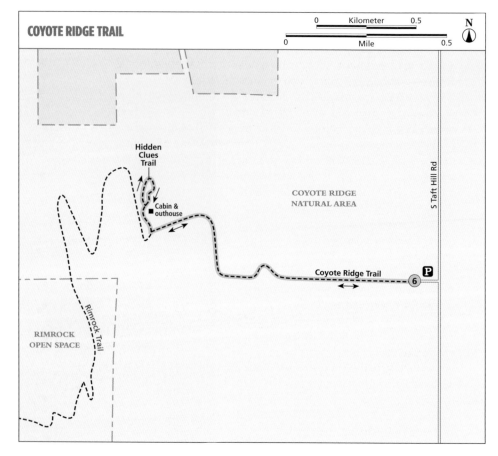

MILES AND DIRECTIONS

0.0   Start from the Coyote Ridge Trailhead, on the west side of the parking lot, and begin hiking downhill on the wide dirt path. Elevation: 4,980 feet.

0.4   Read an interpretive sign about snakes and local wildlife.

0.65 Arrive at an interpretive sign detailing the site's prehistoric significance.

1.0   Walk past the outhouse, and continue hiking toward the cabin.

1.05 Walk across the cabin's deck to get to the Hidden Clues Trail.

1.1   Arrive at the Hidden Clues Trail. The trail is a very short interpretive loop that can be completed in either direction.

1.3   After exploring the Hidden Clues Trail, hike back to the cabin and begin retracing your steps to the trailhead.

1.4   Turn left at the fork near the outhouse to follow the Coyote Ridge Trail back to the trailhead.

2.4   Arrive back at the trailhead.

7 EAST INLET TRAIL

Between the short hiking distance and flat terrain, the trek to Adams Falls via the East Inlet Trail is one of Rocky Mountain National Park's most popular west side hikes for families. Most visitors tour Adams Falls in the summer and fall, but the high-altitude waterfall is a great target for spring hikers, since the trail is equally fun with snowshoes in March and KEENs in May. The water's spray frequently refracts rainbows and double rainbows, and moose can be spotted in the valley beyond the waterfall.

Start: East Inlet Trailhead
Distance: 0.6 mile out and back
Hiking time: 30 minutes–2 hours
Difficulty: Easy
Elevation gain: 80 feet
Trail surface: Dirt, gravel, and rock
Hours: Rocky Mountain National Park is open 24 hours a day, 365 days a year.
Best seasons: Spring through fall
Water: None
Toilets: Vault toilets at the trailhead
Nursing benches: None. Nurse before the hike, or bring your own seating.
Stroller-friendly: Strollers not allowed on the East Inlet Trail
Potential child hazards: Waterfall, moose

Other trail users: Equestrians
Dogs: Prohibited on all trails inside Rocky Mountain National Park
Land status: National Park Service
Nearest town: Grand Lake
Fees and permits: None.
Maps: Rocky Mountain National Park Kawuneeche Valley Trail Guide
Trail contact: Rocky Mountain National Park Backcountry Office, 1000 East US 36, Estes Park 80517; (970) 586-1242; www.nps.gov/romo/index.htm
Gear suggestions: Snowshoes or micro-spikes (for early spring), waterproof shoes, fleece jackets, windbreakers, binoculars (to look for moose in the valley)

FINDING THE TRAILHEAD

The East Inlet Trailhead is at the end of Tunnel Road (CO 278). From US 34 in the town of Grand Lake, take CO 278 east. After 0.3 mile, use the left fork to bypass Grand Lake and drive directly to Adams Tunnel. Follow the paved road to the West Portal of Adams Tunnel. Note that the West Portal is at the East Inlet, which can be a little confusing. At the West Portal, go left on the unpaved road to the trailhead parking area. From the parking lot, look for the East Inlet Trailhead, which is well marked by signs and a bulletin board.

THE HIKE

Rocky Mountain National Park is the third most visited park in the United States, welcoming more than 4.5 million tourists to its trails, lakes, and campgrounds annually. The 415-square-mile reserve is spectacular—but that won't matter if you're stuck in a car with antsy kids, waiting in a long line at an entrance station.

So choose your adventure wisely! There are two ways for families to enter ROMO: on the east side, through Estes Park, and the west side, via Grand Lake. Both sides provide ample opportunity for outdoor recreating. From Denver, Grand Lake is a longer drive, but families who make the haul are rewarded with shorter lines at the gate, especially

during ROMO's busy season, May through October. Utilize the park's west-side trails before 10 a.m. or after 3 p.m., and you're really setting yourself up for a hassle-free experience.

Adams Falls via the East Inlet Trail is enjoyable for families of all ages, as well as those out-of-town families who are still adjusting to the altitude. The trail departs from a bulletin board located in the West Portal, and a wide dirt path takes hikers on a peaceful stroll up a small hill.

FUN FACTOR

STAY AT THE YMCA.

You drove all the way to Grand Lake with your kids, so you might as well stay a night. Tucked between the towns of Winter Park and Granby, YMCA of the Rockies Snow Mountain Ranch delivers memorable, all-inclusive family vacations without the hefty price tag.

The 5,000-acre ranch contains some of Colorado's most kid-friendly hiking trails. One of the best options for families is the Waterfall Trail, a 2.5-mile out-and-back route ending at an on-site waterfall. The Grand View Trail is also popular, featuring an intermediate 1.5-mile (one way) climb up Nine Mile Mountain to a beautiful overlook and "God's Mailbox," where many hikers leave a special message or note. Swing by the Program Building to learn about the site's trails before heading out.

In addition to stellar hiking, guests at Snow Mountain Ranch can try a variety of on-site activities: mountain biking, archery, swimming, rock climbing, fishing, canoeing, miniature golf, yoga, zip lining, roller skating, horseback riding, and tubing on Colorado's first summer tubing hill. Llama treks are also wildly popular with kids, and most activities and events are included at no additional cost.

Day-use passes are available, with per-person fees depending on age. The best deal is to stay overnight in one of the ranch's campsites, yurts, or lodge rooms. Overnight guests have access to the premises and on-site activities during their stay.

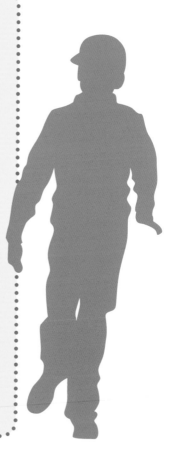

The scenery wows from the get-go as the well-marked and well-maintained trail winds through a mixed forest of conifer and aspen trees.

There are a few steep segments where natural stone stairs help ease the climb. Then, after a quick 0.3 mile, you've arrived at Adams Falls. The hike itself is pleasant, but the falls are a breathtaking sight. Adams Falls is actually a series of waterfalls, dropping 55 feet through a narrow rock gorge. To proceed to an overlook, turn right onto Adams Falls Trail and walk a few more yards.

Remember to be extremely cautious with young children near this trail's edges. Rocks are often slippery from waterfall spray, and the force of the creek can be incredibly swift and powerful, especially in the spring, when snowmelt creates excess runoff.

Hikers who are familiar with Grand Lake history might assume the falls were named for Alva Adams, a former Colorado senator. Instead, they pay tribute to Jay E. Adams, an early Grand Lake settler who threw a blowout party for the entire community on Grand Lake's eastern shore. It must have been some shindig, because midway through the night, all of the guests agreed that the beautiful falls visible in the distance should be named for their host!

Thanks to the way Adams Falls is oriented, the water's spray frequently refracts rainbows. If your child wants to see one, have her view the falls with the sun to her back.

If your family is game, continue down the East Inlet Trail for another 0.25 mile, at which point the trail opens to East Meadow, a large glaciated valley with a river and spectacular views. In addition to colorful mountain flora, the local fauna are usually out and about by late spring. With bighorn sheep, moose, and elk, ROMO's large-animal population draws tourists and photographers from far and wide. There are sixty species of mammals—not to mention oodles of birds, amphibians, fish, and insects—living in the park. In the fall, it's all about hearing bull elk bugle (or call) during their mating season.

Moose can be seen in the valley, so now's the time to dig out those binoculars. If you do spot a moose, remember to keep your distance. Parents should not let children wander

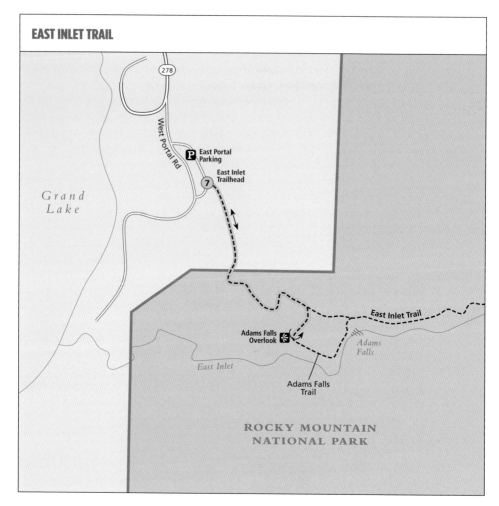

ahead while hiking at ROMO. Because they have very few natural predators, moose don't fear humans the way other animals do.

The hike back from Adams Falls is easy, enjoyable, and scenic, overlooking Grand Lake's mountain-framed ultramarine waters.

With elevations ranging from 7,800 to 12,000 feet, you can bet ROMO will be snow-packed and icy into April. By May, most of the park's 300-plus trail miles should be clear, and the route to Adams Falls will likely be doable in waterproof shoes or hiking sandals.

MILES AND DIRECTIONS

0.0 Start at the East Inlet Trailhead, and begin hiking south on the East Inlet Trail. Elevation: 8,390 feet.

0.3 Arrive at Adams Falls. Admire the area before retracing your steps to the trailhead.

0.6 Arrive back at the trailhead.

8 BLUE AND RED LOOPS

It's a gorgeous day. You're ready to hike, but your kids aren't enthused. The compromise is Philip S. Miller Park, a sprawling 300-acre site located in the heart of Castle Rock, where an 8.6-mile-long trail network surrounds an impressive supply of youth amenities. On the Red and Blue Loops, families get a best-of-both-worlds experience with an entry-level hike ending at a giant adventure playground.

Start: Base of Challenge Hill, the park's 200-step staircase
Distance: 2.8-mile double loop
Hiking time: 1–2 hours on the trail (Don't forget to factor in time for the playground.)
Difficulty: Easy to moderate
Elevation gain: 191 feet
Trail surface: Natural surface
Hours: Sunrise to sunset
Best seasons: Year-round
Water: At the Miller Activity Complex
Toilets: Inside the Miller Activity Complex
Nursing benches: Many spaced out along the trail and around the adventure playground

Stroller-friendly: No
Potential child hazards: None
Other trail users: Mountain bikers
Dogs: Prohibited on Challenge Hill, but welcome throughout the rest of the park
Land status: Town of Castle Rock
Nearest town: Castle Rock
Fees and permits: None
Maps: Town of Castle Rock Philip S. Miller Park Trail Map
Trail contact: Town of Castle Rock, 1375 West Plum Creek Pkwy., Castle Rock 80109; (720) 733-2260; www .crgov.com/2051/Philip-S-Miller-Park
Gear suggestions: Athletic shoes, sunscreen, sun-protective clothing, brimmed hats, sunglasses

FINDING THE TRAILHEAD

From historic downtown Castle Rock, drive south on Perry Street. Turn right onto Plum Creek Parkway, and follow the road across I-25. If you're coming from Denver or Colorado Springs, get off I-25 at exit 181 and drive west on Plum Creek Parkway. The park entrance, marked by a large metal-and-stone sign, appears on the left side of the road in less than 1 mile. Turn left into Philip S. Miller Park and follow the signs to the Miller Activity Complex, where there's plenty of parking.

THE HIKE

Philip S. Miller Park packs a lot of punch by seamlessly combining urban amenities and outdoor recreation. To gain some elevation, begin with a short and steep climb up Challenge Hill, the prominent staircase 0.25 mile south of the Miller Activity Complex. If you're familiar with the Manitou Springs Incline, you'll recognize Challenge Hill's 200 timber steps as a miniature version of that infamous Colorado ascent.

Challenge Hill looks a little intimidating from its base. Although most kids will probably enjoy it, you can skip the climb by turning right at the trailhead and hiking 0.1 mile to reach the park map that appears at 0.5 mile in the directions below.

Otherwise summit Challenge Hill then continue along the Blue Loop, a natural-surface trail with ample switchbacks to ease the upcoming descent.

After rounding a bend, you'll get a bird's-eye view of the entire park. The trail feels more "hikey" by 0.3 mile as you drop into a mixed shrubland dotted with cactus, yucca, flowering gilia, and Indian paintbrush, all of which draw pollinators such as bees, moths, and hummingbirds.

When you reach the park map at 0.5 mile, you have the option to turn right and complete the Blue Loop by hiking another 0.1 mile to the base of Challenge Hill.

Five loops come together to create the park's 8.6-mile trail system, and the Red and Green Loops are the most nature-oriented options. The Red Loop begins at the fork at 0.75 mile. For this hike, we'll bear left (clockwise), although to the right your children will almost certainly spot Epic Sky Trek, a privately operated, three-level challenge course with more than 110 elements.

After rolling through a meadow dominated by shrubs, the trail ascends a modest hill, opening to pretty countryside views.

Notice the zip line platform at 1.5 miles? Castle Rock Zip Line Tours is a privately managed zip line course with ten lines stretched throughout the park's ridgelines. Open year-round (weather permitting), the zip line is the park's most thrilling—and priciest—feature. There are height and weight requirements, and advance reservations are required.

Past the zip line, look for an outdoor amphitheater in the distance. The amphitheater overlooks a quaint pond where families can picnic post-hike.

The next descent is the most scenic and serene segment inside the park. After the trail bottoms out, complete the Red Loop by turning right at the trail post at 2.1 miles. When you reach the five-way trail intersection, walk straight through it to finish your hike. As you wrap up this hike, look ahead for a stellar view of the flat-top rock that inspired the town of Castle Rock's name.

Families wishing to extend their route can tack on the 1.2-mile Green Loop (miles not included in the directions below). The Gold Loop picks up where the Green Loop ends, and the 2.1-mile trail links to Ridgeline Open Space via the Wolfensberger Pedestrian Bridge. With another 13.4 miles of trail, Ridgeline Open Space is a great place to extend your adventure while traveling through open grassland, scenic ridgelines, and dense stands of Gambel oak.

Post-hike, let children burn off any remaining energy on the adventure playground. There's no shame in enjoying urban amenities and nature together, especially if the experience gets your kids excited about hiking.

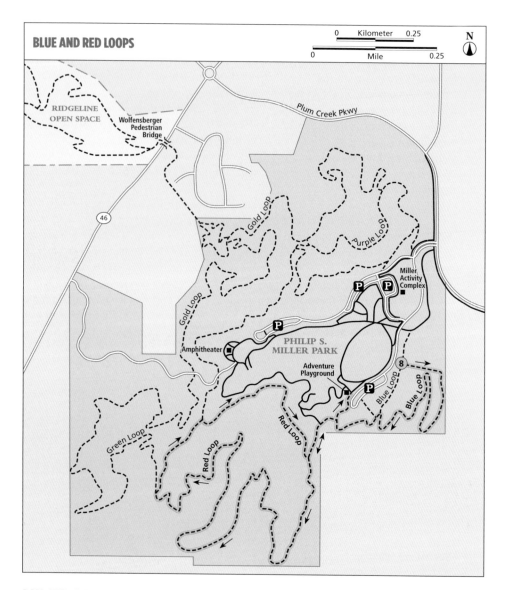

MILES AND DIRECTIONS

0.0 Start from the Challenge Hill Trailhead and climb straight up 200 steps. Elevation: 6,224 feet.

0.08 Turn right at the top of Challenge Hill, and descend on the Blue Loop.

0.5 Arrive at a park map, and turn left onto the Red Loop. A few steps later, look for a trail post with a red arrow. Continue slightly downhill.

0.65 Reach a trail post. Following the red arrow, bear left at a fork. Walk uphill to another marker.

0.75 Stay left at a fork in the trail.

1.5 Pass a zip line platform. Follow the trail around the bend.

FUN FACTOR

EXPERIENCE FAMILY-FRIENDLY CASTLE ROCK.

Settled around "the Rock" in the 1870s, the town of Castle Rock is known for being a great place to raise a family. It's also a great place to visit with a family. On the east side of Philip S. Miller Park, Miller Activity Complex—the MAC, for short—is a massive 64,443-square-foot recreational facility with a variety of fee-based amenities, including a zero-entry leisure pool and water slide, eighteen-hole golf simulator, trampoline court, batting cages, and a play structure for toddlers and preschoolers.

About 20 minutes up the road, families with children ages 10 and up can tour a real castle when they visit Cherokee Ranch and Castle. The site's signature 90-minute tour provides guests with an in-depth look at one of the state's unique treasures. Reservations required, so be sure to call ahead.

You don't have to shell out cash to have fun in Castle Rock. The Philip S. Miller Library is a fun stop-off. Time your trip right, and you might catch one of the organization's story times, youth science programs, or LEGO workshops. Fit families can also hike to the top of the town's namesake rock. From the Rock Park Trailhead, just 2.5 miles northeast of Philip S. Miller Park, a short hike provides quick elevation gain and sweeping town views.

1.6 Cross a narrow service road to arrive at a wooden post. Keep straight.

2.1 Turn right at the trail post. Use an unnamed access trail to complete the Red Loop.

2.3 Arrive at a five-way intersection. Walk past the park map toward a red blaze.

2.6 Bear left at the fork. The trail makes a big U-turn around the Epic Sky Trek challenge course.

2.7 Walk uphill toward the challenge course before turning right onto a broad dirt trail. From here, walk to the playground.

2.8 The trail ends at a sidewalk leading to a series of playgrounds. Challenge Hill and the Miller Activity Complex are visible in the distance. You shouldn't have any trouble finding your car from here.

9 HORSETOOTH FALLS TRAIL

On the outskirts of Fort Collins, Horsetooth Mountain Open Space contains 29 miles of hiking trails spread over 2,711 acres. The site is named for its tallest feature, Horsetooth Rock, towering above the Eastern Plains at 7,256 feet. Native American legend had it that the landmark was the remains of an evil giant's heart, but European settlers thought the rock looked more like a horse's tooth. The out-and-back route to the rock is a popular trek. For families, though, Horsetooth Falls Trail is optimal, with mellow terrain and a water feature.

Start: Horsetooth Mountain Trailhead
Distance: 2.4 miles out and back
Hiking time: 1.5–3 hours
Difficulty: Easy to moderate
Elevation gain: 250 feet
Trail surface: Dirt and rock
Hours: Open 24/7
Best seasons: Year-round
Water: A pump with potable water near the outhouse
Toilets: Drop toilets between the picnic tables and trailhead
Nursing benches: Several along Horsetooth Falls Trail
Stroller-friendly: No
Potential child hazards: Rattlesnakes, sun exposure, a sheer ledge preceding the waterfall (The waterfall itself is minute and poses little danger.)
Other trail users: None on Horsetooth Rock Trail; equestrians and mountain bikers allowed on other trails inside the open space
Dogs: Must be leashed
Land status: Larimer County
Nearest town: Fort Collins
Fees and permits: Entrance fee payable by cash, Visa, or Mastercard
Maps: Larimer County Department of Natural Resources Horsetooth Mountain Open Space Map
Trail contact: Larimer County Department of Natural Resources, 1800 South CR 31, Loveland 80537; (970) 619-4570; www.larimer.org/naturalresources/parks/horsetooth-mountain
Gear suggestions: Sunscreen and/or sun-protective clothing, sunglasses, brimmed hats, waterproof hiking sandals, Nuun tablets, a picnic

FINDING THE TRAILHEAD

From I-25, take exit 265 for Harmony Road/Timnath. Drive west on Harmony Road for 7 miles, at which point it becomes CR 38E at the Taft Hill Road intersection. Continue along CR 38E as it curves around the south side of Horsetooth Reservoir. About 2 miles past the reservoir, look for Horsetooth Mountain Open Space's well-marked entrance, to your right. The parking lot is past the entrance station. When the lot reaches capacity on busy summer weekends, visitors must wait to enter. The catch is that only two cars are allowed to wait at a time. Avoid a major parking nightmare by arriving before 8 a.m. on Saturday and Sunday or hiking on a weekday.

THE HIKE

Horsetooth Mountain Trailhead is easy to spot just east of the picnic tables and outhouse. Two paths depart from the same trailhead. To get to the falls, take the trail to the right, and follow the signs for the Horsetooth Rock and Horsetooth Falls Trails. Watch for rocks, roots, and snakes as you begin a somewhat steep ascent on a well-marked trail.

The open space provides a habitat for several types of snakes. If you see one coiled to strike, it could be a rattlesnake, but there's also a good chance it's a nonvenomous bull snake. Bull snakes have the ability to imitate rattlesnakes, and their coloration and size are almost identical. Always play it safe with snakes by keeping your distance.

FUN FACTOR

BE A LONG WEEKENDER.

A long weekend in Denver's fourth most populous city—FoCo to the locals—is a fun spring getaway with standout dining, kid-friendly attractions, and tons of outdoor offerings.

After working up an appetite at Horsetooth Mountain Open Space, recoup lost calories with made-to-order doughnuts at the Foco Doco, one of many restaurants inside The Exchange. Since they're something between a doughnut hole and a full-size bun, you're totally justified in sampling a few before heading south to Old Town.

If Old Town Square looks familiar, that's probably because downtown Fort Collins was the inspiration for Disneyland's Main Street, U.S.A. From Snooze to Beau Jo's to Next Door Eatery, there's a local restaurant for every type of diner in the town's eclectic shopping district.

The playground at Twin Silo Park is a memorable stop-off with kids, with a series of ropes and cargo nets leading to a giant slide connecting two 48-foot farm silos.

On a hot spring day, cool off at the Fort Collins Museum of Discovery. This city-sponsored museum is a hodgepodge of hands-on exhibits encompassing everything from prehistoric times to modern sound and indigenous creepy crawlers. Somehow it works. Nearby, The Farm at Lee Martinez Park is great for younger children, who can feed chickens, goats, and sheep; ride ponies; and play on tractors.

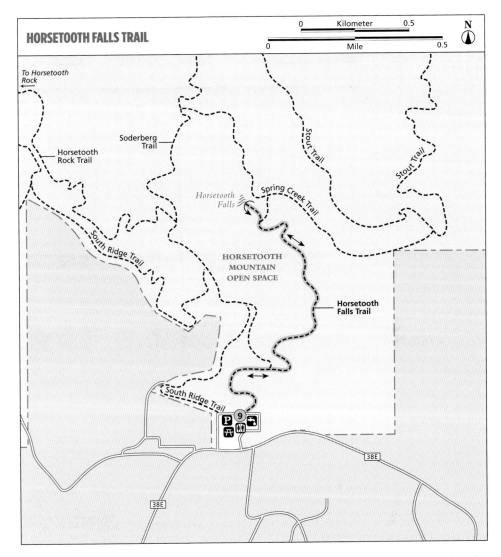

Things get really scenic really fast as the parking lot fades into a beautiful gulch. After circling the gulch and climbing a few stone steps, make sure to look back before rounding the bend for a stellar view.

When the trail splits at 0.32 mile, bear right to take the Horsetooth Falls Trail to the waterfall. A left would put you on Horsetooth Rock Trail, which ends at—you guessed it—Horsetooth Rock. With older adolescents, tweens, or teens, parents can tack on an additional 4.2 miles round-trip by hiking to Horsetooth Rock after visiting the falls. Just be sure to pack plenty of snacks and water for a big adventure.

Several trails inside Horsetooth Mountain Open Space are named for the region's earliest homesteaders, including the Wathen, Herrington, Soderberg, and Culver families, who lived in the area in the early 1900s.

After a solid climb, Horsetooth Falls Trail weaves through a grassy meadow with wild-flowers and cacti. The scenic overlook at 0.68 mile is a great place to capture memories

with a family selfie before the trail drops down to Spring Creek. Continue to watch for rocks as you descend the rugged singletrack.

A bridge gets hikers across the creek, at which point the trail winds uphill, steepening for the final 0.2 mile. There's a ledge with sheer drops to the left, so make sure to keep an eye on young children during this segment.

You'll be able to hear the waterfall by the time you reach the fork in the trail at 1.06 miles. Steer left, and hike another 200 feet to the base of Horsetooth Falls. In April and May the waterfall is usually gushing with spring snowmelt, and the pool in front of the falls is typically full. By the Fourth of July, though, Horsetooth Falls is just a trickle, and the area surrounding it will be bone-dry.

Either way, the waterfall is a fun target. There are plenty of rocks to sit and climb on. So pack a picnic lunch to enjoy while your children splash around and explore.

MILES AND DIRECTIONS

0.0 Start from the Horsetooth Mountain Trailhead, head right onto the well-marked singletrack, and follow the signs for Horsetooth Rock and Horsetooth Falls. Elevation: 5,430 feet.

0.22 Climb a stone staircase.

0.32 Reach a fork in the trail. A right takes you to Horsetooth Falls.

0.36 Pass a wooden barricade; continue hiking along the trail as it winds downhill.

0.68 Pass a bench and scenic overlook.

0.9 Use the bridge to cross Spring Creek.

1.06 Arrive at a trail junction. Bear left to continue down to the base of Horsetooth Falls.

1.2 Reach Horsetooth Falls. After enjoying the area, turn around and retrace your steps to the trailhead.

2.4 Arrive back at the trailhead.

10 MOUNT FALCON PARK UPPER LOOP

Mount Falcon Park has everything a family could possibly need: well-marked trails, beautiful vistas, and several hidden structures for children to discover during a low-mileage hike through a ponderosa pine forest and meadow. Most visitors head straight to the Walker Home Ruins, the site's crumbling castle. But the 2,249-acre park has much more to offer from its West Trailhead.

Start: Mount Falcon Park West Trailhead
Distance: 2.45-mile lollipop
Hiking time: 1.5–3 hours
Difficulty: Easy to moderate
Elevation gain: 641 feet
Trail surface: Dirt and rock
Hours: Open daily, 1 hour before sunrise to 1 hour after sunset
Best seasons: Year-round. Expect slick, icy conditions Nov through Mar.
Water: None
Toilets: Drop toilets 0.1 mile past the trailhead
Nursing benches: Available at a picnic shelter near the trailhead and at the Eagle Eye Shelter
Stroller-friendly: The direct route to the Walker Home Ruins (via Castle Trail) is doable with a stroller.

Potential child hazards: Sheer drops at the Eagle Eye Shelter
Other trail users: Equestrians, mountain bikers
Dogs: Must be leashed
Land status: Jefferson County Open Space
Nearest town: Indian Hills
Fees and permits: None
Maps: Jefferson County Open Space Mount Falcon Park Map
Trail contact: Jefferson County Open Space, 700 Jefferson County Pkwy., Ste. 100, Golden 80401; (303) 271-5925; www.jeffco.us/1332/Mount-Falcon-Park
Gear suggestions: Windbreakers, waterproof shoes that can get muddy, sunscreen, hats, extra water

FINDING THE TRAILHEAD

From the I-70/CO 470 interchange, take CO 470 south to US 285, bypassing Mount Falcon Park East. Go right (south) on US 285, and follow the road for almost exactly 5 miles. After a big bend, turn right (north) onto Parmalee Gulch Road. The road winds through the community of Indian Hills. Soon after passing Parmalee Gulch Park, turn right at the Mount Falcon sign; continue along Mount Falcon Road until it ends at the park.

THE HIKE

When you start this hike, tell your children there are three "secret places" hidden along the trail. It's their job to find them!

Mount Falcon's main event is the Walker Home Ruins, the ragged remains of entrepreneur John Walker's turn-of-the-twentieth-century mountaintop mansion. It's possible to reach the Walker Home Ruins from the park's east entrance via its Morrison Trailhead, offering a tough, 5.8-mile out-and-back hike along Castle Trail. (While the 2,000-foot elevation gain might be too difficult for young children, it's a great trek with older adolescents and teens.)

The most important thing to know about Mount Falcon is that the park has two entrances. At 3.6 miles (each way), Castle Trail connects the park's Morrison and West Trailheads. The route listed here departs from Mount Falcon West Trailhead, located at the end of Mount Falcon Road.

Begin at the upper parking lot on a generous dirt and gravel trail beyond the stone pavilion. After passing a kiosk and outhouse, a Castle-Meadow trail junction appears at 0.4 mile. Turn right onto a narrow dirt path to visit a rocky outcrop opening to pretty views. This short detour is worth it, especially if your children love climbing rocks. Just be careful—there's a big drop on the other side of the outcrop.

Most hikers turn left at the Castle-Meadow junction and head directly to the Walker Home Ruins. With toddlers and preschoolers, this is a great option. But to see all of the park's secret places, hike straight through the intersection and huff it uphill to Eagle Eye Shelter. This is the steepest part of the hike, and it's nothing your kids can't handle.

Eagle Eye Shelter appears on the right, near a boarded-up well. Follow the stamped concrete pathway into the shelter, which was once a summer cabin owned by the Kirchhoff family. For more information, read the interpretive sign describing the shelter, and use a QR code to listen to a song by Austrian composer Franz Schubert.

Eagle Eye Shelter has been beautifully maintained, and it is a great spot for a snack or picnic lunch. When you're ready, continue uphill on the Tower Trail, where hikers escape the heat in a scenic stand of ponderosa pines.

Don't overthink the fork that appears at 0.67 mile. Both ways lead to Lookout Tower. One path is for hikers; the other is for horseback riders. Follow the arrow on the trail post, and do your best to take the designated hiking trail to Lookout Tower, the second secret place on the itinerary.

When you reach the tower, climb the staircase and take in the best views of the day. From here, you'll continue on the Tower Trail by descending the stairs, walking forward several feet, and turning left onto an unmarked trail. In about 250 feet, the trail makes

a U-turn then winds downhill. Eventually it links back up with the Meadow Trail at a four-way intersection at 1.15 miles.

Turn right at this intersection. Then make a quick left to take the Meadow Trail through a beautiful meadow filled with prairie grasses and wildflowers in the spring. Families hiking with older children can add an extra 0.6 mile to their route by checking out the forested Old Ute Trail loop before entering the meadow.

FUN FACTOR

DISCOVER MORRISON'S DINOSAUR MUSEUMS.

If you don't already know it, Colorado is a hotbed of fossil finds, claiming thousands of prehistoric bones. After sharpening your children's archaeology skills inside Mount Falcon Park, drive to Morrison, where they can become paleontologists at the Morrison Natural History Museum. This small-town attraction houses several important dinosaur discoveries and has been featured in *Smithsonian* magazine.

Hour-long museum tours are offered throughout the day. (Reservations for small groups are not required but are appreciated.) Families can also peruse fossils and exhibits at their own pace. Because the museum actively studies paleontology, you'll see modern fossils on display; you might also catch researchers working in the laboratory.

If your children really dig dinos, check out Dinosaur Ridge, a National Natural Landmark claiming the world's first stegosaurus discovery.

MOUNT FALCON PARK UPPER LOOP

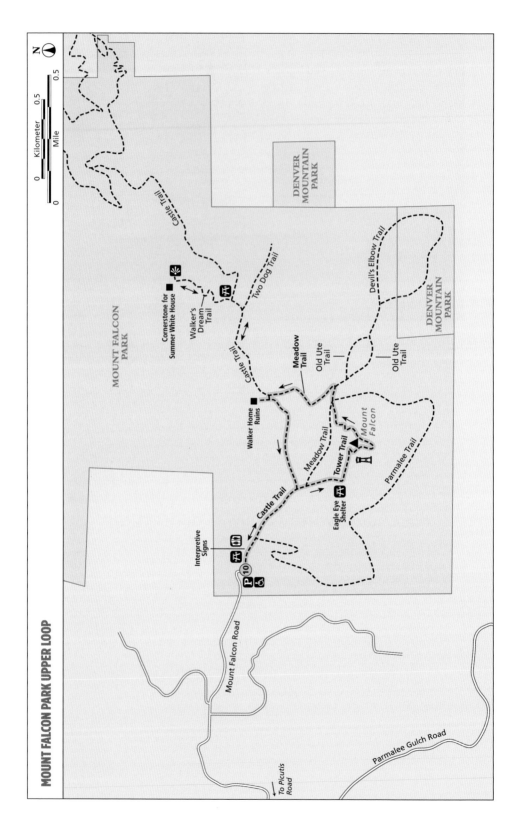

The Meadow Trail ends at an intersection preceding the Walker Home Ruins. Enjoy this fascinating site. And remember, the ruins are fragile. While it's tempting to hop the barricades, good hikers always respect parameters set by park managers, even if others aren't following the rules.

After visiting the Walker Home Ruins, backtrack to the four-way interchange; turn right to take the Castle Trail back to where you started, following the wide dirt path as it tracks around three S-shaped bends before ascending a broad hill. This portion of trail is fully exposed (read: blazing hot).

MILES AND DIRECTIONS

0.0 Start from the upper parking lot, at the end of Mount Falcon Road, and look for the Mount Falcon West Trailhead. Begin hiking on the Castle Trail. Elevation: 6,857 feet.

0.1 Pass a kiosk, and arrive at an outhouse and trail intersection. Hike straight through the intersection. Do not turn right onto the Parmalee Trail.

0.4 Reach a junction of the Castle and Meadow Trails. Go straight through it to merge onto the Meadow Trail.

0.5 Arrive at a three-way trail intersection. Keep going straight to begin hiking the Tower Trail.

0.6 Reach the Eagle Eye Shelter. Follow the Tower Trail as it rounds a bend and tracks uphill.

0.67 Come to a fork in the trail. Both paths lead to Lookout Tower; take the designated hiking trail.

0.75 Arrive at Lookout Tower. Walk forward a few feet and turn left onto a narrow, unmarked trail (Tower Trail). You'll know you've gone the right way when the trail makes a big U-turn in about 250 feet.

1.15 Reach a four-way trail intersection for the Tower, Meadow, and Parmalee Trails. Walk straight through it, pass a bench, and begin hiking on the Meadow Trail.

1.22 Reach a trail post. Turn left to stay on the Meadow Trail.

1.58 Arrive at a four-way trail intersection. Walk uphill to the Walker Home Ruins. When you're finished exploring the area, backtrack to this Meadow-Castle intersection.

1.65 Back at the four-way Meadow-Castle intersection, turn right onto the Castle Trail.

2.05 Reach a three-way trail junction. This should look familiar. Turn right to take the Castle Trail back to the trailhead.

2.45 Arrive back at the trailhead.

11 EAGLE WIND TRAIL

With bountiful wildflowers, unique geological features, and sweeping views of snowcapped summits, the Ron Stewart Preserve at Rabbit Mountain is a serene place for families to unwind. Laid out over miles of rolling terrain, the interpretive signs on Eagle Wind Trail provide insight into the site's human history, as well as the variety of wildlife calling this beautiful area home.

Start: Trailhead near the stone picnic shelter and welcome sign
Distance: 4.0-mile lollipop
Hiking time: 2–4 hours
Difficulty: Easy to moderate
Elevation gain: 385 feet
Trail surface: Dirt and rock
Hours: Open daily, sunrise to sunset. The park occasionally closes to the public on select weekdays for elk management through limited hunting.
Best seasons: Year-round
Water: None
Toilets: Vault toilets near the trailhead
Nursing benches: Several spaced out along the trail
Stroller-friendly: No
Potential child hazards: Sheer drops at the scenic overlooks

Other trail users: Equestrians, mountain bikers
Dogs: Permitted on leash
Land status: Boulder County Parks & Open Space
Nearest town: Longmont
Fees and permits: None
Maps: Boulder County Open Space Ron Stewart Preserve at Rabbit Mountain
Trail contact: Boulder County Parks & Open Space, 5201 St. Vrain Rd., Longmont 80503; (303) 678-6200; www.bouldercounty.org/open-space/parks-and-trails/ron-stewart-preserve-rabbit-mountain
Gear suggestions: Windbreakers, sunscreen, sun-protective clothing, brimmed hats, Nuun tablets

FINDING THE TRAILHEAD

From Boulder, take CO 36 north toward the town of Lyons. Turn right (east) when CO 36 dead-ends at Ute Highway (CO 66). Drive for approximately 1 mile before going left onto North 53rd Street. The Ron Stewart Preserve at Rabbit Mountain can be accessed only via the interchange at Ute Highway and North 53rd Street. After driving along North 53rd Street for 3 miles, make a right at the sign for Ron Stewart Preserve at Rabbit Mountain, and park in the forty-one-spot lot.

THE HIKE

Set in a transition zone between the Great Plains and Southern Rockies, Ron Stewart Preserve supplies hikers with typical foothills scenery and terrain, yet Rabbit Mountain itself is a unique formation.

Back when most of Colorado was below sea level—some 140 million years ago—today's preserve was a tropical lowland. When the sea fell back, tension in rocks around Rabbit Mountain created a fault that extends across the north end of the property. Slippage along that fault resulted in Rabbit Mountain's unusual positioning, 3 miles east of the foothills' main hogbacks.

Hikers get noteworthy views from the parking lot, where an unnamed trail departs between the preserve's welcome sign and a thirty-person group picnic shelter. Walk through a metal gate to begin a gradual ascent through an open meadow. Pay attention at the switchback at 0.2 mile, as the trail changes direction abruptly.

The area's diverse plant communities draw tons of wildlife. While passing through grasslands, shrublands, and a ponderosa pine forest, ask children to keep an eye out for mule deer, black-tailed prairie dogs, and desert cottontails, as well as birds, including magpies, meadowlarks, robins, sparrows, wrens, and hawks. Some elk live inside the preserve year-round; the rest migrate from higher elevations when they need to escape deep snow.

Rabbit Mountain was originally called Rattlesnake Mountain. Even though the preserve was renamed to something more inviting, hikers still need to be snake aware.

The preserve's two main trails are Eagle Wind and Little Thompson Overlook. Soon after passing the first scenic overlook, you'll reach a three-way trail intersection. Turn right to merge onto the Eagle Wind Trail, appealing to families with its gradual grades, interpretive signs, and spectacular views. Cross a dirt road, and watch for rocks as the trail loops around a flat "mountaintop," which is really a mesa.

Stop to read the interpretive sign about the Plains Indians. Until the mid-1800s, the Arapaho made Rabbit Mountain their winter home. Thanks to its location, the mountain's visitors and former inhabitants had 360-degree views for observing game, people—even weather patterns. The unusual landscape blocked cold winter winds, and rock fissures supplied drinking water via natural springs.

Beyond the sign, show your children Longs Peak and Mount Meeker in the distance. The Arapaho called these contiguous mountains Nay-ni-sote-uu-u, or "Twin Guides," and used them for navigation.

Turn left at the next fork. The Eagle Wind Trail is a lollipop, and this is the start of the looped segment of your journey. (It's fine to travel either way around the loop, but you'll get the best views if you go clockwise.)

The sunny trail levels out as it rolls through strands of Rocky Mountain juniper and ponderosa pine. With bountiful wildflowers, the Eagle Wind Trail is a colorful spring hike. It's also a good winter trail, since ample sun exposure keeps snow and ice at bay.

A half mile past the educational sign about local predators and prey, stop for a family picture at the preserve's most photogenic overlook. A nearby bench is a good spot to break for snacks. Stay on the right side of the log barricade that's used to manage vegetation regrowth. From December 15 to July 15, there's no public access beyond the barricade.

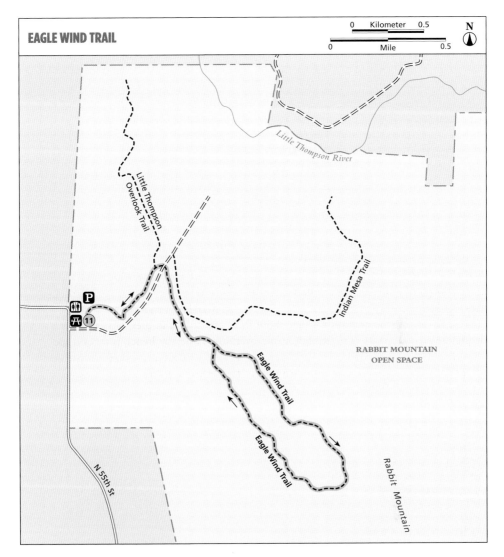

0   Kilometer   0.5

0   Mile   0.5

N

Little Thompson River

Little Thompson Overlook Trail

Indian Mesa Trail

P

11

Eagle Wind Trail

Eagle Wind Trail

RABBIT MOUNTAIN
OPEN SPACE

N 55th St

Rabbit Mountain

At 2.0 miles the trail curves back toward the trail-head. Look right after the bend to admire lichen-covered rocks. If the ground is dry, children can also spy horseshoe impressions.

When the Eagle Wind Trail dead-ends into itself, the looped portion of the hike is complete. Turn left to begin descending to the parking lot where you started. After crossing the dirt road, don't forget to bear left at the fork in the trail. (**Option:** A right at this intersection puts you on the Little Thompson Overlook Trail, which contours north along a steep-faced hogback, adding 2.0 miles round-trip. Miles and directions to Little Thompson Overlook are not included below.)

MILES AND DIRECTIONS

0.0   Start from the trailhead on the north side of the parking lot, near a group picnic shelter and kiosk. Begin hiking on the narrow dirt and gravel path. Elevation: 5,500 feet.

0.35 Pass a bench and scenic overlook.

0.5   Turn right at the trail post to begin hiking on the Eagle Wind Trail.

0.55 Cross a wide dirt road. The Eagle Wind Trail picks back up on the other side.

0.7   Pass an interpretive sign about some of the area's earlier inhabitants.

0.8   Pass another interpretive sign, followed by a bench and a scenic vista.

0.9   Turn left at the fork in the trail.

1.0   Reach another fork. Go left to make a clockwise loop around the mesa.

1.37 Pass an educational sign about predators and prey.

1.4   Continue hiking uphill. Do not turn right onto the flat service road.

1.55 Bear left at the fork in the trail.

1.85 Pass an overlook revealing the trail's most dramatic views.

2.45 Pass another bench and scenic overlook.

2.9   Curious about the faraway peaks you've been ogling? Read an interpretive sign about the mountains.

2.95 Turn left to begin a gradual descent.

3.4   Hike straight across the road, and head back the way you came.

4.0   Arrive back at the trailhead.

FUN FACTOR

BRUSH UP ON REGIONAL HISTORY IN LONGMONT.

If your children enjoyed learning about the human history at Rabbit Mountain, continue your anthropological studies at the Agricultural Heritage Center, open seasonally from April 1 to October 31. Housed in a 1909 farmhouse and stocked with period items, this free museum is all about local agriculture during the first quarter of the twentieth century, when many Boulder families prospered as farmers. In addition to a guided tour, guests can explore interactive exhibits and visit on-site animals, including chickens, pigs, and draft horses.

If learning about history makes you hungry, the Longmont Farmers' Market is a great place to re-up while celebrating modern-day agriculture. Free parking is available at Boulder County Fairgrounds. It's hard to miss the contemporary Longmont Museum, two miles east, with rotating exhibits in history, art, and science, as well as Front Range Rising, a long-term, award-winning exhibit on the region's history and culture.

12 MAY'S POINT LOLLIPOP

Boulder Open Space and Mountain Parks preserves more than 45,000 acres of wild land, and it all started in 1898, when a grassroots group of Boulderites approved a bond issue to purchase 80 acres for "Chautauqua" (pronounced shuh-TAW-kwuh). As times change, Chautauqua Park remains a beloved gateway to the great outdoors. Most visitors access the park via the Chautauqua Trailhead. Avoid the crowds by driving to Realization Point, where the trek to May's Point provides access to unforgettable views of the Continental Divide.

Start: Realization Point Trailhead
Distance: 2.1-mile reverse lollipop connecting the Ute, Boy Scout, and Range View Trails
Hiking time: 1.5–3 hours
Difficulty: Moderate
Elevation gain: 633 feet
Trail surface: Dirt and rock
Hours: Boulder OSMP trails are open 24/7. The Realization Point Trailhead parking lot is open 1 hour before sunrise to 1 hour after sunset.
Best seasons: Spring through fall
Water: None
Toilets: Vault toilets near the Sensory Trailhead
Nursing benches: Picnic tables near the Sensory Trailhead
Stroller-friendly: No
Potential child hazards: Sheer drops at May's Point
Other trail users: Equestrians

Dogs: Control requirements vary from trail to trail; watch for regulation signs at trailheads and intersections.
Land status: Boulder Open Space and Mountain Parks
Nearest town: Boulder
Fees and permits: Park visitors whose cars are not registered in Boulder County must possess an annual permit or purchase a daily permit at the Realization Point parking lot. Bring cash.
Maps: Boulder OSMP Chautauqua Meadow map
Trail contact: Boulder Open Space and Mountain Parks, 1777 Broadway, Boulder 80302; (303) 441-3440; bouldercolorado.gov/parks-rec/chautauqua-park
Gear suggestions: Fleece jackets and/or windbreakers, sturdy athletic shoes, binoculars, a picnic

FINDING THE TRAILHEAD

From US 36, the Denver Boulder Turnpike, turn onto Baseline Road and drive west. In 1.2 miles you'll pass Chautauqua Park's main entrance at the intersection of Baseline Road and 9th Street. Continue west along Baseline Road. At the hairpin turn, Baseline becomes Flagstaff Road. Watch for bikers and deer as you wind up the road for 3.4 miles to reach the Realization Point parking lot, near the intersection of Flagstaff and Flagstaff Summit Roads. There's parking on either side of Flagstaff Road; the trailhead is at the far end of the lot, to the north of Flagstaff Road.

THE HIKE

There are other flatirons in Boulder, but if you hear somebody talking about *the* Flatirons, they're probably referring to Chautauqua Park's most prominent feature: five numbered flatirons running north–south along the eastern slope of Green Mountain (8,144').

The quickest route to these 300-million-year-old formations departs from the Chautauqua Trailhead, one of the site's most congested areas. For a more peaceful experience, begin your hike at the Realization Point Trailhead.

The Ute Trail contours northeast along Flagstaff Mountain (7,283'). Gentle switchbacks weave through an alpine meadow that's blooming with wildflowers by late May. Spring is also the best time to view the park's diverse wildlife.

With a range of landforms—cliffs, canyons, and plateaus—ecosystems like Chautauqua's can support assorted plant communities that provide habitats for many different animals. Mule deer graze alongside rocky dirt trails, and foxes live in Chautauqua's forested areas. In May, look for wild turkey hens with their poults, or baby turkeys.

If your children don't have enough patience for wildlife viewing, ask them to listen for screeching magpies. Weighing in at a mere half pound, Colorado's black-billed magpies are part of the crow family. Like American crows, they're carrion-eating omnivores.

The forest thickens as the Ute Trail shifts north, and suddenly you're surrounded by ponderosa pines. Ask children to take a few deep breaths. When the sun warms the trees, their bark emits aromas of ice cream and chocolate!

A sensory trail picks up just past the five-way trail intersection with a guideline (look for the white rope) and several interpretive signs with interactive activities. The trail descends to the Sensory Trailhead, near an outhouse and stone shelter set past the Flagstaff Summit east parking lot.

Two trails depart from the Sensory Trailhead. Take the trail to the right. You should be traveling downhill. The next segment of the trail is secluded, so enjoy a few quiet moments as you follow several log steps uphill to a trail post.

FUN FACTOR

MAKE A DAY OF IT AT CHAUTAUQUA.

There's a reason the parking lot near Chautauqua Trailhead is always crowded! Chautauqua Park is packed with tons of family-friendly amenities appealing to every type of recreationist. Back on Baseline Road, visit the Ranger Cottage (adjacent to Chautauqua Trailhead). Inside, there are several interesting taxidermy exhibits, and a ranger's always on hand to chat about local flora and fauna and the site's year-round events programming.

Spread out a blanket on the Chautauqua Lawn, the perfect spot for a game of Frisbee and people watching. If your stomach's rumbling, grab a table at the nearby Chautauqua Dining Hall, serving fresh, farm-to-table fare. Dine outside on the wraparound porch. It overlooks an excellent nature-themed playground where younger kids can play before and after their meal.

Time your visit right, and you might catch a show at Chautauqua Auditorium. Constructed in 1898, the wooden building is a venue for lectures and concerts.

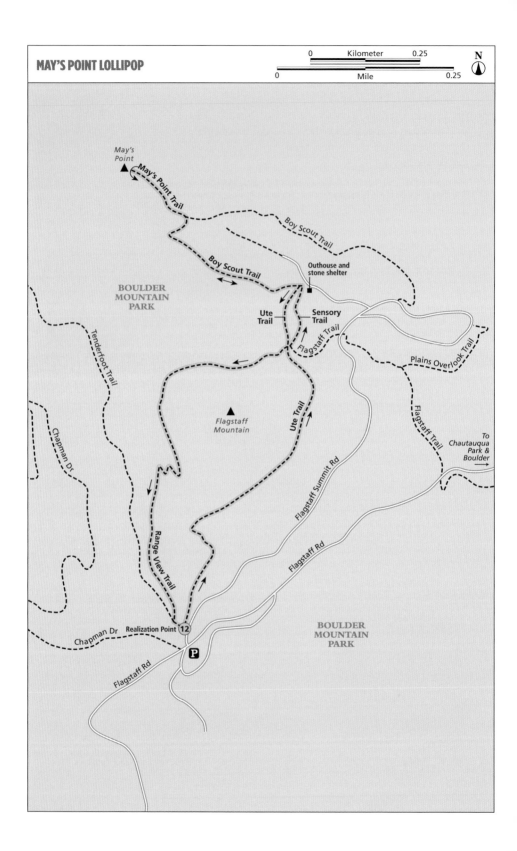

0   Kilometer   0.25

0   Mile   0.25

N

May's Point ▲

May's Point Trail

Boy Scout Trail

Boy Scout Trail

Outhouse and stone shelter

BOULDER MOUNTAIN PARK

Ute Trail

Sensory Trail

Flagstaff Trail

Plains Overlook Trail

Tenderfoot Trail

Flagstaff Mountain ▲

Ute Trail

Chapman Dr

Flagstaff Trail

To Chautauqua Park & Boulder

Flagstaff Summit Rd

Range View Trail

Flagstaff Rd

Chapman Dr   Realization Point 12

P

BOULDER MOUNTAIN PARK

Flagstaff Rd

Turn left, follow a narrow path north, then scramble to the top of the broad rocky outcrop known as May's Point. The 360-degree views are spectacular! But be sure to watch children carefully around the ledges.

When you're ready, retrace your steps to the Sensory Trailhead. Then go back to the five-way trail intersection for the Ute, Flagstaff, and Range View Trails. Turn right onto Range View Trail. This steep, rocky path opens to excellent views of the Indian Peaks Wilderness while traversing the west side of Flagstaff Mountain. As a bonus, there are wildflowers everywhere.

Chautauqua's impressive network of intertwined trails makes it easy for more experienced hikers to extend their route. For a longer trek, park at the Gregory Canyon parking lot, and take Flagstaff Trail straight to May's Point. Families with very young children can skip the Ute and Range View loop altogether by driving up Flagstaff Summit Road to the nature center and beginning the hike from the Flagstaff Summit east parking lot. The nature center is open most weekends.

MILES AND DIRECTIONS

0.0   Start from the Realization Point Trailhead, located behind the self-service parking fee station, and begin hiking uphill on the Ute Trail. Elevation: 6,755 feet.

0.3   Arrive at a fork in the trail. Keep left of the rock.

0.52 Reach a five-way trail junction. Hike straight through it to avoid turning onto the Range View or Flagstaff Trail.

0.54 A short Sensory Loop picks up here. Bear left at the fork, following the white rope (a guideline).

0.6   Walk downhill toward an outhouse and stone shelter. Look for the Sensory Trailhead. Begin hiking downhill toward the Boy Scout Trail.

0.65 Bear right at the sign onto the Boy Scout Trail.

0.86 Reach a May's Point trail post; turn left to hike to May's Point.

0.94 After an easy scramble, the trail resumes.

1.00 The trail ends at the tip of May's Point. Enjoy panoramic views before retracing your steps to the Sensory Trailhead.

1.15 Don't forget to bear right at the post.

1.38 You're back at the Sensory Trailhead. Take the Ute Trail or the Sensory Trail back to the five-way trail intersection for the Ute, Flagstaff, and Range View Trails.

1.47 Turn right at the five-way trail intersection to begin hiking on the Range View Trail.

2.1   Arrive back at the trailhead.

13 WHIPPLE LOOP

Smack-dab in the charismatic town of Buena Vista, the Barbara Whipple Trail System has some of the best entry-level hiking in Colorado. Whipple Main Route is the most popular way to climb Midland Hill. The rocky path travels from the Arkansas River up to an old railroad grade, hovering high enough to afford impressive views of the Collegiate Peaks. Along the trail, young hikers discover kiosks with historic factoids.

Start: Barbara Whipple Trail welcome sign, on the far edge of the River Park parking lot
Distance: 1.95-mile lollipop
Hiking time: 1.5–3 hours
Difficulty: Easy
Elevation gain: 267 feet
Trail surface: Dirt, gravel, and rock
Hours: None posted
Best seasons: Spring through fall
Water: Drinking fountains near the restrooms
Toilets: Flush toilets just past the welcome sign; open seasonally
Nursing benches: At the two scenic overlooks located at 0.8 mile and 1.75 miles
Stroller-friendly: No

Potential child hazards: Rocky trails, a fast-current river
Other trail users: Equestrians, mountain bikers
Dogs: Allowed on-leash
Land status: Bureau of Land Management
Nearest town: Buena Vista
Fees and permits: None
Maps: GARNA Friends of Fourmile Buena Vista Map
Trail contact: Bureau of Land Management Royal Gorge Field Office, 3028 East Main St., Cañon City 81212; (719) 269-8500; www .buenavistacolorado.org/locations/ barbara-whipple-trailhead
Gear suggestions: Sturdy athletic shoes, extra water, sun protection

FINDING THE TRAILHEAD

The simplest way to access Whipple Main Route (6031) is via the pedestrian bridge near the River Park parking lot, located at the end of East Main Street. From US 285, turn right (north) onto Arizona Street. In 2.5 miles, soon after Arizona Street becomes South Court Street, turn right onto East Main Street. (If you're coming from Summit County, take US 24 south, and turn left onto East Main Street.) The parking lot is at the end of the road. Start this hike at the trifold welcome sign.

THE HIKE

The Barbara Whipple Trail System honors a prominent local artist. After relocating to Colorado in the 1970s, Barbara Whipple opened one of the town's first art galleries on East Main Street and cofounded the Arkansas Valley Council on the Arts. She drew inspiration from nature and enjoyed hiking in the Midland Hill area, where her namesake trail is a part of a larger system granting hikers access to 100,000 acres of USDA Forest Service and BLM lands known as Fourmile.

From the trifold welcome sign on the edge of the parking lot, descend a flight of stairs and cross the Arkansas River pedestrian bridge. The bridge was constructed in 1990 to link Buena Vista River Park with the Whipple Trail System. Rails protect children from

falling into the water below. Remind young hikers not to climb the railing, and always keep an eye on children near the river, which is swift in the spring.

After crossing the bridge, look back for a stellar glimpse of Mount Columbia in the distance. About 500 feet down the trail, at a metal trail post, turn left onto the Steep Shortcut. This can be a little confusing, since the trail post is marked "North Loop." The Steep Shortcut is a great option for hikers, because the spur's sharp incline deters bikers. Expect a rocky ascent on a series of switchbacks overlooking Buena Vista. The trail is well marked; be sure to avoid using unofficial trails, blocked with stones.

When the trail dead-ends, turn right to keep hiking along the Steep Shortcut. A left puts you on the North Loop, which will also get you to the old railroad grade. When the Steep Shortcut runs into Whipple Main Route, turn left to follow the Whipple Trail deeper into a piñon pine forest. (For a shorter hike, go right instead and return to the river, where another right turn takes you back to the bridge.)

Whipple Main Route is the widest, most gradual path within the trail system. It's still hard to believe the steep, winding passage was originally created as a stagecoach route and hack road to carry railroad passengers into town.

The Midland Railroad operated from 1887 to 1918. Trains ran high above the river in order to maintain their Leadville-bound elevation. During your 0.75-mile ascent, ask your kids to look back periodically and imagine flying down the bumpy hill in a horse-drawn buggy.

The final push up Whipple Trail is just rugged enough to be fun, and if you need a break, you can stop to read interpretive signs alongside the trail. The sheltered kiosk at 0.5 mile is a great place to grab a photo and hydrate.

The climb is over when you reach the Old Colorado Midland Railroad Grade. Turn left onto a wide dirt road, and follow it toward the North Loop.

FUN FACTOR

PADDLE INTO SUMMER.

From hiking and mountain biking to rock climbing, paragliding, and hot air ballooning, Buena Vista is a hub for outdoor recreation. The town is especially lively in May, when paddling season kicks off.

One of the best ways for families to experience the Arkansas River is at CKS Paddlefest, a free festival held annually over Memorial Day weekend. During Paddlefest, whitewater aficionados converge to rub elbows with big-name paddling manufacturers, top professional athletes, and other industry leaders for a weekend chock-full of education, entertainment, demonstrations, and steeply discounted gear.

If you're new to paddling, start with a flatwater demonstration at the Town Pond at McPhelemy Park, behind the intersection of US 24 and Main Street. Along Main Street you'll find more than a dozen clinics and workshops, covering a range of topics designed to appeal to paddlers of all ages and skill levels. Whitewater courses are available on the river too, home to the Kayak Rodeo, a multiday freestyle competition and one of the festival's most popular spectator events.

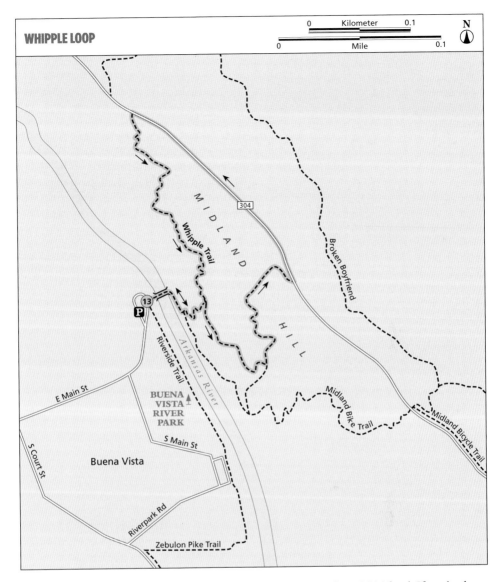

0   Kilometer   0.1

0   Mile   0.1

N

MIDLAND

Whipple Trail

304

Broken Boyfriend

13 P

HILL

Riverside Trail

Arkansas River

E Main St

BUENA VISTA RIVER PARK

S Main St

Midland Bike Trail

Midland Bicycle Trail

S Court St

Buena Vista

Riverpark Rd

Zebulon Pike Trail

Notice any campsites? Dispersed camping is permitted on BLM land. If you've been curious about trying this rugged form of amenity-free camping with your kids, the land alongside the old railroad grade is great for first-timers, since it's close to civilization.

Make a sharp left at 1.25 miles onto the North Loop. The descent to the river is steep, and the undulating North Loop is washed out in several places. Be aware of your surroundings, and you shouldn't have a problem avoiding rocks and unofficial paths.

After hiking along the North Loop for about 0.5 mile, look for the North Loop/ Bridge to Bridge trail post. This should be familiar. Turn right to follow the "Bridge to Bridge" arrow downhill and descend the Steep Shortcut. Back at the river, turn right onto the Whipple Trail and cross the bridge.

For a longer hike, park near Whitewater Park, in the town's funky South Main shopping district. Take Riverside Trail north to reach the pedestrian bridge, then follow the directions below. This option adds 0.5 mile (one way) to the journey. Bonus: You'll pass the Buena Vista Boulder Garden, an enjoyable stop-off for toddlers, preschoolers, and grade-school children.

Every summer, during Gold Rush Days, Buena Vista celebrates its intriguing heritage with a free, multiday festival featuring live music, local art, satisfying food and beer, historical reenactments, toilet seat races, and a legendary burro race called the Burro Race Triple Crown.

MILES AND DIRECTIONS

0.0   Start at the welcome sign. Cross the Arkansas River pedestrian bridge to begin hiking south alongside the water. Elevation: 7,965 feet.

0.08   Turn left at the metal post to climb up the Steep Shortcut.

0.18   Arrive at a three-way trail intersection. Turn right to stay on the Steep Shortcut, which is not identified on the trail post.

0.4   Turn left at the fork in the trail. Begin hiking on the Whipple Main Route.

0.5   Pass a kiosk with several interpretive signs.

0.75   Reach the Old Colorado Midland Railroad Grade. Turn left onto this historic dirt road.

0.8   Pass a scenic overlook and kiosk.

1.24   Arrive at a North Loop trail post. Turn left to descend.

1.76   Pass a bench, then come to the three-way trail intersection you encountered at 0.18 mile. Turn right to merge onto the Steep Shortcut by following the "Bridge to Bridge" arrow.

1.86   When you reach the water, bear right onto Whipple Main Route and hike toward the bridge.

1.92   Cross the Arkansas River pedestrian bridge.

1.95   Climb the stairs and arrive back at the parking lot.

SUMMER

The weather's warm, the days are long, and trails are finally clear of mud and snow. As if that weren't enough, brilliant wildflowers are blooming from the Eastern Plains to the Rocky Mountains. It's no wonder summer is often considered prime hiking season in Colorado! With plenty of sun protection and water, you're ready to thoroughly explore mountain passes, alpine lakes, and hidden waterfalls in Colorado's "High Country," where temperatures are often 20 degrees cooler than on the Front Range. If your kids have a months-long break from school, use summer vacation to your advantage by planning memorable road trips to mountain towns and far-reach destinations like Durango (see Hike 16), Pagosa Springs (see hike 22), and Grand Junction (see hike 33).

14 CASCADE CREEK LOOP

In the Chalk Creek Canyon area, hikers discover an undisturbed backcountry where 14,000-foot peaks frame impeccable aspen-filled valleys. Rerouted in 2019, the new Cascade Creek Loop extends toward Agnes Vaille Falls, a modest waterfall flowing from a rocky shelf below Mount Princeton, one of Colorado's 14ers. For families, the trail delivers a remote hiking experience without excessive mileage.

Start: Cascade Creek Loop Trailhead
Distance: 1.1-mile loop
Hiking time: 1–2 hours
Difficulty: Easy
Elevation gain: 365 feet
Trail surface: Dirt and rock
Hours: None posted
Best seasons: Summer
Water: None
Toilets: None
Nursing benches: A wooden bench at 0.6 mile
Stroller-friendly: No
Potential child hazards: Sliding rocks, waterfall
Other trail users: Equestrians, mountain bikers

Dogs: Must be leashed or under voice command at all times
Land status: USDA Forest Service
Nearest towns: Buena Vista and Salida
Fees and permits: None
Maps: USGS Chalk Lake
Trail contact: Pike & San Isabel National Forests, Salida Ranger District, 2840 Kachina Dr., Pueblo 81008; (719) 539-3591; www .fs.usda.gov/recarea/psicc/ recarea/?recid=12629
Gear suggestions: Layers, fleece jackets and/or windbreakers, waterproof footwear, extra water, binoculars, a paper map and compass

FINDING THE TRAILHEAD

From Buena Vista, take US 285 south toward the unincorporated village of Nathrop. After passing a post office, turn right (west) onto Chalk Creek Drive (a well-maintained dirt road), which is also labeled "CR 162." Continue for approximately 8.7 miles to the Cascade Creek Trailhead; park in the pullout lot to your right.

THE HIKE

The drive up CR 162 is flush with postcard-perfect views of the Sawatch Range. Even if you're moving at a snail's pace on the bumpy dirt road, there's plenty of visual stimulation. Park in the small pullout lot on the right side of Chalk Creek Drive, about 4 miles past Chalk Lake Campground.

Two paths depart, in opposite directions, on either side of the Cascade Creek kiosk. The Cascade Creek Trail makes a loop, so hikers can go either way. The most direct path to the waterfall is an out-and-back trek on the trail to the left. We'll go right to make a counterclockwise loop.

About 650 feet up the trail, the terrain changes abruptly from packed dirt to sand. The trail's a little washed out and can be temporarily tricky to follow. Pay close attention to trail markers as you hike. Because there's no cell phone service, you must pack a paper map and/or download a map to your smartphone in advance. The last thing you want to do is get lost with your kids!

FUN FACTOR

TAKE A SIDE TRIP TO ST. ELMO'S.

Deep at the end of Chalk Creek Drive lies the dusty ghost town of St. Elmo. Despite its notoriety, and spot on the National Register of Historic Places, the abandoned gold and silver mining settlement is so far off the beaten path, it's often eerily quiet.

St. Elmo has the characteristics of a full town. It was founded in 1880 and thrived, only briefly, with completion of the Denver, South Park & Pacific Railroad. After peaking at 2,000 residents, St. Elmo's population rode the last train out of town and never came back, so the story goes.

Start with a quick visit to the Ghost Town Guest House, an authentic and operational three-story bed-and-breakfast at the top of Main Street. It's across from the St. Elmo General Store, selling drinks, snacks, and trinkets seasonally through September.

Families get a sense of what life was like in Colorado during the gold rush while perusing a series of structures and storefronts preserved with classic Main Street finishes. Can't-miss buildings include an old courthouse and the one-room schoolhouse, accessible via a bridge north of "downtown." Step inside to view the interiors of these buildings, staged with 1880s furnishings. It's like a trip to a living history museum, but without the interpreters.

Take a stroll to Iron City Cemetery. To get there, backtrack on CR 162 for 0.25 mile until you reach the turnoff for CR 292. (There's pullout parking where 162 and 292 meet.) Walk down CR 292, and follow the wide dirt road through Iron City Campground until you arrive at the cemetery's enchanting white gate.

Up the fun factor by letting older children use the compass and map to practice orienteering. Kids of all ages can use binoculars to look for mountain goats and bighorn sheep.

At the intersection at 0.65 mile, hikers are funneled right at a Cascade Creek sign. The site's previous trail—Agnes Vaille Falls Trail—was rerouted after a large rockslide event claimed several lives in 2013. While the previous trail led hikers up to the falls, the new loop maintains a safer distance. Obey the parameters. They're for your safety.

A few hundred feet past the trail sign, the creek reappears. With young children, stop at the water and enjoy the gushing stream. Older children can use large stepping-stones to cross the water. Walk a few feet down the trail for a great view of Agnes Vaille Falls, wedged between 14,197-foot Mount Princeton to the north and 14,269-foot Mount Antero to the south.

After backtracking to the Cascade Creek trail sign, turn right at the fork to complete the loop. On your way back to the parking lot, you'll encounter several abrupt turns while traveling downhill toward a prominent stone-and-wood bench. Do your best to stay on-trail and prevent additional erosion.

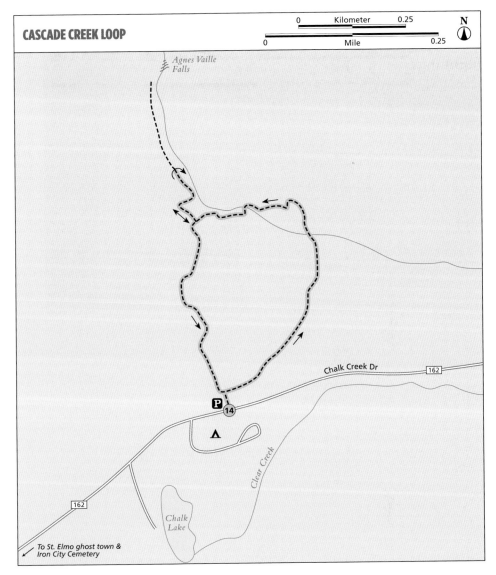

During this final stretch, take in big views of Mount Antero, named for Uintah Ute Chief Antero. With its rich deposits of aquamarine and other gemstones, the towering peak has been called the highest gem field in North America.

Before you reach the parking lot, an interpretive sign reveals the history behind the falls, honoring mountaineer Agnes Vaille. Born in 1890, Agnes was a gutsy woman who joined the Red Cross in France during World War I and later became secretary of the Denver Chamber of Commerce. She had a passion for hiking and planned to explore all of Colorado's highest summits. During a winter ascent of Longs Peak, Agnes slipped on ice and froze to death after surviving the initial fall down the north face of the mountain—a powerful reminder of nature's sovereignty.

Speaking of nature, you're hovering around 9,000 feet on this hike. Chug more water than you think you need, wear sunscreen, and encourage kids to go slowly, watching for signs of altitude sickness, which can include nausea, vomiting, and general malaise.

MILES AND DIRECTIONS

0.0 Start on the dirt trail to the right of the Cascade Creek kiosk. Elevation: 8,750.

0.15 Cross a stream. A more-obvious trail resumes momentarily.

0.2 Pass a trail marker.

0.3 Use stone steps to cross a small ditch.

0.4 Follow stone steps uphill. The trail curves right and makes a hairpin turn at 0.45 mile.

0.5 Cross the stream, and continue ascending.

0.55 Reach a trail sign. Turn right to hike toward the waterfall.

0.6 Pass a wooden bench.

0.65 Arrive at a Cascade Creek Trail sign. Parents with older children can bear right at the sign and, a few hundred feet later, use stepping-stones to cross the stream before scrambling uphill. View the waterfall from a safe distance before retracing your steps to the sign.

0.75 Turn right at the Cascade Creek Trail sign to complete the loop.

0.8 Observe several hairpin turns in the washed-out trail as you travel downhill toward a stone-and-wood bench.

1.0 Reach an interpretive sign about Agnes Vaille.

1.1 Arrive back at the Cascade Creek kiosk.

15 SPRUCE MOUNTAIN TRAIL

Spruce Mountain Open Space is a forested meadow situated in the South I-25 Conservation Corridor, a wildlife passage linking Greenland Ranch to Pike National Forest. The secluded 932-acre property contains several shaded hiking trails that'll keep families cool all summer long. For the best views, ascend Spruce Mountain, and cross the tree-covered mesa to reach Windy Point (7,605 feet).

Start: Spruce Mountain Open Space interpretive kiosk
Distance: 5.0-mile lollipop
Hiking time: 2.5–5 hours
Difficulty: Moderate to difficult
Elevation gain: 494 feet
Trail surface: Natural surface with minimal rock
Hours: Open daily, 1 hour before sunrise to 1 hour after sunset
Best seasons: Year-round
Water: Available at a spigot at the nearby Greenland Open Space Trailhead
Toilets: Portable toilets in the parking lot
Nursing benches: Several spaced out along the route
Stroller-friendly: No
Potential child hazards: Steep ledges with sheer drops, icy trail conditions in winter

Other trail users: Equestrians, mountain bikers
Dogs: Must be leashed
Land status: Douglas County Division of Open Space and Natural Resources
Nearest town: Larkspur
Fees and permits: None
Maps: Douglas County Division of Open Space and Natural Resources Spruce Mountain Open Space Trail
Trail contact: Douglas County Division of Open Space and Natural Resources, 100 3rd St., Castle Rock 80104; (303) 660-7495; www.douglas.co.us/dcoutdoors/open-space-properties/spruce-mountain-open-space-and-trail
Gear suggestions: Windbreakers, sturdy athletic shoes or hiking boots, trekking poles, binoculars, extra water, snacks, a picnic

FINDING THE TRAILHEAD

From I-25, take exit 167 (Greenland Road), and drive west. In 0.25 mile turn left (south) onto Noe Road. Bypassing the Greenland Open Space Trailhead, continue right on the main gravel road. Drive over two sets of railroad tracks. In 1 mile, turn left (south) onto Spruce Mountain Road. The parking lot for Spruce Mountain Open Space will be on your right. Alternatively, exit at Larkspur and drive south 6 miles along Spruce Mountain Road to reach this entrance. The trailhead is at the far end of the parking lot.

THE HIKE

The climb up Spruce Mountain's eastern flank is a physically demanding trek that's flush with tranquil scenery laid out below a ponderosa pine and Douglas fir forest. With kids, take the ascent slowly, and use the Oak Shortcut (included in the directions below).

The first scenic lookout appears at 0.2 mile, but to reach the first spectacular lookout you'll have to complete a tough, 0.85-mile climb to the top of the mesa.

After crossing Pine Junction, the trail winds past monolith rock formations before arriving at Greenland Overlook, revealing breathtaking views of Greenland Open Space, along with Pikes Peak, the Palmer Divide, Carpenter Creek, and thousands of acres of

protected wilderness. Break for water and snacks, and spend some time enjoying the fruits of your labor. If you're hiking with young children, Greenland Overlook makes a great "summit." When you're ready, simply turn around and retrace your steps to the trailhead for a 1.7-mile adventure.

Otherwise, continue to Windy Point (7,605'). There are huge drops to the left: Be cautious with children while moving across the mesa. Paddock's Point comes into view just beyond the trail marker at 1.1 miles.

The looped segment of the hike begins at the fork in the trail at 1.25 miles. It's fine to go either way. We'll make a clockwise circle around the mesa by walking straight past the marker and merging onto Upper Loop Trail.

Take in aerial views of Palmer Lake before passing a picnic area to the left. From here it's another 0.2 flat and easy mile to Windy Point, a rocky outcropping opening to incredible views of Mount Herman (9,063') and Pikes Peak (14,115').

Past Windy Point, the trail makes a hairpin turn to begin tracking back toward Greenland Overlook. Bear right at the junction at 2.8 miles, and hike slightly uphill on the Spruce Mountain Trail. Don't turn left onto the service road unless you'd like to extend the prescribed route by hiking back on the Eagle Pass Trail. If you're thinking about giving this a try, keep in mind that the service road is steep and often rutted, making it potentially difficult for children.

After circling the mesa, you're back at Upper Loop Junction. Go straight through the trail intersection, and return to Greenland Lookout. It's all downhill from here—but downhill doesn't necessarily mean easy on a steep trail like this one! Remind children to watch out for rocks and roots, and when you come to Pine Junction, don't forget to take the Oak Shortcut back to your car.

FUN FACTOR

WALK INTO A REAL-LIFE FAIRY TALE.

Larkspur was once a major lumbering site for railroad ties, telegraph poles, and firewood, but today the tiny town is known for its massive Renaissance Festival, a popular fair set in a sixteenth-century Tudor village, held over several weekends between June and August.

Part living history experience, part blowout bash, the annual festival is a life-size replica of a rollicking European festival day. Hundreds of interpreters and volunteers stroll the streets decked out in authentic costumes, delighting kids and kids-at-heart with games and live entertainment, including jousting competitions, fire blowing, and acrobatics. Other highlights include the exotic live carousel, a giant swing, and an internationally renowned mime.

From roast turkey legs and "steak on a stake" to fresh baked goods, the food at the festival is fit for kings and queens. Village streets are lined with shops offering handmade wares such as jewelry, clothing and costumes, weapons, pottery, and shoes. What is really fascinating are the live blacksmithing, pottery, woodworking, and glassblowing demonstrations. Get tickets online, where you'll find scheduling information for the current season.

SPRUCE MOUNTAIN TRAIL

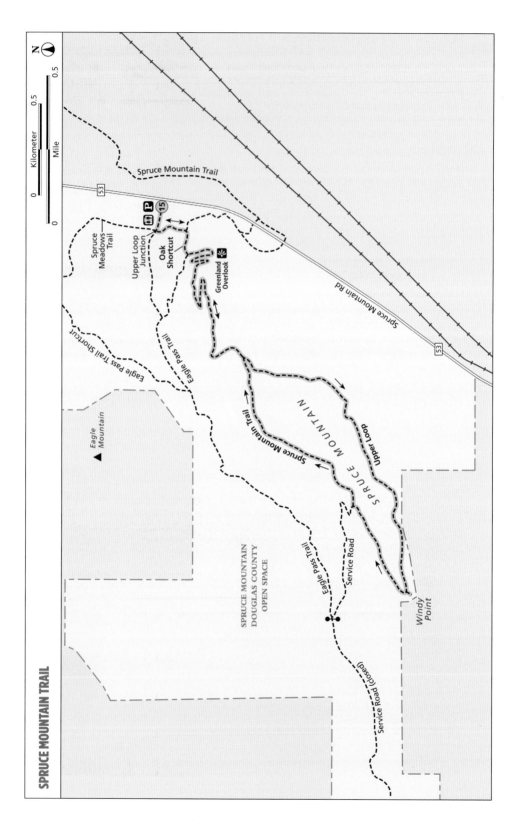

N

Kilometer
0   0.5

Mile
0   0.5

Spruce Mountain Trail

Spruce Meadows Trail

Upper Loop Junction

Oak Shortcut

Greenland Overlook

Eagle Pass Trail

Eagle Pass Trail Shortcut

Eagle Mountain

SPRUCE MOUNTAIN
DOUGLAS COUNTY
OPEN SPACE

Spruce Mountain Trail

S P R U C E   M O U N T A I N

Upper Loop

Service Road

Eagle Pass Trail

Service Road (Closed)

Windy Point

Spruce Mountain Rd

53

MILES AND DIRECTIONS

0.0 Start at the Spruce Mountain Open Space kiosk and welcome sign, and walk toward the obvious trailhead at the far end of the parking lot. In 150 feet, pass a trail marker. Turn left to take the Oak Shortcut. Elevation: 6,727 feet.

0.2 Pass a bench and scenic overlook.

0.3 Reach a three-way trail intersection. Turn left, following the arrows on the sign toward Mountain Top and Greenland Lookout.

0.85 Arrive at Greenland Lookout.

1.1 After passing a trail marker, arrive at Paddock's Point.

1.25 Pass another marker. Keep straight to begin the Upper Loop Trail.

2.1 Pass a scenic overlook and picnic tables.

2.4 Arrive at the turnoff for Windy Point. Follow a narrow dirt pathway to this scenic overlook. Admire the views before returning to the main trail.

2.8 When you reach the three-way trail intersection, turn right to take the Spruce Mountain Trail back to the trailhead.

3.5 You're back at the Upper Loop Junction. Stay straight at the trail marker, and retrace your steps to Greenland Overlook.

4.55 After descending the mesa, bear right at Pine Junction to return to the trailhead via the Oak Shortcut.

5.0 Go right at the fork, and arrive back at the trailhead.

16 SPUD LAKE TRAIL

Although it's listed as an "easy" hike on the USDA Forest Service website, the ascent to Spud Lake can be a challenge if you don't live 9,000 feet above sea level. The target—a pristine alpine lake—is worth the effort, especially in the summer, when the weather's pleasant and wildflowers adorn the rugged scenery. Pack a picnic and laze by the lake before returning to the trailhead, where a beaver pond delivers real-world ecology lessons.

Start: Spud Lake Trailhead, marked "661" on the San Juan National Forest recreation map
Distance: 2.2 miles out and back
Hiking time: 2–4 hours
Difficulty: Moderate
Elevation gain: 380 feet
Trail surface: Dirt, rock, and gravel
Hours: None posted
Best seasons: Summer and fall
Water: None
Toilets: None
Nursing benches: None
Stroller-friendly: No
Potential child hazards: Altitude sickness, sheer drops, a large lake
Other trail users: Equestrians, mountain bikers

Dogs: Should be leashed or under voice control at all times
Land status: USDA Forest Service
Nearest town: Durango
Fees and permits: None
Maps: USGS Geologic map of the Durango quadrangle, southwestern Colorado
Trail contact: USDA Forest Service, San Juan National Forest, 15 Burnett Ct., Durango 81301; (970) 247-4874; www.fs.usda.gov/recarea/sanjuan/recreation/hiking/recarea/?recid=43242&actid=50
Gear suggestions: Waterproof hiking sandals, trekking poles, sunscreen and/or sun-protective clothing, Nuun tablets, high-energy snacks, a picnic

FINDING THE TRAILHEAD

From Durango, travel 29 miles north on US 550 to FR 591 (Old Lime Creek Highway), located on the right side of the road immediately after a hairpin curve. After passing a sign for Spud Lake, follow Old Lime Creek Highway uphill for a bumpy 3 miles. A high-clearance vehicle is highly recommended. The trail appears just past a large lily pond. Look left to spot the USDA Forest Service trailhead, labeled "661." Parking is available near the trailhead and along the old dirt road.

THE HIKE

You're in for a bumpy drive up Old Lime Creek Road, part of the original passage from Durango to Silverton. After a few rough miles, a trailhead appears on the left side of this road, at the bottom of a draw.

This USDA Forest Service trail isn't actually labeled "Spud Lake," or even "Potato Lake," its nickname. It's simply listed as Trail 661 on the San Juan National Forest recreation map. To the right of the map, a narrow, rocky path picks up between two wooden posts. This is the Spud Lake Trail.

You're hiking in an area that has been preserved and protected since 1905, when Theodore Roosevelt signed a Presidential Proclamation designating nearly 2 million acres of land for a national forest in southwestern Colorado. Over the years, the federal land has been known by a variety of names, including the Montezuma National Forest. Today it's

the San Juan National Forest, where hundreds of trail miles weave across a landscape that ranges dramatically, from high-desert mesas to barren alpine peaks.

The hike to Spud Lake is pure rock at first. Before long, difficult terrain gives way to a friendlier dirt trail passing through thick aspen glades.

You don't have to go far—just 0.4 mile—to get your first aspen-framed view of Mount Engineer, a distinctive 12,000-foot summit rising southwest of Silverton. Gray-rock Peak and Spud Mountain are also visible from the Spud Lake Trail, along with the Needle Mountains to the east. With so much to see, it's easy to forget about what's below. Remind children to watch for rocks and roots while hiking.

Past the 0.5-mile mark, hikers who aren't used to the altitude get some relief when the trail levels out and meanders through a pretty meadow. By June, wildflowers dominate the grassland; many also bloom alongside the trail, which skirts large outcroppings while following a small creek that drains from the lake ahead.

Don't be disappointed by the small body of water that appears through the trees at 1.05 miles. This is not your final destination. (But if you want to tease your kids, now's the time to act disappointed!)

Keep following the Spud Lake Trail, and you'll come to an immaculate alpine lake with a broad shore in the shadow of Spud Mountain, sometimes referred to as Potato Hill, rising to 11,871 feet directly over the water. Look for the Twilight Peaks towering to the east at more than 13,000 feet. North Twilight is the highest summit in the West Needles Range of the San Juan Mountains.

The lake is stocked with trout, and fishing is fair. But the best thing to do is skip a few rocks with your children before exploring the looped path wrapping Spud Lake. There's a good chance your kids will find wild strawberries and raspberries growing around the banks. Take some time to listen for birdcalls you wouldn't normally hear:

FUN FACTOR

TRY A HANDS-ON ECOLOGY LESSON.

Did you notice the lily pad pond across the road from the Spud Lake Trailhead? Walk to the edge of it, and instruct your children to quietly observe their surroundings.

Exploring this unique habitat, kids can learn all about beavers. Weighing in at 40 to 60 pounds, the continent's largest rodents are related to rats, mice, and squirrels. The beaver's most noticeable feature is its broad tail, used to steer while swimming, similar to how we humans use a boat's rudder.

Beavers are hard to spot in the wild because they're shy and nocturnal. The entrance to a beaver's lodge is underwater, so even if you visit the pond near dawn or dusk, you probably won't see the critters with your naked eye.

Listen for them instead. If you hear a loud slapping sound against the water, that means a beaver has spotted you. It's using its tail to sound a warning to its buddies.

Beavers have many body parts that are shaped for a specific purpose. Huge front teeth, used for cutting logs, are another example of an adaptation. During the day, ask children to feel for beaver tooth marks in aspen stumps alongside the pond. Then look around for a beaver lodge. Beavers build lodges, or homes, out of sticks, logs, rocks, and mud.

Back in Durango, take children to the Powerhouse, an interactive science center built inside a coal-fired steam-power AC generating plant. The museum's rotating exhibits are designed to appeal to all ages, and an on-site MakerLab is the perfect place to release some STEAM creativity.

The area provides tremendous opportunities for four-season birding. Dispersed campsites are found near the lake, and permits aren't required.

After enjoying the lake, turn around and relish a quick descent to the trailhead. If you're hiking with older children and need a longer route, park at the first parking lot you pass on your right, when you come in on Old Lime Creek Highway. It's a straight shot to the trailhead across the dirt road, with plenty of enjoyable scenery. This option adds 5.0 extra miles to the hike, for a total 7.2 miles round-trip.

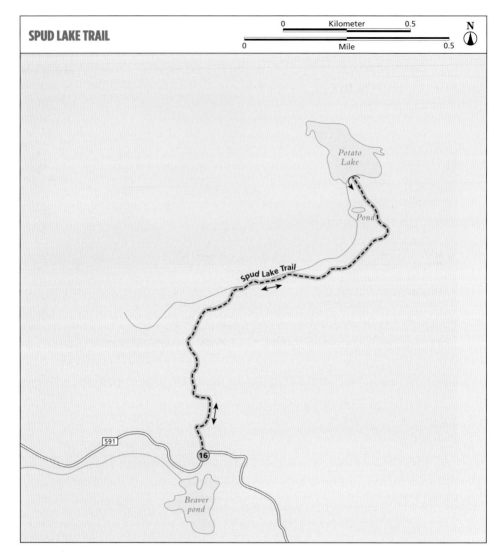

MILES AND DIRECTIONS

0.0   Start from the Spud Lake Trailhead (661), and walk through two wooden posts onto a very rocky trail. Elevation: 9,360 feet.

0.3   Pass a clearing to the left; continue hiking straight on the main trail.

0.4   Look left for a stunning view of Mount Engineer.

1.05   Arrive at a small body of water. Keep following the trail until you come to the larger lake.

1.1   Reach Spud Lake, the terminus of the Spud Lake Trail, and enjoy the majestic landscape before backtracking to the trailhead.

2.2   Arrive back at the trailhead.

17 PETROGLYPH POINT TRAIL

Mesa Verde National Park is a bucket list destination with eight trails laid out among nearly 5,000 known archaeological sites, including 600 cliff dwellings. The hardest thing about a day trip to Mesa Verde is deciding what to do! A guided tour is a must. You'll also want to explore portions of the 52,000-acre site on your own. For young hikers, Petroglyph Point Trail packs a lot of punch with excellent views of Spruce and Navajo Canyons plus a well-preserved petroglyph panel.

Start: Petroglyph Point Trailhead, below Spruce Tree House
Distance: 2.6-mile loop
Hiking time: 1.5–3 hours
Difficulty: Moderate
Elevation loss: 206 feet
Trail surface: Dirt
Hours: Park road open 24/7. Trail hours vary by season; check the park's website for up-to-date information.
Best seasons: Mesa Verde National Park is open year-round, but some areas are closed in winter.
Water: Inside Chapin Mesa Archeological Museum
Toilets: Flush toilets inside Chapin Mesa Archeological Museum
Nursing benches: None along the trail
Stroller-friendly: No

Potential child hazards: Dehydration, sun exposure, steep drops along the canyon wall
Other trail users: None
Dogs: Not permitted on trails within national park boundaries
Land status: National Park Service
Nearest towns: Cortez and Mancos
Fees and permits: Park entry fee; National Parks and Federal Recreational Lands Pass accepted
Maps: NPS Petroglyph Point Trail
Trail contact: Mesa Verde National Park, PO Box 8, Mesa Verde 81330; (970) 529-4465; www.nps.gov/meve/index.htm
Gear suggestions: Sunscreen, sun-protective clothing, sunglasses, brimmed hats, extra water, Nuun tablets, binoculars, Dramamine for children who get carsick

FINDING THE TRAILHEAD

From Cortez, drive east on US 160 for 10 miles to reach the turnoff for Mesa Verde National Park. Take Chapin Mesa Road south for 21 winding miles. After driving for approximately 45 minutes, you'll reach the Chapin Mesa Archeological Museum. Petroglyph Point Trail takes off just below the museum, in front of the Spruce Tree House Overlook.

THE HIKE

With its fascinating human history and geology galore, Mesa Verde is one of those great summertime destinations where parents can sneak in educational tidbits while enjoying the outdoors with their kids.

The first thing to do is check your gas tank. You'll drive for at least 50 miles inside this massive park, and the only place to buy gas on-site is at Morefield Campground.

GPS is not reliable, and cell service is very limited past the entrance sign. So next, drop by the Mesa Verde Visitor and Research Center for a paper map and to purchase tickets for Cliff Palace, Balcony House, and/or Long House tours (discussed at the end of this hike). With interactive exhibits, informational signs, and restrooms, the visitor center is

FUN FACTOR

TAKE A CLOSER LOOK.

You drove this far; you might as well shell out a few bucks for a guided tour of Cliff Palace, Balcony House, or Long House. Offered seasonally, tours are the only way to get up close to the ruins of ancient cliff dwellings. The park's interpretive guides know a lot about the area, which means you and your kids will know a lot too by the end of your adventure.

The hour-long tour of Balcony House is a good option for families craving adventure. During the tour, visitors climb a 32-foot ladder, crawl through an 18-inch-wide and 12-foot-long tunnel, and then climb up a 60-foot open cliff face with stone steps and two 10-foot ladders to exit.

Mesa Verde's largest dwelling, Cliff Palace, is a better bet for cautious guests. On the hour-long, 0.25-mile journey, you'll still get some thrills while descending uneven stone steps and climbing four ladders.

There aren't any height or age restrictions for tours, so technically they're "all ages." But children must be capable of climbing ladders by themselves to participate. If not, they'll have to be carried in a backpack or baby carrier. Purchase timed-entry tickets at the Mesa Verde Visitor and Research Center.

a good place to stretch before driving across the park toward Spruce Tree House, the third-largest and best-preserved cliff dwelling.

Spruce Tree House was closed to the public in 2015 due to unstable rocks, but it's easy to view the 130-room dwelling from Petroglyph Point Trail and overlooks outside the Chapin Mesa Archeological Museum.

The museum contains exhibits, dioramas, and a short film tracing the lives of the Ancestral Puebloan people who inhabited the area between 600 and 1300 CE. In the museum gift store, re-up on snacks and water, and check in with an attendant. Hikers are required to register before using the Petroglyph Point Trail.

Petroglyph Point and Spruce Canyon Trails share a trailhead, and both trails begin on a paved path that fades to dirt at 0.1 mile, right before the routes split. Follow the signs to continue on the Petroglyph Point Trail.

At 0.5 mile look slightly right to spot cliff dwellings in the distance, across Spruce Canyon, below charred remnants of 2002's Long Mesa Fire.

By now, the trail is narrow, rugged, and rocky. In another 0.5 mile, you'll discover a cave known as a grotto. If your kids are tempted to climb on the cave's masonry walls, this is a great time to remind them how important it is to tread lightly, especially in historically significant areas. If kids do their part by staying on designated trails, future hikers can enjoy Mesa Verde for generations to come.

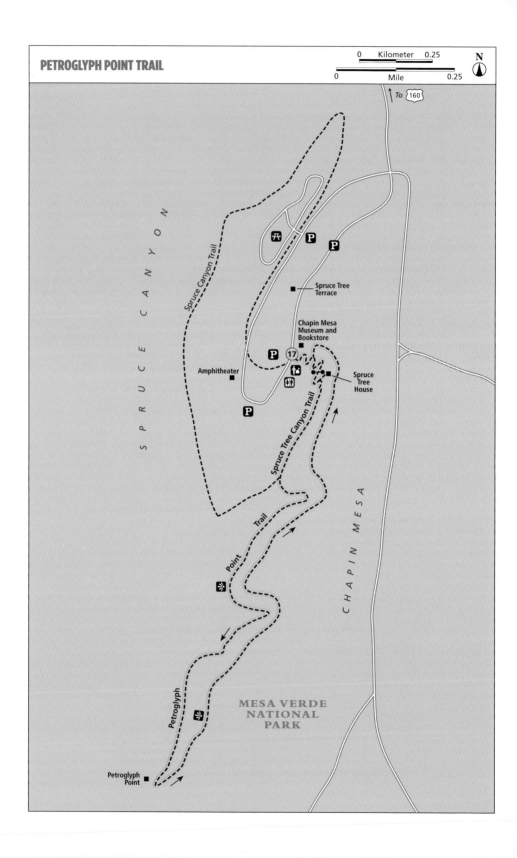

PETROGLYPH POINT TRAIL

0   Kilometer   0.25

0   Mile   0.25

N

To 160

SPRUCE CANYON

Spruce Canyon Trail

Spruce Tree Terrace

Chapin Mesa Museum and Bookstore

17

Amphitheater

Spruce Tree Canyon Trail

Spruce Tree House

CHAPIN MESA

Point Trail

Petroglyph

MESA VERDE NATIONAL PARK

Petroglyph Point

Another 0.4 mile down the trail, look for the trail's namesake, a large petroglyph panel that you really can't miss. Ask children to decipher the art carved into the rocks. In 1942, four Hopi men visited Mesa Verde National Park and interpreted some of the petroglyphs. The modern-day interpretations are provided in the "Petroglyph Trail Guide," available at the trailhead for a donation. How does your family's reading stack up?

Past the petroglyph panel, prepare for a short scramble up a large stone staircase. Kids won't mind using their hands and feet to get to the top, where hikers are rewarded with aerial views and an easy return to the museum. Careful during this last stretch: There are steep drop-offs along the canyon wall.

Mesa Verde National Park gets tons of foot traffic in July and August. Roll through in September for a less-crowded experience.

MILES AND DIRECTIONS

0.0	Start on the paved path at the Petroglyph Point Trailhead, just below the Chapin Mesa Archeological Museum. Elevation: 6,950 feet.
0.1	Arrive at a trail intersection; continue straight to stay on the Petroglyph Point Trail. Do not turn onto the Spruce Canyon Trail.
0.5	Ask your children to look through the trees to their right. Can they spot the cliff dwellings across the canyon, below the ledge? Binoculars are helpful.
1.1	Reach a grotto containing the remains of a small cliff dwelling.
1.5	Look for a long panel filled with petroglyphs. Begin a short but steep scramble up a series of large stone steps. At the top, follow the gravel trail back to the museum.
1.7	Pass trail marker #33, then look across the canyon. An alcove on the highest rock ledge provides another opportunity to view ruins.
2.6	Arrive back at the museum and parking lot near the trailhead.

18 MOUNT SANITAS HISTORY HIKE

Mount Sanitas is shrouded in local history. The 3.3-mile trek to the top of its rocky summit delivers a challenging ascent ending in a series of scrambles that are tough enough to be fun without requiring technical mountaineering skills or equipment.

Start: Mount Sanitas Trailhead
Distance: 3.3-mile lollipop
Hiking time: 2–4 hours
Difficulty: Moderate to difficult
Elevation gain: 1,150 feet
Trail surface: Dirt and gravel; very rocky near the summit
Hours: Boulder OSMP trails open 24/7; Centennial Trailhead parking lot open 5 a.m. to 11 p.m.
Best seasons: Summer and fall
Water: None
Toilets: An outhouse on the far end of the Centennial Trailhead parking lot
Nursing benches: Available 1.2 miles into the described route
Stroller-friendly: With a stroller, try an out-and-back hike on the Sanitas Valley Trail.

Potential child hazards: Falling on the scramble to the summit
Other trail users: Equestrians
Dogs: Allowed; control requirements vary from trail to trail.
Land status: Boulder Open Space and Mountain Parks
Nearest town: Boulder
Fees and permits: None
Maps: Boulder OSMP Centennial / Sanitas
Trail contact: Boulder Open Space and Mountain Parks, 1777 Broadway, Boulder 80302; (303) 441-3440; bouldercolorado.gov/osmp/mount-sanitas-trailhead
Gear suggestions: Sturdy athletic shoes or hiking boots, trekking poles, sunscreen, sun-protective clothing, high-energy snacks, Nuun tablets, ample water, walkie-talkies

FINDING THE TRAILHEAD

From Boulder, take Broadway north to Mapleton Avenue. Turn left (west) onto Mapleton Avenue and drive for 0.9 mile to the Centennial Trailhead parking lot, located on the left (south) side of the street. From this lot, you'll backtrack on foot to reach the trailhead. Two pullout lots precede the Centennial Trailhead parking lot. To begin your hike from one of the pullouts, walk west until you reach the trailhead.

THE HIKE

At the Mount Sanitas welcome sign, ask school-age children to read the name of the area's towering summit aloud. If they pronounce the mountain "san-EE-tis," placing emphasis on a long "e" sound, give them a quick social studies lesson while hiking along the wide gravel trail wedged between Mount Sanitas and the Hogback Ridge.

John Harvey Kellogg—you know him from his cereal!—was a Seventh Day Adventist practicing medicine at the turn of the twentieth century, proffering the then–novel idea that diet plays a role in one's overall health. In 1894 Dr. Kellogg opened the Boulder-Colorado Sanitarium and Hospital. Tuberculosis sanatoriums were cropping up across Colorado, but treatment at Kellogg's sanitarium was spa-like. By 1904, people with communicable diseases were prohibited at the Boulder-Colorado Sanitarium and Hospital, which operated its own dairy and a natural food factory.

KYLE VELTE

Because the name Sanitas is derived from the word "sanitarium," the correct pronunciation is "SAN-eh-tis," emphasis on the first syllable. There's much more to learn at Boulder's Carnegie Library, where you'll find information about the sanitarium's history, including bulletins, photographs, and personal histories.

At the intersection of the Sanitas Valley and Dakota Ridge Trails, see if your kids can nail the mountain's correct pronunciation before ascending Dakota Ridge via a rocky course offering bird's-eye views of the draw below.

You're using the same trail sanitarium guests once roamed. In an effort to get his clients outdoors, Kellogg built several stone structures throughout the area. Look for a smokestack past the trail junction at 0.4 mile. It was part of the original sanitarium, along with a nearby stone shelter and the remains of an arch.

Dakota Ridge Trail continues for another 0.8 mile, passing interesting rock formations before reaching a scenic overlook and three-way intersection of the Dakota Ridge and Sanitas Valley Trails.

Brochures for Kellogg's sanatorium promoted not just the hospital's facilities but also its activities, including burro rides up Mount Sanitas. A brochure from 1902 read: "Nearly everyone can reach the peak by simply taking his time."

That's still true today! But if your kids aren't ready for a burro-free ascent, turn left at the trail post and enjoy an easy, 1-mile-long stroll down the Sanitas Valley Trail. Turn right at Mapleton to get back to your car.

If you're following the directions below, go right on the Sanitas Valley Trail to begin climbing to the 6,863-foot summit. The Sanitas Valley Trail becomes the East Ridge

FUN FACTOR

ROGER THAT.

Our friends the Hartleys suggested the hike up Mount Sanitas for this book, and they joined us on the trek. For school-age kids, everything's more fun when friends are involved. But what really made this hike an adventure were the walkie-talkies.

The Hartleys carry two-way radio transceivers when they hike, and their son is encouraged to hike slightly ahead of his parents, keeping in touch on his walkie-talkie. After years of trying to get my kids to "keep up," I couldn't believe how much faster they moved when they were the ones blazing the trail.

Children should hike ahead of their parents only if they're old enough to follow directions and you trust them to stay on the trail and remain within eyeshot. Give kids a whistle in case they need to call for help, and teach them what to do if they get lost.

Once they realize they're lost, children should stay put by hugging a tree or making a nest—whatever activity will get them to stop walking. Then your child should use a whistle and their voice to call out frequently until help arrives.

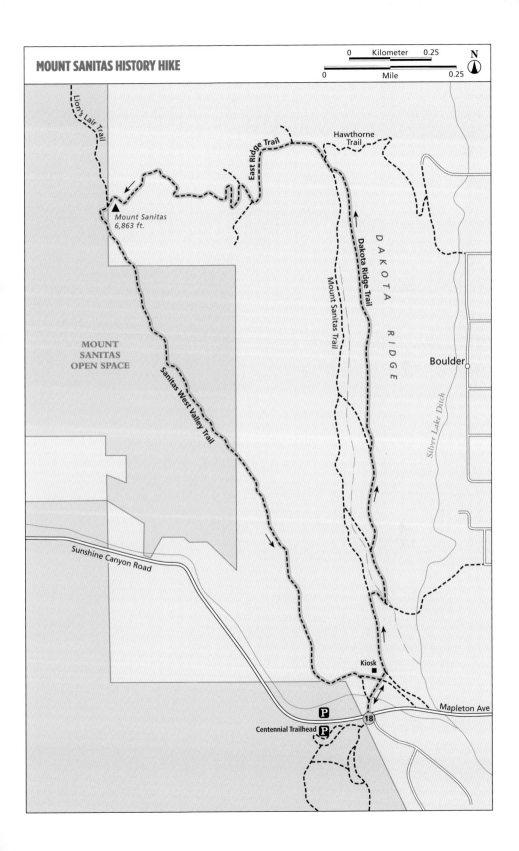

0   Kilometer   0.25

0   Mile   0.25

N

Lion's Lair Trail

East Ridge Trail

Hawthorne Trail

Mount Sanitas
6,863 ft.

Dakota Ridge Trail

Mount Sanitas Trail

D A K O T A   R I D G E

Boulder

MOUNT
SANITAS
OPEN SPACE

Sanitas West Valley Trail

Silver Lake Ditch

Sunshine Canyon Road

Kiosk

Mapleton Ave

P

18

Centennial Trailhead

P

Trail, a fully exposed path gaining nearly 1,000 feet of elevation in under a mile. Near the summit, portions of the trail are difficult to follow. Things get hairy at around 1.75 miles as the trail winds through big rocks and boulders. Pay attention, and look for the metal markers. This popular route is heavily trafficked, so when in doubt, just follow other hikers who seem to know where they're going.

Most kids will love climbing across rocks and passing through a semi-squeeze. There's a short scramble near the top, and by 2.0 miles you've summited. Take a well-earned snack break, and ask children what they think sanatorium patients felt like hiking the same trail over one hundred years ago.

To get back to your car, walk across the peak and descend on the Mount Sanitas Trail. Make sure you're on the Mount Sanitas Trail, not Lion's Lair, a much longer path down the back of the mountain.

The last leg of this loop features scenic overlooks and gorgeous views of Sunshine Canyon and the Continental Divide. Aside from a clip over a sheet of red sandstone, the vast majority of the descent is easy and safe thanks to a new series of staircases completed by Boulder OSMP trail crews. By 2.6 miles, the trail levels out substantially and the steepest part of the descent is behind you.

MILES AND DIRECTIONS

0.0   Start from the Centennial Trailhead parking lot, and look for a green sign near the main road reading "Trail to Pedestrian Crossing for Mt. Sanitas." Following the arrow on the sign, walk past the outhouse. In 200 feet, turn left. Carefully cross Mapleton Avenue at the pedestrian crosswalk. Elevation: 5,550 feet.

0.1   Pass a Mount Sanitas trail marker. Walk through the opening in the fence, and follow the trail up a hill. Hike straight through the four-way intersection.

0.15   Arrive at the Mount Sanitas welcome sign. Walk straight through the trail intersection to stay on the Sanitas Valley Trail.

0.32   Turn right onto the Dakota Ridge Trail.

0.4   Turn left at a trail junction.

0.5   Turn right at the trail marker, and walk up a stone-and-wood staircase.

0.7   Bear right at the fork.

1.15   The narrow path branching off to the right leads to a rocky outcropping.

1.2   Pass a bench and scenic overlook on your right. The Dakota Ridge Trail dead-ends at the Sanitas Valley Trail. Turn right. As you round the bend, the Sanitas Valley Trail becomes the East Ridge Trail.

1.6   Watch for an abrupt switchback marked by a metal post.

2.0   Arrive at the top of Mount Sanitas (6,863'). Walk across the summit, and descend via the Mount Sanitas Trail.

3.0   Reach a natural stone-and-wood staircase.

3.1   Cross a bridge, and come to a fork in the trail. Go either way; the trails link back up.

3.2   The dirt trail becomes a sidewalk. Turn right at a four-way intersection. Walk toward Mapleton Avenue, where you'll turn right and backtrack to the pedestrian crosswalk.

3.3   After crossing Mapleton Avenue and turning right, arrive back at the Centennial Trailhead parking lot.

19 TROLLSTIGEN TRAIL

From Breckenridge's captivating main street, straight into an enchanted forest with a giant wooden troll, this short hike is pure magic for young children. The 1.3-mile route combines entry-level hiking on the Illinois Creek trail system with a larger-than-life example of upcycling, scoring major brownie points for passing a free outdoor museum and mining-themed playground.

Start: Breckenridge Brewery
Distance: 1.3-mile double loop
Hiking time: 1–2 hours
Difficulty: Easy
Elevation gain: 128 feet
Trail surface: Paved sidewalk, dirt, flagstone, and a wooden walkway
Hours: None posted
Best seasons: Summer and fall
Water: At the playground
Toilets: Flush toilets at Breckenridge Brewery and the playground
Nursing benches: At the playground and near the troll sculpture
Stroller-friendly: Yes
Potential child hazards: None

Other trail users: Mountain bikers
Dogs: Allowed on leash
Land status: Breckenridge Open Space and Trails
Nearest town: Breckenridge
Fees and permits: None
Maps: Breck Trails 3-D Breckenridge/Summit County Trails
Trail contact: Breckenridge Open Space and Trails, PO Box 168, Breckenridge 80424; (970) 453-3189; gobreck.com/experience-breckenridge/arts-and-culture/how-to-find-the-breckenridge-troll
Gear suggestions: Sun protection, windbreakers, water

FINDING THE TRAILHEAD

There's no troll parking at the Trollstigen trailhead. From the Breckenridge Welcome Center, located at 203 South Main Street, walk 0.3 mile south, toward the end of town, until you reach Breckenridge Brewery at the corner of South Main and Ridge Streets.

THE HIKE

Here's a pro tip: Always choose the hike with the giant wooden troll. There are hundreds of miles of trail extending from Breckenridge's adorable downtown shopping district. If you're having trouble narrowing the options, ask, "Does one of the trails include a 15-foot-tall wooden troll?" Yes? That's the route for you!

This hike departs from Breckenridge Brewery because one, I like their beer, and two, Breckenridge is a walking town. Park your car in the South Gondola lot, and help preserve the town's historic charm by minimizing traffic and pollution.

From the two-story pub at 600 South Main Street, cross Ridge Street and head out of town, using the sidewalk on the east side of South Main Street. Boreas Pass Road appears quickly. Turn left, and cross the road at the crosswalk at South French Street.

The real fun begins at Breckenridge's High Line Railroad Museum, a free outdoor museum housing Engine No. 9, one of the few remaining narrow-gauge locomotives that once traveled over treacherous mountain passes. Open June through September, 10 a.m. to 3 p.m., this cute stop-off has a rotary snowplow, a replica C&S caboose, and a flatcar.

For young kids, the adjacent mining-themed playground is even more enticing. If stopping at a playground doesn't feel like "real hiking," remember that the whole idea is to deliver a fun, memorable experience that'll instill in your kids a lifelong love of hiking. With that goal in mind, let your children play before embarking on the next leg of the journey: a troll hunt!

Rodeo Trail picks up on the south side of the playground, opposite Engine No. 9, at 0.3 mile. There are several game paths leading to the unmarked trail. Hike toward the Stephen C. West Ice Arena, and look right for pleasant mountain views.

After curving around the ice arena, cross a bridge to access the Illinois Creek Trail. Now we've hit the real hiking. Follow the flat trail east. The ice arena will be visible to the left. When you reach the clearing at 0.5 mile, ask children to find the wood trail post with a picture of a troll. Follow the arrow toward the stone path constituting the "out" segment of the Trollstigen Trail, a one-way directional path for pedestrians.

The stroll along the Trollstigen Trail is enchanting in the early evening, when sunlight flickers through a canopy of trees. This short loop was built for Isak Heartstone, a larger-than-life troll sculpture created by Danish artist Thomas Dambo, who specializes in upcycled artwork.

FUN FACTOR

TRY A LIVING HISTORY HIKE.

Ten minutes north of the Trollstigen Trail, on the Iowa Hill Trail, a 0.9-mile lollipop takes families through a historic hydraulic mining site dating back to the Pikes Peak gold rush. On the looped segment of this easy-to-follow trail, kids discover a series of preserved ruins and interpretive signs detailing the key placer mining innovations honed on Iowa Hill. A few highlights include a decaying undercurrent sluice, a water flume, and an old derrick that was used to move boulders and tree roots.

After a mellow ascent past a blacksmith exhibit, the route tops out near 10,000 feet at the Iowa Hill boardinghouse, an 1870s-era log cabin restored with period-appropriate furnishings. Peek through the cabin's windows to get a glimpse into the past. For a guided tour of the site, contact the Breckenridge Heritage Alliance.

To access this hike from downtown Breckenridge, drive north on CO 9. Turn left onto Valley Brook Street, and right onto Airport Road. About 0.25 mile down Airport Road, a dirt road branches off to the left. Follow it to the trailhead.

It's hard to miss Isak Heartstone at the end of the Trollstigen Trail. The big guy draws large crowds of tourists, so be prepared to wait in line for a picture. Children aren't allowed to climb on Isak Heartstone, but it's totally fine to get close enough for a family snapshot.

Use the raised wooden walkway to return to the trailhead, where a four-way trail intersection offers a few options. Families with very young children might be ready to retrace their steps to Breckenridge Brewery. In the directions below, we'll extend the hike by venturing deeper into the forest via the Illinois Creek High Trail.

After making a wide U-turn, Illinois Creek High descends to Illinois Creek Low. Walk straight through a four-way trail intersection to reach the Rodeo Trail marker. This should look familiar. Cross the wooden bridge, walk back to the playground, and return to South Main Street the way you came.

Stop at Breckenridge Brewery for sustenance. Bring a portable game like Spot It!, and grab a seat upstairs if you can.

MILES AND DIRECTIONS

0.0   Start from Breckenridge Brewery, and walk south on the paved sidewalk alongside South Main Street (CO 9). Elevation: 9,600 feet.

0.1   Turn left at the stoplight on Boreas Pass Road.

0.2   Reach South French Street. Use a pedestrian crosswalk to cross Boreas Pass Road. Visit Breckenridge's High Line Railroad Museum, home to Engine No. 9, and let your children play on the adjacent playground.

0.3   Rodeo Trail picks up on the south side of the playground. Turn left onto the Rodeo Trail to hike toward the Stephen C. West Ice Arena. After passing the ice arena, cross a wooden bridge and go left on the Illinois Creek Low Trail.

0.5   Reach a clearing in the woods. The trail post with a picture of a troll will help you locate the Trollstigen Trail.

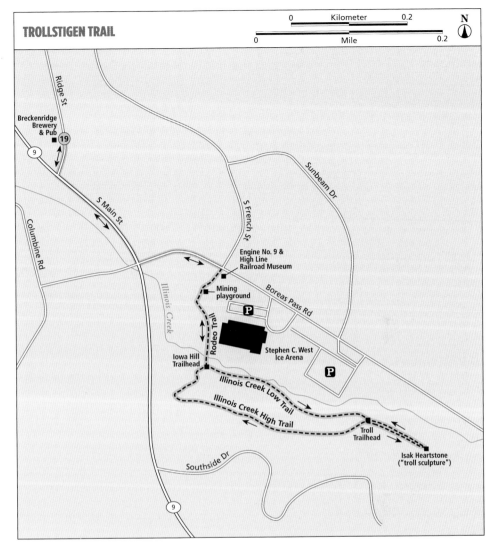

0   Kilometer   0.2

0   Mile   0.2

N

Ridge St

Breckenridge
Brewery
& Pub

19

9

S Main St

Columbine Rd

Sunbeam Dr

S French St

Engine No. 9 &
High Line
Railroad Museum

Boreas Pass Rd

Mining
playground

P

Illinois Creek

Rodeo Trail

Iowa Hill
Trailhead

Stephen C. West
Ice Arena

P

Illinois Creek Low Trail

Illinois Creek High Trail

Troll
Trailhead

Isak Heartstone
("troll sculpture")

Southside Dr

9

0.6 Reach Isak Heartstone, Breckenridge's 15-foot troll sculpture. Admire the art before following a raised wooden walkway back to the Trollstigen Trailhead.

0.7 Arrive at a four-way trail intersection. Turn left onto the Illinois Creek High Trail. A few feet later, bear left at a fork. In 500 feet, turn right at a trail marker. (It's not as complicated as it sounds.)

0.8 Stay straight at the fork in the trail. You should be hiking parallel to the ice arena below.

0.9 Make a sharp left turn to merge onto Illinois Creek Low. Walk straight through the four-way trail intersection, cross the wooden bridge, and retrace your steps to the playground.

1.0 You're back at the playground. Return to South Main Street the way you came in.

1.3 Arrive back at Breckenridge Brewery. If you like beer, the fun's just beginning.

20 PINE VIEW TRAIL

Anchored by Pine Lake, Pine Valley Ranch Park is an 883-acre treasure enclosing 5.9 miles of secluded trail shaded by thick stands of conifers growing along the north edge of Pike National Forest. All the park's trails are well maintained and easy to follow, but Pine View is especially fun for families looking for a low-mileage hike with a backcountry feel.

Start: Pine Valley Ranch Park Trailhead
Distance: 2.5-mile loop
Hiking time: 1.5–3 hours
Difficulty: Moderate
Elevation gain: 809 feet
Trail surface: Dirt and rock
Hours: Open daily, 1 hour before sunrise to 1 hour after sunset
Best seasons: Spring through fall. Pine Lake is a popular winter destination for ice-skaters and anglers.
Water: None
Toilets: Outhouses at the trailhead and on the west side of the lake
Nursing benches: At both scenic overlooks and the picnic shelter preceding Pine Lake
Stroller-friendly: Pine Lake Loop and Narrow Gauge Trail are doable with a jogging stroller, and the site is wheelchair-compatible.

Potential child hazards: A large lake, steep ledges coming up the Park View Trail
Other trail users: None on the Park View and Pine Lake Loop Trails; equestrians and mountain bikers allowed on other trails inside the park
Dogs: Must be leashed
Land status: Jefferson County Open Space
Nearest towns: Bailey and Conifer
Fees and permits: None
Maps: Jefferson County Open Space Pine Valley Ranch Park
Trail contact: Jefferson County Open Space, 700 Jefferson County Pkwy., Ste. 100, Golden 80401; (303) 271-5925; www.jeffco.us/1428/Pine-Valley-Ranch-Park
Gear suggestions: Trekking poles, sun protection, binoculars, a blank journal and colored pencils (for drawing by the lake)

FINDING THE TRAILHEAD

From Conifer, take US 285 south for approximately 6.7 miles. When you reach the Pine Junction Country Store, turn left (south) onto Pine Valley Road. Cell phone service is spotty here. In 6 more miles, turn right onto Crystal Lake Road, and follow the signs to Pine Valley Ranch Park. If you reach the unincorporated community of Pine, you've gone too far. Inside Pine Valley Ranch Park, drive past the first two parking lots, and park in the third lot at the end of the road. The trailhead is near the outhouse at the far end of this lot.

THE HIKE

First things first: Snap a photo of your kids on the truss bridge just beyond the parking lot. Thanks to the picturesque mountain scenery to the east, even an amateur with an iPhone can get a frame-worthy shot.

Following the wheelchair-access sign, merge onto the Pine Lake Loop; stroll alongside the stream until the paved sidewalk becomes dirt singletrack. Before long, you'll see a staircase to the left. Turn and begin a steep ascent up the Park View Trail. Watch your kids

FUN FACTOR

MAKE A DAY OF IT IN PINE.

The unincorporated community of Pine is a rustic former railroad town with a few noteworthy enterprises. One mile north of town, the Phantom Falls Disc Golf Course is a fun fairway with twenty-seven holes progressing through heavily wooded and hilly terrain. Tee times are required and can be booked in advance on the company's website. BYO discs if you're planning to play.

Grub like a local at the Buck Snort Saloon, an authentic mountain bar drawing motorcyclists, mountain bikers, and sightseers. (At the very least, stop in for chips and salsa so your kids can paste a dollar bill to the bar's graffiti-covered walls.)

If you visit Pine Valley Ranch Park in June, time your hike around the annual Pine Grove Rhubarb Festival, usually held at North Fork Fire Station. Between the pancake breakfast, rhubarb cook-off, and baking contests, this small-town celebration showcases all the ways people get rhubarb into their bellies.

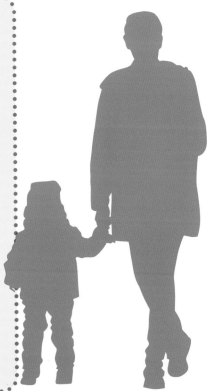

closely. Park View Trail is narrow with a steep ledge. If you're feeling breathless, stop at either of the back-to-back overlooks offering aerial views of Pine Lake.

Just past a series of natural stone staircases, several switchbacks ease the final push toward the top. The Park View Trail flattens out significantly at 0.8 mile, and by 0.95 mile you've hit the highest point on the route, just past the trail map.

The trail dips into Pike National Forest, a massive 1,106,604-acre space managed by the USDA Forest Service. There are several 14ers surrounding Pine, including Mount Lincoln (14,286'), Mount Bross (14,172'), and Mount Democrat (14,148'), and recreation is undeveloped, accessible mainly by four-wheel drive, horseback, and foot. This is your chance to enjoy Colorado's beautiful backcountry.

When the Park View Trail ends at 1.1 miles, bear right onto the Strawberry Jack Trail to loop back to Pine Valley Ranch. For a super-short option, make this an out-and-back hike by turning around at the Strawberry Jack Trail and following the Park View Trail back to the lake.

Families with older children can add mileage to the described route. Turn left onto the Strawberry Jack Trail, and head deeper into the national forest. The Strawberry Jack Trail continues south for miles, crossing over the Skipper and Homestead Trails before ending at the Miller Gulch Trail. After exploring the trail for another mile or two, turn around and return to the intersection of the Strawberry Jack and Park View Trails, then stay straight and continue following the directions below.

The next segment is all downhill on the Strawberry Jack and Buck Gulch Trails. You'll feel a little sun on your back before coming to a big U-turn. The trail drifts gently downhill before dropping into a dense aspen grove. This part's a real treat.

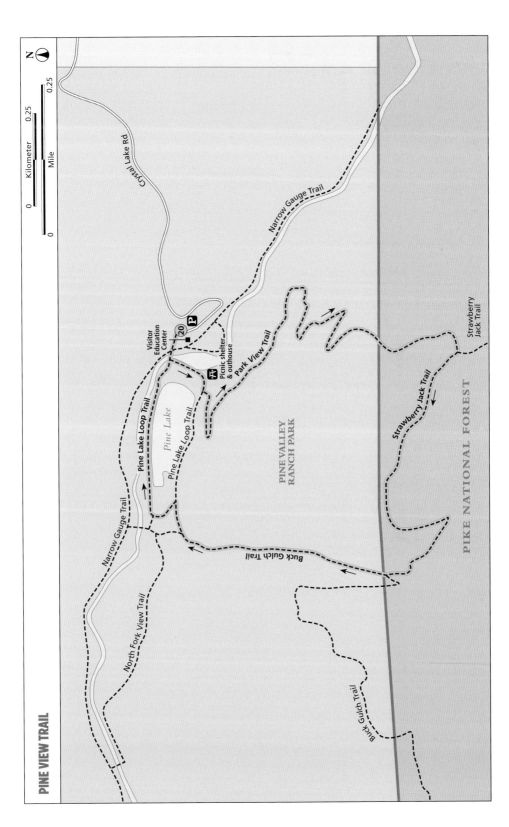

PINE VIEW TRAIL

Visitor Education Center

Picnic shelter & outhouse

Pine Lake

Pine Lake Loop Trail

Pine Lake Loop Trail

Narrow Gauge Trail

Narrow Gauge Trail

North Fork View Trail

Buck Gulch Trail

Buck Gulch Trail

Park View Trail

Strawberry Jack Trail

Strawberry Jack Trail

Crystal Lake Rd

PINE VALLEY RANCH PARK

PIKE NATIONAL FOREST

N

0   0.25   Kilometer
0   0.25   Mile

When you reach the junction at 2.15 miles, it's fine to go either way around the lake. The directions here take you on a path wedged between Pine Lake and a babbling stream.

Pine Lake is a popular stop for anglers. If you have a pole, cast a line on one of the piers post-hike. A Colorado state fishing license is required. The beautiful stone pavilion overlooking the lake is an ideal place for a picnic.

Open seasonally, the Visitor Education Center at Pine Valley Ranch Park is housed in the small cottage between the parking lot and truss bridge. Inside, you'll discover park maps, a few exhibits, and a short historical video with information on the park and its four-legged inhabitants. Outside the cottage, picnic benches overlook the river, and rangers occasionally post up here with nature-based activities and games: looking at bugs under a microscope and identifying scat, for example.

MILES AND DIRECTIONS

0.0 Start from the Pine Valley Ranch Park Trailhead, walk across the bridge, and use the concrete sidewalk to access the Pine Lake Loop. Bear left onto the Pine Lake Loop. Elevation: 6,785 feet.

0.1 Turn left onto the Park View Trail. Climb the stairs.

0.4 Reach another staircase.

0.47 Pass the first of two back-to-back scenic overlooks.

0.54 Bear right at the top of the stairs, and hike along the washed-out dirt path. A clear trail resumes shortly.

0.8 Arrive at a trail marker. Turn left to continue hiking uphill.

0.95 Reach a trail map. The trail dips into Pike National Forest.

1.1 After passing a Park View Trail sign, turn right onto the Strawberry Jack Trail.

1.72 Come to a sign for the Strawberry Jack Trail. Return to Pine Valley Ranch Park by turning right onto the Buck Gulch Trail.

2.1 Turn right to begin hiking on the Pine Lake Loop.

2.15 Pass a picnic shelter and an outhouse. Turn left at the junction for the Pine Lake Loop, and hike around the lake.

2.22 Bear right at a trail intersection. Pine Lake should be on your right as you round the bend.

2.44 Turn left. Take the stairs downhill toward the river, and look for the dirt trail.

2.5 Arrive back at the bridge where you started.

21 MOUNT BIERSTADT TRAIL

Hiking to the top of a 14,000-foot mountain is a rite of passage for many Coloradans, and a handful of the state's 14ers are family-friendly. Even after exiting tree line and picking its way up scree, the Mount Bierstadt Trail is rated an "easy" Class 2 ascent that many children can attain. Keep in mind, though, that no 14er is actually easy. This is by far the most difficult hike in this guide.

Start: Guanella Pass Trailhead
Distance: 7.1 miles out and back
Hiking time: 6–8 hours
Difficulty: Difficult
Elevation gain: 2,850 feet
Trail surface: Dirt, rock, and scree
Hours: None posted
Best seasons: Mid-June through mid-Sept
Water: None
Toilets: Vault toilets between the parking lot and trailhead
Nursing benches: This hike is not recommended for babies and toddlers.
Stroller-friendly: No
Potential child hazards: Altitude sickness, overexertion, dehydration, scree, sheer drops
Other trail users: None
Dogs: Must be on hand-held leashes at all times
Land status: USDA Forest Service

Nearest town: Georgetown
Fees and permits: A free self-issuing permit is required for the Mount Evans Wilderness. Free permits are available at the trailhead.
Maps: USGS Mount Evans; National Geographic Trails Illustrated Idaho Springs, Georgetown, Loveland Pass
Trail contact: Arapaho and Roosevelt National Forests, Clear Creek Ranger District, 2060 Miner St., Idaho Springs 80452; (303) 567-4382; www.fs.usda.gov/recarea/psicc/recreation/hiking/recarea/?recid=12973&actid=50
Gear suggestions: Trail running shoes or hiking boots, layers, sunglasses, gloves, warm hats, compressed oxygen (canisters available at REI), trekking poles, high-energy snacks, Nuun tablets, CamelBaks. Carry up to 3 liters (100 ounces) of water for each hiker in your group.

FINDING THE TRAILHEAD

From I-70, take exit 288 and head south through Georgetown. Following the signs for Guanella Pass, go south on Argentine Street for 0.6 mile, turn left (east) onto 6th Street, and right (south) onto Rose Street. Drive south on Rose Street for 4 blocks before turning right on 2nd Street, which becomes Guanella Pass Road. Follow Guanella Pass Road for 10 miles to reach the pass. The trailhead is on the left side of the road, 2 miles past Guanella Pass Campground. Overflow parking is available on the right side of the road. Parking along the roadside in undesignated locations is prohibited.

THE HIKE

A 14er is a peak that's 14,000 feet or taller and more than 0.25 mile from the next nearest peak. There are roughly ninety in the United States. While Alaska contains the highest (Denali), Colorado has the most. Depending on how you count, the Centennial State claims fifty-three to fifty-eight 14ers.

Colorado's 14ers are special because many are accessible to novice hikers, with well-marked and maintained trails leading to summits that can be tackled in a single day. On

an entry-level 14er, you won't need advanced climbing skills or mountaineering equipment, just performance clothing, good shoes, and the ten essentials.

Entry-level doesn't mean easy. It takes physical and mental stamina to summit a high-altitude peak. But with enough water and breaks, most hikers can get up Bierstadt.

First things first: Summit-seekers must head out early, by 7 a.m. at the latest. Check the weather report before departing. Summer is prime season for climbing 14ers—and for afternoon thunderstorms. Mountaintop weather conditions can change rapidly in the afternoon. If you haven't summited Bierstadt by noon, turn around and call it a day.

The most popular route up Bierstadt is the West Slope, from the Guanella Pass Trailhead. The first mile is tame. In fact, the trail starts on a decline, dropping hikers into "The Willows," a wetland willow thicket providing habitat for snow

quail. Thanks to a series of raised boardwalks built by the Colorado Fourteeners Initiative, your children won't be complaining about wet feet after winding through this willow carr, or fen.

Cross Scott Gomer Creek, pass two alpine lakes, and begin a steady climb into the alpine tundra. While scattered trees can grow in some tundra regions, they don't exist in alpine tundra because the soil inhibits tree growth. High-altitude vegetation consists of low-lying plants such as dwarf shrubs, sedges, perennial grasses, forbs, mosses, and lichens.

Pass the time with make-believe games and stories—and wildlife viewing. Look for pikas scurrying alongside the trail. Marmots are also visible on the rocks, and you'll likely hear their piercing chirps. As you advance above tree line, listen for the rock ptarmigan's subtle calls, which sound like *kuk-kuk-kuk*. Your kids will need binoculars to see a ptarmigan, since the medium-size game birds are camouflaged by piles of gray rock.

Some hikers spot elk toward the scrub oak. Bighorn sheep hang out on the mountain's broad slopes, and very observant hikers might spy mountain goats on ledges. Contrary to popular belief, mountain goats are not native to Colorado. They were originally brought to the state in the mid-1900s as game animals.

The trail steepens significantly at 1.7 miles, and by 2.2 miles you're officially hiking above tree line. The barren, postapocalyptic backdrop can be a little jarring for those who aren't used to it.

Watch for signs of altitude sickness in children. Staying hydrated might help ward off this illness, but if somebody in your group falls victim, the only cure is to descend. Be prepared to bail if needed. There's no shame in coming back another day.

The grade intensifies, and the wide dirt trail becomes increasingly rugged. But the saddle just below the mountain peak is a false summit. Bear left, and keep trekking.

Mountain Bierstadt Trail is very well marked until you reach the scramble at the end. Use your hands to climb up steep, uneven rock fragments. There's no clear path. Pick a route that goes uphill, and stay on rocks to avoid trampling vegetation. If in doubt, look for cairns or follow other hikers.

The mountain's small summit gets crowded, but there should be plenty of room to grab some photos and celebrate your achievement with top-of-the-world views of the Sawtooth Formation extending toward Abyss Lake, as well as Mounts Evans and Spalding, and Grays and Torreys Peaks to the west. Temperatures at the summit could be 40 degrees cooler than temperatures at the trailhead.

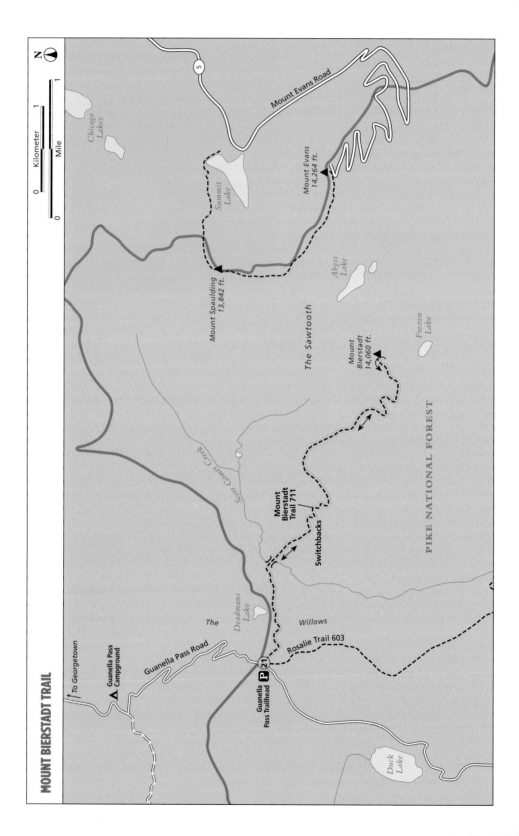

MOUNT BIERSTADT TRAIL

N

Kilometer

Mile

To Georgetown

Guanella Pass Campground

Guanella Pass Road

Chicago Lakes

Mount Evans Road

5

Summit Lake

Mount Spaulding 13,842 ft.

Mount Evans 14,264 ft.

Abyss Lake

Scott Gomer Creek

The Sawtooth

Mount Bierstadt 14,060 ft.

Frozen Lake

Mount Bierstadt Trail 711

Switchbacks

PIKE NATIONAL FOREST

The
Deadmans Lake

Willows

Rosalie Trail 603

Guanella Pass Trailhead

21

Duck Lake

You made it to the top, but the adventure isn't over. You still have to get back to your car. The descent can be tedious with kids who are exhausted and bored by the redundant scenery. Remember that easy start you had several hours ago? The last 0.3 mile of this hike is uphill.

Back at the car, give your child a big hug and a high five. Climbing a 14er requires hours of physical exertion, and summitting one is a huge accomplishment. Before you attempt a 14er, ask yourself if your child is ready for an intense adventure. If you haven't mastered low-altitude hiking yet, start there.

You don't actually have to summit a 14er to enjoy the Mount Bierstadt Trail. To turn a difficult expedition into an easy hike, stop at the trail's low point, at Scott Gomer Creek, then turn around and retrace your steps to the trailhead.

MILES AND DIRECTIONS

0.0 Start at the Guanella Pass Trailhead, and begin hiking east toward Mount Bierstadt. Elevation: 11,650 feet.

0.2 The trail becomes a series of boardwalks as you stroll through The Willows.

0.3 A dirt trail picks back up; follow it. Look for Deadmans Lake to the left.

1.1 After an easy first mile, the grade increases. Switchbacks help with the initial ascent.

2.2 Exit tree line, and begin hiking southeast.

2.9 Reach a bend in the trail. Hike east toward Mount Bierstadt's rocky summit. Do your best to follow any obvious path.

3.55 Arrive at the top of Mount Bierstadt, and look for the permanent trail marker. After enjoying top-of-the-world views, turn around and descend via the same route.

7.1 Arrive back at the trailhead.

FUN FACTOR

UNLEASH YOUR CHILD'S INNER ARTIST.

Mount Bierstadt was named for landscape painter Albert Bierstadt, who might have made one of the first ascents of the mountain, in the 1860s. His massive, 12 x 7-foot painting, *Storm in the Mountains,* was developed with sketches he created while exploring the stunning area surrounding his namesake peak.

Pack a few simple art supplies (nothing that will weigh you down), and encourage children to sketch their own landscapes during initial water breaks and/or after completing the hike. Later, admire your child's masterpieces over lunch in Idaho Springs. The city's downtown historic district, located on Miner Street, is home to a variety of shops, restaurants, and breweries.

22 TREASURE FALLS TRAIL

There's something oddly rewarding about following a primitive trail through a misty forest to a powerful 105-foot-tall plunge waterfall. In addition to flaunting one of the state's highest waterfalls, this short trek in the San Juan Mountains is packed with enchanting scenery, obscure history, and a local legend about buried treasure that's still waiting to be recovered.

Start: Treasure Falls Trailhead
Distance: 0.7-mile loop
Hiking time: 30 minutes–2 hours
Difficulty: Easy to moderate
Elevation gain: 432 feet
Trail surface: Dirt and rock
Hours: None posted
Best seasons: Year-round. Use extreme caution if the trail is muddy, icy, or packed with snow.
Water: None
Toilets: None
Nursing benches: Along the non-primitive trail and near the falls
Stroller-friendly: The non-primitive trail is doable with a jogging stroller.
Potential child hazards: Waterfall, standing water
Other trail users: None

Dogs: Leash recommended; unleashed dogs must be under voice control at all times.
Land status: USDA Forest Service
Nearest town: Pagosa Springs
Fees and permits: None
Maps: USGS Scientific Investigations Map 3419: Geologic Map of the Pagosa Springs 7.5' Quadrangle, Archuleta County, Colorado
Trail contact: San Juan National Forest Service, Pagosa Ranger District, 180 Pagosa St., Pagosa Springs 81147; (970) 264-2268; www.fs.usda.gov/recarea/sanjuan/recarea/?recid=43266
Gear suggestions: Hiking sandals or waterproof shoes, windbreakers, trekking poles, binoculars

FINDING THE TRAILHEAD

From downtown Pagosa Springs, head east on US 160 for 15 miles. Pullout parking and the trailhead for Treasure Falls will be visible off the shoulder of the highway, on the right (east) side of the road. The parking area accommodates only about eighteen vehicles and often fills to capacity during the summer. The hike is very short; if you're able to wait, a spot will be available soon. While the trailhead is open year-round, the entrance is sometimes blocked by plowed snow in winter.

THE HIKE

There's plenty of noteworthy hiking around the funky town of Pagosa Springs. But many of the local routes—Cimarrona Trail (#586), for example, and the 10-mile out-and-back trek along Coal Creek Trail (#581)—are long, steep, and difficult. For families, Treasure Falls is an easy-to-reach waterfall in the rugged San Juan National Forest.

The path leading to Treasure Falls is Trail #563 on the San Juan National Forest recreation map. You can almost see the waterfall from the parking lot. With reluctant hikers, having one eye on the prize can be motivating.

Two trails depart in opposite directions from the trailhead on the southeast edge of the pullout lot. Assuming the forecast is clear and the trail is mud-free, take the "primitive" trail shooting out to the right. If the trail is muddy, heed the warnings and use the easier,

"non-primitive" route to access Treasure Falls. The primitive trail is extremely treacherous in mud and/or falling rain.

The directions below combine the primitive and non-primitive routes to make a loop. Begin a beautiful trek uphill on soft dirt singletrack weaving through a lush forest. The trail is steep, crude, and rocky. It's also very short, and most kids will enjoy the challenge. Pretend you're exploring a tropical jungle. The sound of gushing water will enhance the game.

As you hike toward the waterfall, tell your children how Treasure Falls got its name. Legend has it, there's a chest of gold buried in the area. According to local lore, a group of Frenchmen hid their booty right before their capture by a band of pursuing Spaniards. To this day, the treasure remains undiscovered.

FUN FACTOR

VISIT A NATIONAL MONUMENT.

National monuments are the National Park Service's best-kept secrets. Twenty miles southwest of Pagosa Springs, Chimney Rock National Monument is a quiet destination showcasing Ancestral Puebloan dwellings; open May 15 through September 30.

The monument spans 7 square miles preserving 200 ancient homes and ceremonial buildings, some of which have been excavated for viewing. There's no entry fee into the archaeological site, but to really explore, you'll have to pay for a tour at the visitor cabin past the main entrance.

Only tourgoers are permitted to make the white-knuckle drive up a steep gravel road to a high mesa, where guided and self-guided tours begin. While the self-guided option is interesting, the real thrills happen with the group as you walk in the footsteps of the Ancestral Puebloans of the Chaco Canyon, following a rugged pathway that hasn't changed for 1,000 years. A 0.5-mile hike features a great kiva, a pit house, and Chacoan-style great house pueblo, plus spectacular 360-degree views of Colorado and New Mexico. Reservations aren't required; all tours are first-come, first-served.

By the time you've finished the story, you should be at the bridge. Turn right, and follow the trail as it switches uphill toward an observation area, Misty Deck, where you can feel the waterfall's horsetail spray.

Treasure Falls is one of Colorado's highest waterfalls. It's considered a plunge waterfall because it drops vertically without touching underlying rocks on the way down, a phenomenon occurring when a river spills water over a ledge.

You might see other hikers attempting to get closer to the waterfall. Don't follow them—it's unsafe to ascend past Misty Deck.

After viewing the waterfall, turn around and backtrack to the trail junction. To complete a loop, turn right and follow the main (non-primitive) trail downhill. A series of switchbacks make this the gentlest option, though if you loved the primitive trail, that route also works.

During winter, Treasure Falls freezes. It's possible to access the frozen waterfall with snowshoes or spikes, but you must use caution in icy conditions.

Fifteen minutes past Treasure Falls, Pagosa Springs is a no-fuss destination for active families. The laid-back town is surrounded by 2.5 million acres of national forest and wilderness, so you won't have to travel far to pick up some additional trail miles. There's great entry-level hiking within town limits at Reservoir Hill Park, located near the pirate ship playground at Dr. Mary Fisher Park. The San Juan River Walk winds along the trout-filled San Juan River.

Pagosa Springs is built around a geothermal hot spring. More than 1,002 feet deep, the Mother Spring aquifer has been Guinness World Records certified as the world's deepest. Post-hike, soak in the mineral-rich waters at The Springs Resort & Spa, The Overlook Hot Springs, or Healing Waters Resort & Spa, all open to the public for day use.

MILES AND DIRECTIONS

0.0   Start at the Treasure Falls trail marker, on the southeast edge of the parking lot. If the weather's good and the trail's clear, go right to begin hiking on the primitive trail. Elevation: 8,112 feet.

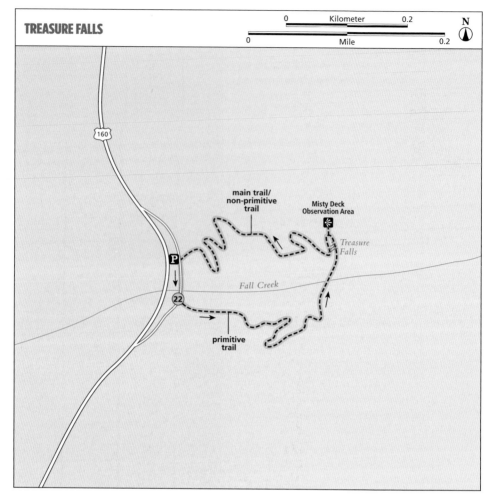

TREASURE FALLS

0.22 Cross a stream, and continue uphill.

0.25 Pass an interpretive sign.

0.28 Reach a stairwell. Continue hiking uphill toward the base of the waterfall.

0.32 Cross a bridge to arrive at a trail map. Bear right at the fork, and walk uphill to the Misty Deck.

0.36 Enjoy the upper observation deck, then turn around and hike back to the trail map. Be extremely careful with children near the waterfall.

0.42 You're back at the trail map. Bear right at the fork to take the main (non-primitive) trail back to your car.

0.5 Pass an interpretive sign.

0.58 Turn left at the trail marker.

0.7 Arrive back at the parking lot.

23 SHRINE MOUNTAIN TRAIL

Do not—I repeat: Do not—forget to pack a good camera for this picturesque high-country hike. The trail leading to Shrine Mountain is filled with wildflowers by mid-July, and orange, blue, and yellow blooms continue dotting the hillside through August. If the scenery doesn't take your breath away, the altitude will! Families willing to huff it are rewarded with top-of-the-world views of the Gore, Ten-mile, and Sawatch Ranges, some of central Colorado's most expansive sierras.

Start: Bulletin board near the vault toilets in the parking lot
Distance: 4.2 miles out and back
Hiking time: 2–4 hours
Difficulty: Moderate to difficult
Elevation gain: 743 feet
Trail surface: Dirt
Hours: None posted
Best seasons: July through Sept
Water: None
Toilets: Flush toilets at the Vail Pass Rest Area, a vault toilet near the trailhead
Nursing benches: None
Stroller-friendly: No
Potential child hazards: Altitude sickness, sheer drops on the ridge
Other trail users: Equestrians
Dogs: Must be leashed or under voice command at all times

Land status: USDA Forest Service
Nearest town: Vail
Fees and permits: None
Maps: ORIC Summit County Region Day Hiking Trails
Trail contact: USDA Forest Service, Eagle–Holy Cross Ranger District, 24747 US 24, Minturn 81645; (970) 827-5715; www.fs.usda.gov/recarea/whiteriver/recreation/hiking/recarea/?recid=41399&actid=50
Gear suggestions: Trail running shoes or hiking sandals, sunscreen, sun-protective clothing, sunglasses, brimmed hats, fleece jackets and/or windbreakers, Nuun tablets, CamelBaks, compressed oxygen (canisters available at REI), binoculars

FINDING THE TRAILHEAD

From I-70 take exit 190 for Vail Pass and drive toward the Vail Pass Rest Area. Restrooms are available at the rest area, but there isn't any potable water. Turn right (west) on the dirt road marked "Shrine Pass and Red Cliff" (FR 709). This bumpy road is open June 21 through mid-November. Drive for approximately 2.3 miles to the top of Shrine Pass; park in the lot on the left (south) side of the road, near the gravel driveway for the Shrine Mountain Inn.

THE HIKE

It's no wonder the trail to Shrine Ridge Mountain is a popular summertime destination. The out-and-back route is eye-catching, beginning with a beautiful ascent through a pine-studded meadow filled with brightly colored wildflowers. It's almost like you're hiking through the poppy scene in *The Wizard of Oz*.

Unless you're a seasoned botanist, you'll probably struggle to identify the colorful blooms appearing everywhere along the first segment of trail. Bring along a field guide to wildflowers, or just ogle home-state varietals, including bistort, willows, Jacob's ladder, daisies, chiming bells, monkshood, and red elephants.

When you hike along the Shrine Mountain Trail, you're trekking through history. The passage was originally used by the Ute people. Later, silver miners and settlers walked the route.

About 1.0 mile in, the trail crosses over a modest creek bordered by bright pink paintbrush and Parry's primrose. By this point, you've seen the best display of wildflowers. Families hiking with toddlers, preschoolers, or children sensitive to altitude can use the creek as their turnaround point. It's better to have a short enjoyable trek than to risk pushing kids beyond their physical limits. (Remember, the goal isn't to make it to the top of every pass, but rather to create fun experiences.)

If you decide to continue to Shrine Mountain, cross the creek and keep climbing. The trail turns west and creeps steadily uphill into a denser pine forest before emerging from the trees at 1.4 miles. On a clear day, you might catch a glimpse of Flat Top Mountain (12,361'), the highest summit in the Flat Tops Wilderness.

Enjoy a relatively easy segment of trail before a steep push to the saddle. See the snowbanks alongside the trail? Now's the time to watch out for stray snowballs. It's not uncommon for a summer snowball fight to break out among hikers at the drift below Shrine Ridge. And it's totally fine if your kids want in on the action.

During the final ascent, the trail weaves around interesting rock formations. The giant, flat rock at 1.5 miles is a great place to stop for a drink.

At the top of the ridge, your efforts are immediately rewarded with incredible 360-degree views of the Gore Range to the north (the border between Eagle and Summit Counties) and the Flat Top Mountains and Uneva Peak directly east.

Southeast, there's Copper Mountain ski area. Look left to see the Sawatch Range and Mount of the Holy Cross (14,009'). If there's still snow in its cracks, it'll be easy to spot the 14er named for the distinctive cross-shaped snowfield on its northeast face. It was this awe-inspiring geological feature that inspired the "Shrine" in Shrine Mountain.

Between 1929 and 1950, the mountain was Holy Cross National Monument; it was returned to the USDA Forest Service and thus lost its national monument status. The mountain has been the subject of painters, photographers, and even a poem by Henry Wadsworth Longfellow, "The Cross of Snow."

A trail sign marks Shrine Mountain Ridge, the turnaround point for this hike. If your kids are game, walk along the ridge for another 0.25 mile to gain additional views. When you're ready, simply turn around and retrace your steps to the trailhead. It's all downhill from here.

FUN FACTOR

RACE AROUND COLORADO'S LARGEST SKI MOUNTAIN.

Vail might be renowned for its slopes, but the bustling ski town also has an endless stockpile of summertime activities, events, and festivals. In addition to Vail Resort's popular mountaintop theme park, Epic Discovery, there's Piney River Ranch, Vail Stables, the Vail Nature Center, and a unique instrument petting zoo—not to mention kid-approved playgrounds at Ford Park, Pirate Ship Park, Donovan Park, and Bighorn Park.

The town also hosts one of the coolest youth contests on the planet. Kids Adventure Games is a can't-miss annual event held in August. Working in teams of two, participants ages 6 to 14 must bike and trek across a 3-mile obstacle-adventure course filled with natural and man-made elements, including mud pits, ziplines, cargo nets, and rappelling. Even if your children don't feel like competing, they can still get in the action at the Family Adventure Zone, featuring climbing walls, slack lines, and cheer card stations.

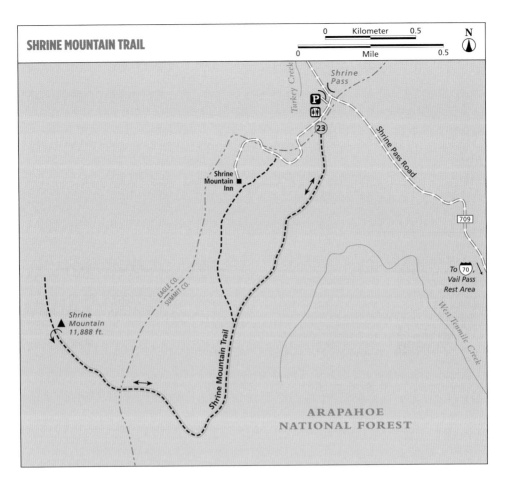

MILES AND DIRECTIONS

0.0 Start at the bulletin board near the vault toilets in the parking lot; merge onto the dirt road and begin hiking southwest. Elevation: 11,089 feet.

0.05 Turn left at the Shrine Ridge Trail sign.

0.68 You might notice a fork in the trail. Go either way; both paths will reconnect momentarily.

0.95 Reach a trail junction. Walk straight past the wooden post.

1.4 The trail emerges from the forest to climb up the ridge.

1.5 See that big flat rock to the right? It's a perfect place to break for water and snacks.

1.75 Turn right at the top of the ridge, and continue ascending Shrine Mountain.

1.9 Pass an unofficial trail coming in from the left. Walk straight through it while enjoying a spectacular view of Mount of the Holy Cross to the west.

2.1 Arrive at a trail sign. Turn around and head back the way you came. (**Option:** Walk along the ridge for another 0.25 mile before turning around, adding 0.5 mile round-trip to the hike.)

4.2 Arrive back at the trailhead.

24 GLACIER HIKE TRAIL

Commonly referred to as St. Mary's Glacier Trail, the rocky path extending from Fall River Road to St. Mary's Lake is a good place for families to experiment with high-altitude hiking before embarking on longer alpine adventures. After a quick climb, the trail opens to a sparkling lake framed by snow-capped alpine peaks. The nearby "glacier" isn't a glacier at all: It's a snowfield attracting snowboarders and sledders all summer long.

Start: St. Mary's Glacier sign off Fall River Road, between the parking lots
Distance: 1.2 miles out and back
Hiking time: 1–3 hours
Difficulty: Moderate to difficult
Elevation gain: 695 feet
Trail surface: Rock, boulder, and dirt
Hours: None posted
Best seasons: Summer
Water: None
Toilets: Portable toilets in the first parking lot
Nursing benches: None
Stroller-friendly: No
Potential child hazards: Rocky/uneven trail conditions, altitude sickness, a large lake, perennial snowfield
Other trail users: None
Dogs: Must be leashed
Land status: USDA Forest Service

Nearest town: Idaho Springs
Fees and permits: Self-pay fee
Maps: Clear Creek County Tourism Bureau, Clear Creek County Recreation & Trails Map
Trail contact: USDA Forest Service Clear Creek Ranger District, 2060 Miner St., Idaho Springs 80452; (303) 567-4382; www.fs.usda.gov/recarea/arp/recreation/hiking/recarea/?recid=28372&actid=50
Gear suggestions: Trekking poles, waterproof shoes or hiking sandals, fleece jackets, gloves, warm hats, compressed oxygen (canisters available at REI), Dramamine for children who get carsick (**Note:** While some families bring toboggans, sledding on the snowfield is at your own risk.)

FINDING THE TRAILHEAD

From Denver, take I-70 west to exit 238 (Fall River Road). Turn right (north) onto Fall River Road, and begin a 9-mile drive through the town of Alice. Two parking areas service this trail—a large lot south of the trailhead and a smaller one to the north. Both lots require a cash-only parking permit. Parking along Fall River Road is prohibited, and fines are frequently imposed. From the south parking lot, walk along the shoulder of Fall River Road until you reach the trailhead, marked by a "Glacier Hike" sign. From the north parking lot, use the shoulder of Fall River Road to backtrack to the trailhead.

THE HIKE

Other guides and websites rate this hike as easy. Despite the short distance, I always find it to be demanding due to the grade, rocky terrain, and high altitude.

The nearby town of Idaho Springs is 7,526 feet above sea level. From there, you'll gain almost 3,000 additional feet of elevation during the drive up Fall River Road. If anyone in your party gets carsick, have a bag ready.

There's parking on both sides of the trailhead. Use the first/larger lot, if possible. Whatever you do, don't park along the road. Your car might be towed.

There are portable toilets in the first lot, but they're notoriously dirty. It's better to make a pit stop in Idaho Springs before driving up Fall River Road.

Both parking areas are self-pay, and here's something important to know: You need cash and a pen to complete a permit, obtainable at one of the pay stations. Forest service permits are small envelopes with attached forms. Fill out the form, drop the posted fee into the envelope, and stuff it in the bin. Don't forget to leave the detachable portion of the permit on your dashboard.

From either lot, access the trailhead by carefully walking a few feet along the shoulder of Fall River Road. You can't miss the large "Glacier Hike" sign with the big arrow. When the sign appears, hop on the trail and hike straight uphill to St. Mary's Lake.

The trail is extremely rocky. Be patient with children as they negotiate their footing. And be prepared to pay close attention to your surroundings—the Glacier Hike Trail is not marked past the sign at the trailhead.

At first the path is wide enough to accommodate a jeep, but it's still hard to believe the route is an old service road. Today the trail is closed to vehicles, including all-terrain vehicles (ATVs).

Shortly after merging onto the trail, you'll come to a fork. Left is the most intuitive way; follow your intuition. There's another fork a few feet down the trail. Once again, bear left. Don't overthink it: just follow the crowds of people.

After passing the forks, it's a straight shot uphill. If in doubt, ask another hiker for directions. Descending hikers are especially helpful, since they just visited the lake and should have a clear idea of where it's located.

As you travel through Arapaho National Forest's subalpine woods, do your best to stay on the designated trail. Much of the surrounding land is privately owned.

After hiking for 20 to 40 minutes, depending on your group's pace, the trail opens to a beautiful lake ringed by willow and bristlecone pine, the latter of which thrives in extreme alpine environments. Look for wildflowers dotting the tundra and panoramic views near tree line.

The directions provided here end at the lake. Once you've arrived, it's an explore-at-your-own-pace situation. If you go left at the lake, you'll eventually reach an impasse—but along the way, there are many places to dip your toes in the ice-cold water.

Look to the right. See that massive white patch of packed snow climbing up the hill? That's St. Mary's Glacier.

To visit the "glacier," turn right at the lake and follow the trail to a metal bridge. Cross Silver Creek, and continue hiking. When you come to a three-way fork, take the middle trail, the most direct path to the base of the snowfield.

The term "glacier" is a misnomer here. What you're actually seeing is a perennial snowfield that feeds into the lake. Winter sports enthusiasts will be skiing, snowboarding, tubing, and sledding down the snowfield. Exploring it can be dangerous. Join in on the fun at your own risk, and exercise caution and good judgment. Injuries and fatalities occur every year at St. Mary's Glacier.

Because this hike is close to Denver and accessible from I-70, it's easy to forget that the entire route is above 10,000 feet. Watch for signs of altitude sickness in children. When hiking above tree line, always start your adventure early. Check the weather report before heading out, and keep an eye on the sky, since conditions can change rapidly at high elevation. To avoid a parking nightmare, hike on a weekday and arrive at the lot by 8:30 a.m.

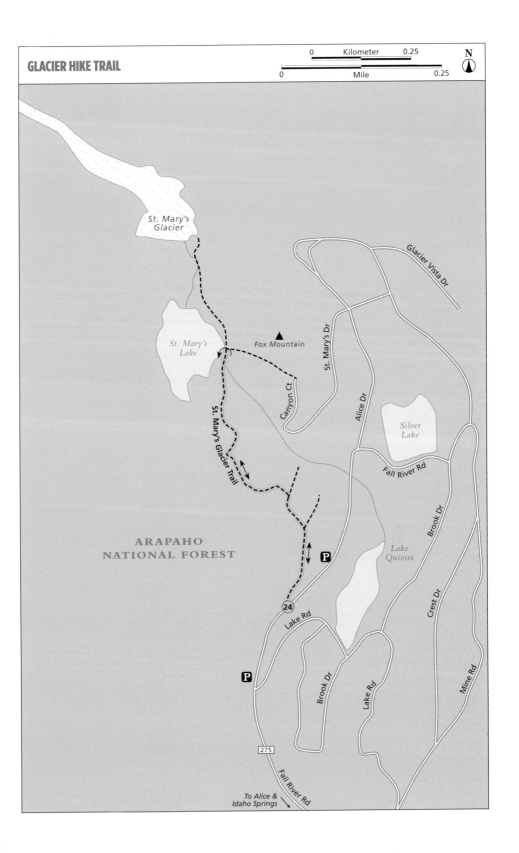

St. Mary's
Glacier

St. Mary's
Lake

Fox Mountain

Canyon Ct

St. Mary's Dr

Alice Dr

Glacier Vista Dr

Silver
Lake

St. Mary's Glacier Trail

Fall River Rd

Brook Dr

Lake
Quivira

ARAPAHO
NATIONAL FOREST

Crest Dr

Mine Rd

24

Lake Rd

Brook Dr

Lake Rd

275

Fall River Rd

To Alice &
Idaho Springs

0   Kilometer   0.25
0   Mile   0.25

N

FUN FACTOR

DISCOVER NEW ADVENTURES IN THE HISTORIC WEST.

Situated in the I-70 corridor, Clear Creek County is composed of several historic mining communities. The area's first gold strike took place in the mid-1800s, and modern-day tourists can visit working mines and pan for gold while exploring the Victorian mining towns of Georgetown, Idaho Springs, Silver Plume, and Empire.

A ride on the Georgetown Loop Railroad is always fun for families. Or drive along the Mount Evans Scenic Byway, the highest paved road in the Northern Hemisphere, ending at the 14,265-foot-high summit of Mount Evans.

Take I-70 to exit 240, and follow the signs to CO 103 and Mount Evans. Drive south for 14 miles, and turn onto CO 5. Just before reaching CO 5, look for the Echo Lake Lodge Restaurant and Gift Shop, your last stop for water and restrooms before reaching the summit. Don't forget to pay a per-vehicle summit fee at the USDA Forest Service Welcome Station.

Over the next 14 miles, you'll pass several mountain lakes while winding through alpine meadows and bristlecone pine forest. Keep your eyes peeled for mountain goats, mule deer, elk, bald eagles, and marmots. The summit of Mount Evans is usually open the Friday before Memorial Day through Labor Day.

Farther down I-70, between Lawson and Silver Plume, the Georgetown Wildlife Viewing Station offers permanent viewing scopes and educational exhibits. Weekends in November and December, trained guides from the Colorado Division of Wildlife are on hand to help visitors locate bighorn sheep.

MILES AND DIRECTIONS

0.0   Start at the trailhead marked by a giant sign reading "Glacier Hike." Begin hiking straight uphill on a very rocky service road. Elevation: 10,350 feet.

0.2   Come to a fork in the trail. Bear left, continuing uphill.

0.3   Arrive at another fork. Bear left, continuing uphill.

0.45 The trail levels out momentarily at a third fork. Go either way. I usually take the trail to the right because it's not quite as rocky.

0.6   Arrive at St. Mary's Lake. It's another 0.2 mile to the base of the snowfield. Additional mileage to/from the snowfield is not included here. After exploring the area, turn around and retrace your steps to the trailhead.

1.2   Arrive back at the trailhead.

25 THE COLORADO TRAIL AT JUNCTION CREEK

Similar to "bagging" a 14er (see hike 21), exploring the Colorado Trail (CT) is a quintessential experience for many hikers. Stretching from Denver to Durango, this narrow, 485-mile path passes through some of the state's best backcountry while crossing eight mountain ranges, six national forests, six wilderness areas, and five major river systems. The CT's southern terminus in Durango is especially fitting for families.

Start: Junction Creek Trailhead
Distance: 5.1 miles out and back
Hiking time: 2–4 hours
Difficulty: Moderate to difficult
Elevation gain: 533 feet
Trail surface: Dirt and rock
Hours: None posted
Best seasons: Summer and fall
Water: None
Toilets: An outhouse on the far edge of the parking lot
Nursing benches: None
Stroller-friendly: No
Potential child hazards: Sheer drops, poison ivy, heat exhaustion, dehydration. Flash floods have occurred in floodplains near the CT's southwestern terminus.
Other trail users: Equestrians, mountain bikers

Dogs: Must be leashed or under voice control
Land status: USDA Forest Service
Nearest town: Durango
Fees and permits: None
Maps: USDA Forest Service San Juan National Forest—Junction Creek Campground
Trail contact: USDA Forest Service, San Juan National Forest, 15 Burnett Ct., Durango 81302; (970) 247-4874; www.fs.usda.gov/recarea/sanjuan/recreation/recarea/?recid=42996&actid=50
Gear suggestions: Sunscreen, sun-protective clothing, brimmed hats, sunglasses, trekking poles, waterproof hiking sandals, swimsuits, high-energy snacks, Nuun tablets, CamelBaks

FINDING THE TRAILHEAD

From downtown Durango, drive north on Main Avenue. The numbers on the cross streets—East 10th Street, East 11th, etc.—should be increasing. Turn left onto East 25th Street, which quickly becomes Junction Creek Road (CR 204). In 2.9 miles, stay left at the fork in the road. Then, in another 0.6 mile, turn into a dirt parking lot leading to the Junction Creek Trailhead. If you drive another mile down CR 204, you'll come to Junction Creek Campground, administered by the USDA Forest Service.

THE HIKE

With its relatively low elevation and proximity to Durango, the Junction Creek Trailhead provides easy access to one of Colorado's most iconic landmarks. In this guide we're exploring the last 2.5 miles of "Segment 28," widely considered the final portion of the CT. Despite some rugged terrain, the bridge that crosses Junction Creek is an attainable target for most hikers, regardless of age and ability level.

A few feet past the parking lot, you'll see how the trailhead got its name as you wander alongside a clear mountain stream. Everyone in your group needs to watch their step

while admiring the water. Loose stones and rocks will trip you if you aren't careful, and bikers share the narrow multiuse trail.

July, August, and September are the best months for exploring the CT. Before this three-month "season" begins, users can encounter severe snowpack; past September, fall storms bring new powder.

The route provided here is mostly exposed. Avoid hiking in the heat of the day, and remember to break frequently for water. It's easy to become dehydrated in Durango's arid climate.

Aside from its impressive length, what really makes the CT unique is the story behind its development. Thousands of volunteers from the Colorado Trail Foundation built the

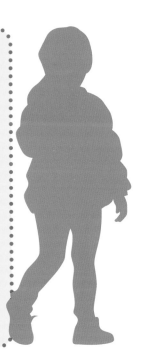

FUN FACTOR

TAKE A LOAD OFF.

Durango was founded in 1880 by the Denver and Rio Grande Railroad, which transported precious metals out of high-country mines. Over the years, the Durango & Silverton Narrow Gauge Railroad carried $300 million in precious metals, but today the coal-fired, steam-powered train only hauls tourists.

With young children, your first stop should be the original 1882 train depot. The railroad's signature Silverton train tour departs daily from the depot in summer months, taking passengers on a scenic 3½-hour ride through the San Juan National Forest to Silverton, where you'll have time to eat and shop before returning to Durango.

If a 9-hour day trip is too much, take a family-friendly yard tour instead. Visit the free train museum behind the depot. It's open every day the train operates. The depot is believed to be haunted, so if your kids are into spooky stuff, ask a guide about the station's ghostly guests.

trail. The USDA Forest Service is the foundation's primary partner, helping with management and publicity.

During the first 1.0 mile, you'll pass several river access points. Let your children stop to skip rocks on the way out if they'd like, but wait until the end of your hike to get wet. Splashing around in the creek will be a great reward, especially on a hot day.

Across the creek, a stunning cliff appears at 0.5 mile. See if your kids notice the trees shooting up from the rocky ledge, then enjoy some intermittent shade as the trail dips briefly into a forest.

When you arrive at a trail intersection and map at 1.1 miles, walk straight through the junction. Over the next 0.2 mile, avoid turning left onto game trails. If you're hiking with very young children, or anybody who isn't acclimated to the altitude, the trail map is a good place to call it a day and head back to the trailhead.

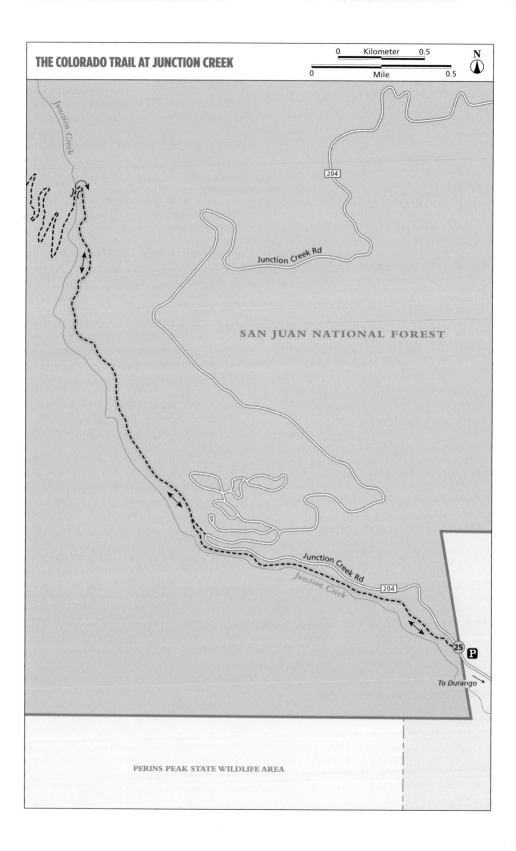

THE COLORADO TRAIL AT JUNCTION CREEK

0   Kilometer   0.5

0   Mile   0.5

N

Junction Creek

204

Junction Creek Rd

SAN JUAN NATIONAL FOREST

Junction Creek Rd

Junction Creek

204

25
P

To Durango

PERINS PEAK STATE WILDLIFE AREA

The easy section of this out-and-back hike is officially over. Up next: a steep ascent with spectacular views of cliff faces and wooded hillsides. Watch children closely while climbing a narrow ledge with sheer drops.

After reaching a crescendo, the trail slopes down to the creek. Keep following it until you arrive at a cute little bridge and a shallow bank. Take a break in the shade, grab some photos, then turn around and retrace your steps to the trailhead.

Adventurous families might opt to continue across the creek. From here the trail switches up to Gudy's Rest, named for Gudy Gaskill, the so-called mother of the Colorado Trail. Gudy's Rest is a beautiful place to sit down and take in panoramic views of Durango and the San Juan Mountains, but the difficult climb adds an extra 3.0 miles round-trip.

MILES AND DIRECTIONS

0.0   Start from the Junction Creek Trailhead map, and follow the dirt trail east toward the river. Elevation: 6,983 feet.

0.22   Arrive at a primitive wood bridge. Bear left after crossing the stream.

0.3   Pass the first of several river access points.

1.1   Reach a trail map. Continue hiking straight through the intersection. Over the next 0.2 mile, avoid turning left onto game trails extending from the main route.

2.2   Reach a particularly rocky patch of trail, and begin walking downhill.

2.4   There's a big dip in the trail. Keep going: You're almost to the bridge.

2.55   Arrive at the bridge. After lounging near the water, turn around and hike back the way you came.

4.0   You're back at the trail map and intersection you passed at 1.1 miles. Bear right, then hike downhill toward the river.

4.85   Turn right at the primitive wood bridge.

5.1   Arrive back at the trailhead.

26 JUD WIEBE MEMORIAL TRAIL

Accessible from Telluride's historic business district, this short but steep trek gives families a taste of what Telluride hiking is all about: babbling brooks, steep ascents, panoramic views, quaking aspen trees, wildlife viewing, and waterfalls—all in a couple of miles.

Start: Jud Wiebe Memorial Trail welcome sign at the top of North Aspen Street
Distance: 2.2 miles out and back
Hiking time: 1–3 hours
Difficulty: Difficult
Elevation gain: 905 feet
Trail surface: Dirt and rock
Hours: None posted
Best seasons: Summer and fall
Water: None
Toilets: None
Nursing benches: At the scenic overlook at 1.1 miles
Stroller-friendly: No
Potential child hazards: Steep ledges

Other trail users: Equestrians, mountain bikers
Dogs: Must be leashed
Land status: USDA Forest Service
Nearest town: Telluride
Fees and permits: None
Maps: USDA Telluride Area Trails
Trail contact: USDA Forest Service, Norwood Ranger District, 1150 Forest St., Norwood 81423; (970) 327-4261; www.fs.usda.gov/activity/gmug/recreation/hiking
Gear suggestions: Sunscreen, sun-protective clothing, brimmed hats, sunglasses, trekking poles, waterproof hiking sandals, swimsuits, snacks, Nuun tablets, extra water

FINDING THE TRAILHEAD

Two trailheads provide access to the Jud Wiebe Trail, but you can't park at either of them. Drive to Telluride, and park on one of the streets in the downtown business district. Many streets offer free 2-hour parking and/or metered parking for up to 3 hours. If you think you'll be out longer, free all-day parking is available at the Carhenge parking lot on West Pacific Street. From the business district, head to North Aspen Street and begin walking north to reach the intersection of North Aspen Street and West Dakota Avenue. From there, continue uphill to the large Jud Wiebe Trail welcome sign.

THE HIKE

The Jud Wiebe Trail is a local favorite for a reason! A relatively short climb delivers an excellent workout plus panoramic views of Telluride, all the way from Bridal Veil Falls (Colorado's tallest free-falling waterfalls) to the Valley Floor, that 3-mile-long protected corridor you passed on your way into town, featuring meadows, the San Miguel River, and wildlife galore.

Because it's so well loved, the Jud Wiebe Trail is well marked, well worn, and easy to follow. Two trailheads service the pathway. The trailheads are located a few blocks apart, at the tops of North Aspen and North Oak Streets.

Hikers can begin at either trailhead. In fact, many hikers make a 3.0-mile loop by hiking from one trailhead to the other. With kids, we'll start at the North Aspen Street trailhead and tackle a portion of the loop in a clockwise direction.

From the Jud Wiebe welcome sign, walk uphill to Cornet Creek, then cross the bridge to begin a steep climb on a narrow dirt path. Look left as you ascend. Postcard-perfect

views of Telluride appear almost immediately, and you'll have plenty of opportunities to observe aerial panoramas of the town's bustling business district and popular ski mountain.

The Jud Wiebe Trail ascends 900 feet in the first 1.0 mile. If your kids aren't ready for such a massive climb, don't sweat it. By starting at the North Aspen Street trailhead, hikers gain the best views in the first 0.5 mile. If necessary, you can turn around at the bend at 0.5 mile without sacrificing on views.

In this guide, we'll continue on into a thick grove of quaking aspens—a real treat if you're hiking during fall's leaf-peeping season. Before long, you're in a dense pine forest. Keep going uphill!

Look for deer and porcupines scurrying through the woods, and watch for rocks and roots below your feet. After passing a Jud Wiebe Trail marker at 0.8 mile, the trail emerges from the woods and you travel along a ridge. The grade decreases, and the views get better and better as you go.

For families, the bench and scenic overlook at 1.1 miles is a perfect "summit." Look for a small boulder with a plaque. The trail is named for a forest service snow ranger who planned it in the 1980s. Wiebe's vision for Telluride was to bring nature directly to residents and visitors by making authentic nature experiences more accessible. Wiebe passed away from cancer a year before this trail's completion, but thankfully his vision lives on today.

Enjoy a snack at the bench before turning around and hiking back the way you came. (**Option:** If you get to the bench and you're up for more, complete the full loop. The trail eventually intersects Tomboy Road. Follow Tomboy downhill to reach the other trailhead, at the top of North Oak Street.)

The best thing about the out-and-back route is that it ends at Cornet Creek, a wonderful reward for young hikers. Play in the water before heading up the Cornet Creek Trail, the vague trail to the right of the stream. In 0.2 mile you'll discover the 80-foot-tall Cornet Creek Falls. The additional mileage to/from the waterfall is not included in the detailed directions below.

FUN FACTOR

RIDE THE GONDOLA IN TELLURIDE.

Telluride has a lot going for families! The former Victorian mining town is set in a box canyon, a special type of canyon with such steep-sided walls that there's only one entrance/exit.

Telluride is known for its vibrant summer festival scene and its alpine skiing. Fall and spring are also good times to visit. The town's historic shopping district claims several landmarks, including the Telluride Historical Museum, which showcases local history in a converted hospital from 1896. Town Park has an excellent playground, and tubing on the San Miguel River is always fun with kids, but the best place for families to start is with a free ride on the Telluride/Mountain Village gondola.

This 8-mile, wind/solar-powered transportation system runs daily, from 7 a.m. until midnight, providing connectivity between Telluride and the nearby community of Mountain Village.

The "G," as locals call it, consists of four stations. Begin at Telluride Station and ride to the 10,540-foot summit at San Sophia Station, featuring hiking and biking trails, Allred's Restaurant, and the ski resort. From San Sophia, gondola riders can descend into Mountain Village. Once you've reached Gondola Plaza, go down the stairs to Mountain Village Core, or keep riding the gondola to access the Mountain Market and Mountain Village Town Hall.

Back in Telluride, there's plenty of family-friendly dining laid out along West Colorado Avenue and throughout the downtown district. For pizza lovers, Brown Dog Pizza is a must-try. The Detroit-style joint has won several awards for its pies, and competes at the World Pizza Championship.

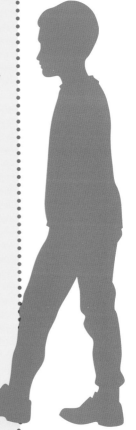

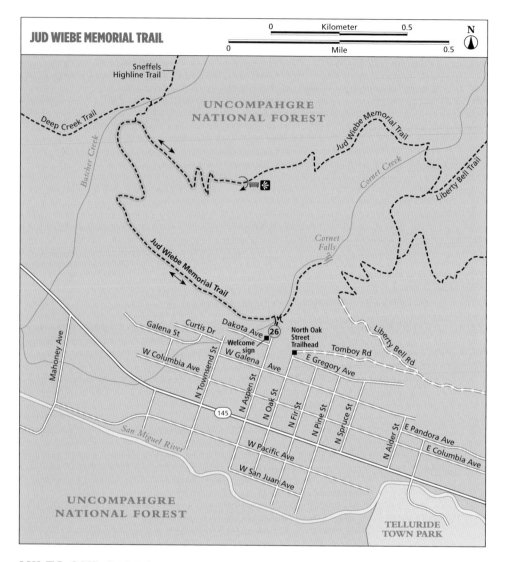

MILES AND DIRECTIONS

0.0 Start from the Jud Wiebe Memorial Trail welcome sign, and walk uphill toward the water. In 150 feet, turn left. Use the bridge to cross the river. Elevation: 8,919 feet.

0.5 After rounding a bend, the trail enters a forest.

0.8 Come to a Jud Wiebe Trail marker. Keep hiking uphill.

1.1 Arrive at a bench and scenic overlook. After enjoying the view, return the way you came.

2.2 Arrive back at the trailhead.

FALL

By September, local hikers are talking about one thing only: leaf-peeping. And for good reason! Quaking aspen trees grow especially well in the acidic soil found at higher elevations. In preparation for winter, their green summer leaves turn bright yellow, creating a vivid display in forests across Colorado. Summit County is an especially beautiful place to peep leaves, which is why you'll find several hikes in Silverton and Breckenridge listed in this section. With its cooler temperatures, autumn is also an ideal time to explore some of the state's hottest hiking destinations, including Paint Mines Interpretive Park (see hike 39). Keep in mind that fall comes quickly in the Centennial State, and it doesn't last long. September and October are the best times to view foliage and wildlife scurrying about in a pre-hibernation frenzy. If you put off your hiking until later in the season, all those colorful leaves will be covering the ground.

27 LOWER CATARACT LOOP TRAIL

Tucked inside the Eagles Nest Wilderness, Lower Cataract Lake is an inspiring place for total nature immersion. A loop trail rings the water, delivering a flat trek suitable for all ability levels. The route might be easy, but the setting is dreamlike, with unforgettable views of Cataract Falls set beyond a breezy meadow filled with butterflies and dragonflies. Architectural elements, including a large beaver dam and a long bridge, provide fodder for young builders.

Start: Lower Cataract Loop Trailhead
Distance: 2.3-mile loop
Hiking time: 1.5–3 hours
Difficulty: Easy
Elevation gain: 180 feet
Trail surface: dirt
Hours: None posted
Best seasons: Summer and fall
Water: None
Toilets: Vault toilets near the trailhead
Nursing benches: None
Stroller-friendly: No
Potential child hazards: Large lake, rapids, mosquitoes (during wet season)
Other trail users: None

Dogs: Must be on a leash no longer than 6 feet
Land status: USDA Forest Service
Nearest towns: Silverthorne and Kremmling
Fees and permits: None
Maps: Dillon Ranger District Cataract Lake (Lower) Hiking Trail—FDT 57
Trail contact: USDA Forest Service, Dillon Ranger District, 680 Blue River Pkwy., Silverthorne 80498; (970) 468-5400; www.dillonrangerdistrict .com/trails/Cataract_Lake_Lower.pdf
Gear suggestions: Windbreakers and/or fleece jackets, pants or convertible pants, waterproof hiking sandals, sunscreen, mosquito repellent, extra water

FINDING THE TRAILHEAD

From Silverthorne, drive north on CO 9. Pass mile marker 118, then turn left (east) onto Heeney Road (CR 30). In 5.3 miles, make another left onto Cataract Creek Road. In 2.5 miles—after passing Cataract Campground and the Surprise Lake Trailhead—the bumpy dirt road ends at a parking area. The Lower Cataract Loop Trailhead is on the other side of the USDA Forest Service gate. Do not block the gate with your car.

THE HIKE

Welcome to paradise. If the altitude doesn't take your breath away, the alpine scenery surrounding Cataract Lake certainly will. Through August, beautiful wildflowers fill the lakeside meadows—but it's the fall aspens that are truly worthwhile.

After walking past the forest service gate, look for a vague trailhead marked by several interpretive signs and a welcome kiosk. Three trails depart from this area. The middle path takes families straight to the lake for picnicking and fishing (license required); the outer tracks form the Lower Cataract Loop Trail.

It's fine to go either way. We'll turn left at the signs and walk away from the outhouse to begin a clockwise circuit through the Eagles Nest Wilderness.

As the dirt trail tracks slightly downhill, look ahead for views of Cataract Falls in the distance. After crossing Cataract Creek, the trail skirts the lake before weaving gently

uphill through sunny sagebrush fields with stands of aspen. Instruct children to keep an eye out for dragonflies and butterflies as you near a small pond. Ducks can be seen wading in the shallow water.

Farther down the trail, on the lake's west shore, you'll enter a mixed-conifer forest where red columbine grows on the shadowy hillside. Not quite the state flower, but close.

Look right at 1.05 miles to find the massive beaver dam created by nature's premier engineers. You really can't miss it! (If you get to the long wooden bridge at 1.15 miles, you've gone too far.) Although the falls aren't visible from the bridge, some hikers follow the gushing creek uphill to reach them. Hiking to the falls from the bridge is not part of the forest service trail, and it's a bad idea—the hillside is steep and slippery.

Watch rapids crash below the bridge before continuing on to the lake's north shore. The trail is washed out beyond the bridge. Steer straight, and follow the most obvious path slightly uphill into a wet meadow, where a clear trail resumes.

FUN FACTOR

DISCOVER ONE OF SUMMIT COUNTY'S BEST-KEPT SECRETS.

Constructed between 1938 and 1943 as a part of the Colorado–Big Thompson Project, Green Mountain Reservoir provides Colorado's Western Slope community with water from the Colorado River. The humongous, 2,125-acre reservoir also supplies residents and tourists with easy access to the great outdoors.

To fully experience the reservoir, you'll have to get on the water. On the northwest bank, Heeney Marina is a one-stop shop for pontoon and paddleboard rentals. The reservoir is popular with anglers, who catch rainbow, lake, and brown trout and kokanee salmon. If you want to cast a line, fishing equipment and bait are available at the nearby bait-and-tackle store.

Hikers can explore any of the paths below the high-water mark around the lake. Here's something you won't read anywhere else in this book: Go ahead and go off-trail to reach any of the fish coves.

If ever there was a time for your family to take up birding, this is it. For years, Green Mountain Reservoir has been a nesting site for a pair of eagles, and western ospreys hunt for fish around the water. Whether you're boating, hiking, or birding, be sure to carry binoculars—and bug spray.

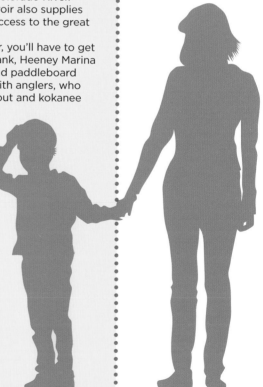

For the next 0.5 mile, enjoy aerial views of the site's main attraction as the trail ascends to a ridgeline hovering above Cataract Lake. After passing a forest service marker, bear left at a fork and hike away from the water. The trail dips into a lush forest. In what seems like too short a time, you're out of the woods, and the trail dead-ends into a service road. Turn left onto the dirt-and-gravel drive.

Back at the trailhead, use the middle trail to access the lake's rocky shore, with several picnic benches and a wading area. Fishing on the lake is good. Anglers reel in brown, rainbow, and brook trout—though the big browns tend to congregate further west, where there's vegetation in the water. Additional mileage to/from the lake is minimal, and not included in the directions below.

With older kids, it's possible to continue to Upper Cataract Lake, but you'll have to backtrack to the Surprise Lake Trailhead (FDT 62). While the lower portion of the route is a pleasant walk through open aspen groves, the grade intensifies as the trail climbs through fir-and-spruce forest during a strenuous 5.0-mile out-and-back trek.

MILES AND DIRECTIONS

0.0 Start at the USDA Forest Service gate. Walk through the gate, bear left at the three-way intersection, and hike slightly downhill. Elevation: 8,656 feet.

0.1 Cross the creek, then pass through another gate.

0.2 Come to two back-to-back trail markers. Bear left at both junctions, and follow the arrows.

0.35 Walk across a small footbridge.

0.9 Enter a dense forest. Look for red columbine growing along the shaded hillside.

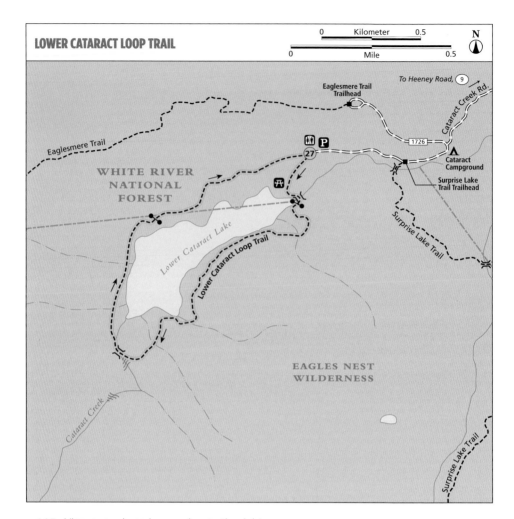

1.05 View a very large beaver dam to the right.

1.15 Cross Cataract Creek on a long wooden bridge. Keep a close eye on young children near the rapids.

1.3 The trail is washed out for the next 0.1 mile. Stay straight, following the most obvious path uphill.

1.85 Pass a forest service sign. Continue walking straight along the Lower Cataract Loop Trail.

1.9 When you come to a fork in the trail, bear left and hike away from the lake.

2.15 The Lower Cataract Loop Trail ends at a service road. Turn left, and follow the road back to the trailhead.

2.3 Arrive back at the forest service gate.

28 LILY PAD LAKE HIKING TRAIL

Lily Pad Lake Hiking Trail (FDT 50) makes it easy for families to enter into the Eagles Nest Wilderness during a gentle trek to the sparkling lake lazing below Buffalo Mountain (12,777'). On this short hike, you'll pass an open meadow, several scenic vistas, and a beaver pond while exploring a peaceful forest of towering lodgepole pines. Colorful wildflowers dot the landscape in summer, yet fall is a particularly vibrant time to tackle this route.

Start: Meadow Creek Trailhead
Distance: 3.0 miles out and back
Hiking time: 1.5–3 hours
Difficulty: Moderate
Elevation gain: 766 feet
Trail surface: Dirt, loose gravel, and rock
Hours: None posted
Best seasons: Apr through Oct
Water: None
Toilets: None
Nursing benches: At Lily Pad Lake
Stroller-friendly: No
Potential child hazards: Large lake, a stream
Other trail users: None

Dogs: Permitted, but must be leashed at all times in the Eagles Nest Wilderness
Land status: USDA Forest Service
Nearest town: Frisco
Fees and permits: None
Maps: National Geographic Trails Illustrated Vail, Frisco, Dillon
Trail contact: USDA Forest Service, Dillon Ranger District, 680 Blue River Pkwy., Silverthorne, 80498; (970) 468-5400; www.dillonrangerdistrict .com/trails/Lilypad_Lake.pdf
Gear suggestions: Sunscreen, hats, sunglasses, warm jackets, sturdy waterproof boots or hiking sandals, a picnic, binoculars, magnifying glass

FINDING THE TRAILHEAD

From I-70, take exit 205 for Silverthorne and Dillon; travel north on CO 9 to the roundabout. Take the second exit off the roundabout, and follow CR 1231 until it ends at a large parking lot set to the highway. Look for a large trail map near the northeast corner of the parking lot marking the Meadow Creek Trailhead.

THE HIKE

The Lily Pad Lake Hiking Trail stretches from the Buffalo Mountain Trailhead down toward the Meadow Creek Trailhead. The trail's main attraction—Lily Pad Lake—is roughly the halfway point between the two trailheads. Families can start their hike from either trailhead. We'll begin at the Meadow Creek Trailhead on the Meadow Creek Trail (FDT 33).

The narrow dirt trail departs from a large USDA Forest Service map near the northeast corner of the parking lot. Traveling north, the rocky path passes through stands of lodgepole pine and aspens that really come to life during leaf-peeping season.

The first segment of the Meadow Creek Trail is steep. About 500 feet into the climb, bear left at a fork to stay on the Meadow Creek Trail, bypassing a thin unofficial trail leading to the creek. After crossing a wooden bridge, the trail levels out momentarily, giving hikers a chance to catch their breath before the grade intensifies. When you come to a fork, turn right, following the arrow on the trail post toward the Lily Pad Hiking Trail.

The trail passes through a thick forest, and you'll notice a significant number of fallen trees. Ask children to look for woodpeckers. Even if they can't see the omnivorous birds, they will likely hear the birds' telltale pecks as they probe for insects in bark and chisel nest holes in deadwood.

You'll also hear rushing water as you approach Meadow Creek. After crossing the creek via a rickety bridge, the Lily Pad Hiking Trail enters the Eagles Nest Wilderness, which preserves the majority of the north–south oriented Gore Range. From here, mountain bikes are prohibited, and dogs must be leashed.

The trail snakes around a ridge and winds through a meadow. A mile into the route, enjoy a perfectly framed view of Dillon Reservoir, sometimes referred to as Lake Dillon.

After a solid trek, you arrive at a small alpine lake covered in pond lilies. In June, the yellow lilies are in full bloom, and you might spy mother ducks crossing the lily pads with their ducklings. Don't stop at this pond. Lily Pad Lake is a little farther down the trail. This first body of water is one of several beaver ponds that attracted fur trappers to the area between 1810 and 1840.

The snowcapped Buffalo Mountain frames Lily Pad Lake to the west. Originally the lake was called Pond Lily, back when the Giberson family owed 720 acres of waterside land and paid the US government to graze their cattle near the lake. The lake's name has always been a bit of a misnomer. You won't see many lilies on Lily Pad Lake; they don't thrive on the big lake.

FUN FACTOR

SEE WHAT FRISCO LAKE LIFE IS ALL ABOUT.

It is no wonder Frisco is nicknamed "The Main Street of the Rockies." Located in the heart of Summit County, book-ended by Mount Royal and the Frisco Marina, the town's Main Street contains more than fifty locally owned restaurants, coffee shops, bookstores, and boutiques.

Dillon Reservoir anchors Frisco. For an out-of-the-ordinary mountain town experience, visit the Frisco Bay Marina, a certified clean marina situated on the shores of the 3,300-acre reservoir. Flatwater activities include kayaking, canoeing, and stand-up paddleboarding. If your family hasn't tried sailing yet, sign up for a 2-hour introductory lesson with one of the ASA-certified instructors at Windrider of Breezerider.

Or try catching your dinner. The reservoir teems with kokanee salmon, arctic char, and brown and rainbow trout, and companies such as Alpine Fishing Adventures offer guided fishing tours for families on pontoon boats that accommodate young children and those with special needs. The high-altitude boating season is weather dependent, typically running from June through mid-September.

If you don't make it up in time to experience lake life, check out the eighteen-hole Peak One Disc Golf Course at Frisco Adventure Park. The public course is free. BYO Frisbee, or borrow one at the on-site lodge. After a round, order takeout on Main Street, and enjoy a picnic lunch at Walter Byron Park, located along Ten Mile Creek, offering a gazebo, picnic tables, and a playground.

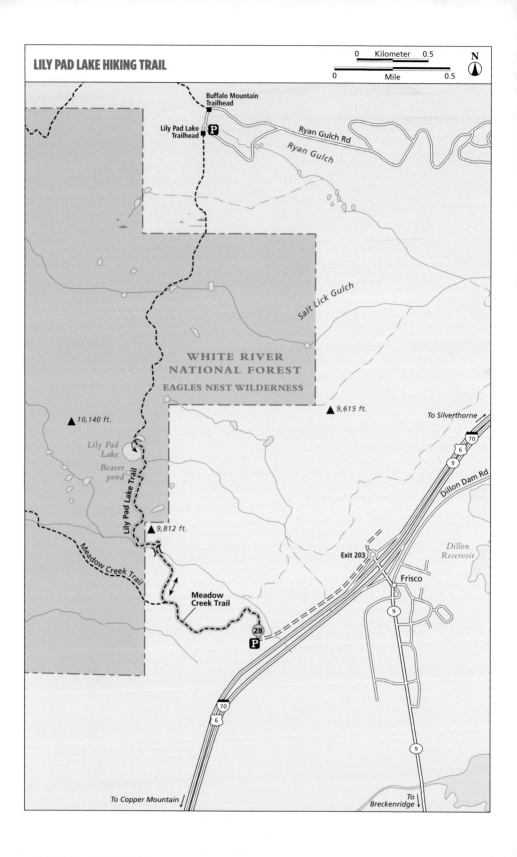

LILY PAD LAKE HIKING TRAIL

0 Kilometer 0.5
0 Mile 0.5

N

Buffalo Mountain
Trailhead

Lily Pad Lake
Trailhead   P

Ryan Gulch Rd

Ryan Gulch

Salt Lick Gulch

WHITE RIVER
NATIONAL FOREST
EAGLES NEST WILDERNESS

▲ 10,140 ft.

▲ 9,615 ft.

To Silverthorne

70
6
9

Dillon Dam Rd

Lily Pad
Lake

Beaver
pond

Dillon
Reservoir

▲ 9,812 ft.

Exit 203

Frisco

Meadow Creek Trail

Meadow
Creek Trail

28

P

9

70
6

9

To Copper Mountain

To
Breckenridge

Follow the trail to a small beach on the lake's rocky shore—the perfect place for a picnic or hearty snack. Past the lake, the Lily Pad Lake Hiking Trail continues on to the northern trailhead on Ryan Gulch Road, which is another 1.4 miles one way. October blizzards are typical in Summit County, so be sure to put this route on your early-fall itinerary.

MILES AND DIRECTIONS

0.0 Start at the large trail map at the Meadow Creek Trailhead (FDT 33), and begin a steep ascent on rocky dirt singletrack. Elevation: 9,825 feet.

0.15 Cross a wooden bridge.

0.6 Bear right at the fork in the trail, and follow the arrow on the trail post toward Lily Pad Lake.

0.8 Cross Meadow Creek via a rickety bridge.

1.5 Arrive at Lily Pad Lake. After enjoying the scenery, turn around and retrace your steps.

2.3 This time, turn left at the trail intersection, and follow Meadow Creek Trail back to your car.

3.0 Arrive back at the trailhead.

29 COYOTE TRAIL

The lush trails inside Rifle Falls State Park will have you feeling like you've been transported to a tropical paradise south of the equator. That's all thanks to the park's pivotal feature: an 80-foot triple waterfall flowing over a travertine dam on East Rifle Creek. In addition to viewing the falls and exploring several small limestone caves, families will discover that autumn is the perfect time for a waterside picnic and a mellow trek to a fish hatchery.

Start: North parking lot, on the far side of Rifle Falls State Park
Distance: 1.5-mile loop
Hiking time: 1–2 hours
Difficulty: Easy
Elevation gain: 70 feet
Trail surface: Dirt
Hours: 6 a.m. to 10 p.m. Campers have 24-hour access to the site.
Best seasons: Summer and fall
Water: A pump with potable water near the walk-in camping area
Toilets: Vault toilets near the walk-in camping area and in the north parking lot
Nursing benches: Several along Coyote Trail
Stroller-friendly: No
Potential child hazards: Waterfall
Other trail users: None

Dogs: Permitted on all three trails inside the park
Land status: Colorado Parks & Wildlife
Nearest town: Glenwood Springs
Fees and permits: Per-vehicle day-use fee or Colorado Parks & Wildlife Annual Pass
Maps: Colorado State Parks Rifle Falls State Park
Trail contact: Colorado Parks & Wildlife, 5775 Hwy. 325, Rifle 81650; (970) 625-1607; cpw.state.co.us/placestogo/parks/riflefalls
Gear suggestions: Waterproof hiking sandals, pants or convertible pants, sunscreen, sunglasses, brimmed hats, bug repellent, binoculars, a flashlight, fishing gear (if fishing)

FINDING THE TRAILHEAD

From Rifle, which is directly north of I-70, take Railroad Avenue through town. After passing the Garfield County Courthouse, Railroad Avenue runs into CO 13 (Government Road). Continue driving north, and in 1.3 miles turn right onto CO 325. When you reach the Rifle Gap Reservoir, veer right to stay on CO 325. In approximately 5.5 miles, reach Rifle Falls State Park, on the right side of the road.

THE HIKE

Rifle Falls has been a tourist attraction since at least 1884, when entrepreneur James Watson charged visitors admission to see a triple waterfall at "Rifle Falls Ranch." When the nearby town of Rifle built its hydroelectric plant in 1910, the falls became a source of hydroelectric power until the late 1950s. It wasn't until 1966 that Rifle Falls became a state park, and the focus shifted back to recreation.

Now the secret's out, and Rifle Falls is a busy place during the summer months. If you're able to plan a fall getaway once school's back in session, you'll be able to hike without all the crowds.

Three trails weave through the 48-acre site. Coyote Trail is especially lush, since spray from the falls continuously waters the surrounding greenery.

The trail departs from the north parking lot, at the far end of the park. To get there, follow a paved road all the way through the campground. Park, and walk up the wide trail toward the waterfall. You'll pass several picnic benches on the way to Rifle Falls. Near the base of the falls, look for the Coyote Trail sign.

Turn left onto Coyote Trail, and begin hiking uphill. Within the first 0.1 mile, you'll come to two limestone caves. It's fine to explore the small caves with children. Consider bringing flashlights for enhanced viewing, and remind everyone in your group to tread lightly through this delicate space.

Coyote Trail continues uphill, past the caves, and is extremely easy to follow thanks to maintenance efforts by park staff in the late 1990s. After a short ascent, you're at the top of the falls. Look for a 0.1-mile detour (each way) to an enclosed overlook granting thrilling views of the waterfall. Then retrace your steps to the main trail, and turn left to complete a loop. The rocky dirt trail winds downhill on the other side of the falls, ending near the parking lot where it started.

Keep an eye out for wildlife as you hike. The area's deciduous riparian forest and wetlands are home to a variety of animals, including turkey vultures, mule deer, and great blue herons.

Rifle Falls is a popular destination for anglers. Fish up to 19 inches long have been reeled in, and rainbow, brown, and cutthroat trout are found in East Rifle Creek, flowing through Rifle Falls.

If your family fishes, or you'd like to add an additional 2.0 miles round-trip to your hike, turn right onto the Bobcat Trail, jutting out from the Coyote Trail not far from the scenic overlook.

The narrow dirt trail travels along East Rifle Creek, through an open meadow, into an alluring box elder and cottonwood forest. After passing several stocked trout ponds, the Bobcat Trail ends at the Rifle Falls State Fish Hatchery, one of the largest trout production hatcheries in Colorado. The hike to the hatchery is not included in the directions below.

Squirrel Trail is another fun add-on. The 1.5-mile dirt path departs from the south end of the north parking lot and follows Rifle Creek through a Gambel oak forest and the park's walk-in tent campsites before ending near the entrance station.

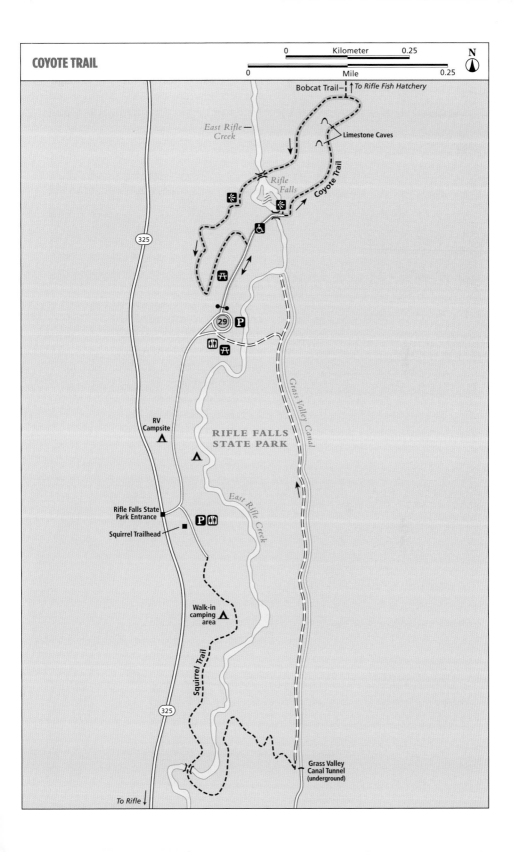

COYOTE TRAIL

0 Kilometer 0.25

0 Mile 0.25

N

To Rifle Fish Hatchery

Bobcat Trail

East Rifle Creek

Limestone Caves

Rifle Falls

Coyote Trail

325

29 P

RV Campsite

RIFLE FALLS STATE PARK

Grass Valley Canal

East Rifle Creek

Rifle Falls State Park Entrance

Squirrel Trailhead

P

Walk-in camping area

Squirrel Trail

325

Grass Valley Canal Tunnel (underground)

To Rifle

If you need any assistance, the Rifle Falls State Park Visitor Center is approximately 4 miles south of Rifle Falls State Park, at the entrance to Rifle Gap State Park.

MILES AND DIRECTIONS

0.0 Start from the north parking lot, on the far side of the park, and walk up the wide trail to view Rifle Falls, then continue on to the Coyote Trail sign. Elevation: 6,500 feet.

0.1 Turn left onto the Coyote Trail and begin hiking uphill.

0.5 Arrive at the top of the falls, where a 0.2-mile out-and-back detour will take you to a viewpoint.

1.5 Arrive back at the Coyote Trail sign.

FUN FACTOR

EXPERIMENT WITH HIKE-IN CAMPING IN A LOW-STAKES ENVIRONMENT.

In addition to its thirteen drive-in campsites with RV hookups, Rifle Falls State Park has seven walk-in campsites stationed along the babbling East Rifle Creek. The walk-in campsites feel secluded, yet you're never very far from the car. It's the perfect introductory experience for families who want to try hike-in camping.

Reserve your campsite early. Space is limited at Rifle Falls, and tent sites fill up on beautiful fall weekends. Always check for fire bans before heading out on an overnight adventure. If a ban is in place, plan ahead by packing peanut butter sandwiches. Then teach your kids that "raw" s'mores are almost as delicious as the cooked variety!

30 SALLIE BARBER MINE ROAD

Colorado was built on mining, and abandoned shafts from Cripple Creek to Summit County tell a powerful story of grit and determination. The French Gulch was an important gold rush area in the late 1800s. Today it's a popular hiking destination managed by the USDA Forest Service, featuring an extensive trail system that includes Sallie Barber Mine Road, a wide dirt-and-gravel path following a babbling stream to the ruins of a historic mining site. In addition to stellar mountain views, endless stands of aspens make this mellow trek extra vivid in September and October.

Start: White River National Forest kiosk
Distance: 2.8 miles out and back
Hiking time: 2–4 hours
Difficulty: Moderate
Elevation gain: 381 feet
Trail surface: Dirt, gravel, and rock
Hours: None posted
Best seasons: May through Oct
Water: None
Toilets: None
Nursing benches: Just past the mine
Stroller-friendly: No
Potential child hazards: A mine shaft
Other trail users: Equestrians, mountain bikers
Dogs: Must be leashed or under voice control

Land status: USDA Forest Service
Nearest town: Breckenridge
Fees and permits: None
Maps: National Geographic Trails Illustrated Breckenridge Tennessee Pass
Trail contact: White River National Forest, Dillon Ranger District, 680 Blue River Pkwy., Silverthorne 80498; (970) 468-5400; www .dillonrangerdistrict.com/trails/ Sallie_Barber_Mine_Road.pdf
Gear suggestions: Fleece jackets and/or windbreakers, waterproof hiking shoes, sunscreen, brimmed hats, sunglasses, binoculars

FINDING THE TRAILHEAD

From I-70, take exit 203 for Frisco/Breckenridge. Travel south on CO 9 through Frisco, and continue toward Breckenridge. Before reaching Breckenridge's downtown shopping district, turn left at the 7-Eleven at the intersection of CO 9 and CR 450. The road forks in 0.4 mile. Taking the right fork for Reiling Road, head into the subdivision. In 0.7 mile come to a stop sign. Turn left onto French Gulch Road (CR 2). Drive for 2.75 miles, then look for a pullout parking area to your right. There is a White River National Forest kiosk and trail map at the far end of the dirt lot. We're starting at this kiosk, since there's no public parking beyond the lot. If you get to the "No Public Parking" signs, you've gone too far.

THE HIKE

The trail leading to the Sallie Barber Mine can be tricky to find. After driving down French Gulch Road for 2.75 miles, you'll come to a small dirt parking area on the right side of the road. There's a White River National Forest kiosk and trail map at the east edge of the pullout, and you'll notice a narrow dirt trail departing from a trailhead. This trail is not Sallie Barber Mine Road (FDR 559).

To get to Sallie Barber Mine Road, park in the pullout and walk farther down French Gulch Road, past the "No Public Parking" signs. In about 0.1 mile, walk through the metal forest service gate, and head downhill. Now you're on the right trail.

The trek to the Sallie Barber Mine ascends a groomed service road. The trail crosses French Creek before making a hairpin turn. After continuing past a clearing, you're in for a gradual climb through a picturesque pine forest studded with colorful aspens. Listen to the tranquil sound of the creek, and look for moss and lichen growing near the water.

When you reach the intersection for Turk's Trail, take in panoramic views of Breckenridge Ski Resort to the west. After crossing a metal drainage tube, the trail narrows slightly as towering trees thicken. Cross a boundary line at 0.8 mile and continue uphill, past the Weber Gulch Trail marker. You really can't miss this hike's summit—the expansive ruins of the Sallie Barber Mine at the top of a hill.

Ask children to imagine what it would have been like mining for gold 10,728 feet above sea level. If it seems like a daunting task, it was. After traveling more than halfway across the country, many East Coast prospectors turned around when they saw what they were up against in Colorado!

The 365-foot-deep Sallie Barber Mine produced zinc ore from 1880 until 1909. Even though it was relatively small, the mine was an important addition to Colorado's gold rush era.

Amazingly, most of the site's original mining equipment is still intact. Preserved items are on display alongside several interpretive signs. Explore this delicate area while enjoying incredible views of Mineral Hill, Brewery Hill, and Humbug Hill. The trail continues beyond the mine ruins, but additional miles are not included in the directions below.

To get back to your car, retrace your steps to the metal forest service gate. Then backtrack on French Gulch Road. Much of the land surrounding Sallie Barber Mine Road is privately owned, so be sure to stay on the trail during this adventure.

FUN FACTOR

SPEND A WEEKEND IN BRECKENRIDGE.

Located at the base of the Tenmile Range, Breckenridge is one of Colorado's most charming mountain towns. Any time is a great time to visit, but early fall is magical, with long days, nice weather, and plenty of leaf peeping.

Beyond the local shopping and dining scene laid out along Main Street, with its colorfully painted Victorian storefronts, Breckenridge has a wide variety of amenities for families. Start at Blue River Plaza, offering a toddler sandbox and miniature play area. Nearby, the town's welcome center houses a small interpretive museum about Breckenridge's evolution from gold-mining mecca to ski village.

Other great in-town experiences include the rock-themed playground at Prospector Park and story time at South Branch Library, featuring musicians and/or magicians.

There's plenty of in-town hiking for active families, including a trek to an upcycled troll sculpture (see hike 19). Other easy hikes from downtown Breckenridge include Sawmill Trail, beginning at the bottom of the Snowflake Lift, and Burro Trail, accessed from the Lehman Ski Trail, located at the base of Peak 9.

On your drive to Sallie Barber Mine Road, did you notice the massive piles of smooth rock on the right side of French Gulch Road? They're remnants of gold dredging operations, and you can get a closer look by taking a quick detour on your drive home.

Park at the B&B Mine Trailhead. After snapping a few photos of your kids in the tepee (you can't miss it), look for the Reiling Dredge, Turk's Trail, and B&B Trail marker. Follow the arrow to the Reiling Dredge Trail, and hike through an aspen grove to reach a long bridge leading to a decaying dredge stuck in a small body of water. It's something

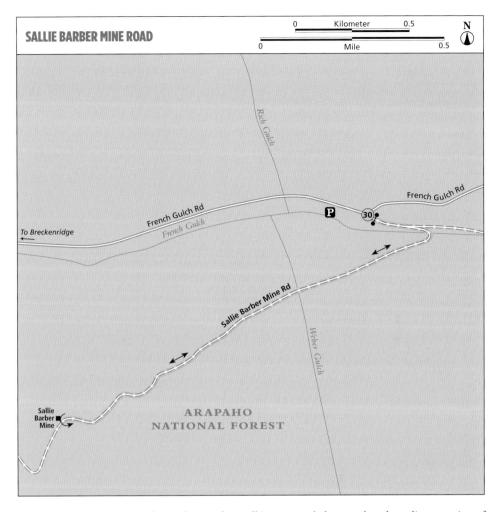

to see! Learn more about the site by walking around the pond and reading a series of interpretive signs.

MILES AND DIRECTIONS

0.0   Start at the White River National Forest trail map and kiosk, and walk east along French Gulch Road, past the "No Public Parking" signs. Elevation: 10,297 feet.

0.1   Come to a metal forest service gate. Walk through the gate and bear right at a fork in the road. Hike downhill to merge onto Sallie Barber Mine Road (FDR 559).

0.4   Pass a trail marker; continue hiking straight through the trail intersection.

0.9   Pass a trail marker for the Weber Gulch Trail. Continue on Sallie Barber Mine Road.

1.4   Arrive at the Sallie Barber Mine Historic Site. When you're done exploring, retrace your steps to the metal forest service gate.

2.7   Walk through the gate, and follow French Gulch Road back to your car.

2.8   Arrive back at the kiosk where you started.

31 HOT SPRINGS TRAIL

The Japanese buzz term "forest bathing" can be taken literally on this classic Steamboat Springs adventure. A pastoral streamside hike ends at a rustic hot springs resort featuring a series of cascading mineral pools nestled among dramatic peaks inside the Routt National Forest. While it's possible to reach Strawberry Park Hot Springs by car, hiking is a simple way to admire and protect the landscape.

Start: Large Routt National Forest Trailhead sign posted alongside Elk River Road
Distance: 6.2 miles out and back
Hiking time: 3–5 hours
Difficulty: Moderate to difficult
Elevation gain: 718 feet
Trail surface: Dirt, gravel, and rock
Hours: None posted
Best seasons: May 2 through Oct 31. The Hot Springs Trail is closed in winter and during mud season, Nov 1 until May 1.
Water: Bottled water and sports drinks available at Strawberry Park Hot Springs; bring cash.
Toilets: Vault toilets near the Mad Creek Trailhead, flush toilets at the base of Strawberry Park Hot Springs
Nursing benches: At Strawberry Park Hot Springs
Stroller-friendly: No
Potential child hazards: Sheer ledges, a fast-flowing creek, mountain lions

Other trail users: Mountain bikers
Dogs: Leashed dogs permitted on the Hot Springs Trail; pets not allowed inside Strawberry Park Hot Springs
Land status: USDA Forest Service
Nearest town: Steamboat Springs
Fees and permits: None
Maps: National Geographic Trails Illustrated Steamboat Springs, Rabbit Ears Pass
Trail contact: USDA Forest Service, Medicine Bow–Routt National Forests, 2468 Jackson St., Laramie, WY 82070; (307) 745-2300; www.fs.usda.gov/recarea/mbr/recarea/?recid=22762
Gear suggestions: Windbreakers, hiking sandals, sunscreen, sun-protective clothing, sunglasses, swimsuits, high-energy snacks, a picnic, water, cash

FINDING THE TRAILHEAD

From Steamboat Springs, take Lincoln Avenue (US 40) out of town. At the major intersection, turn right onto Elk River Road (CR 129), and follow it northwest for 5.5 miles to reach the Mad Creek Trailhead parking lot, on the right (east) side of the road. As you turn into the lot, look for the large Routt National Forest Trailhead sign posted alongside Elk River Road. The directions for this hike will begin at this sign. Do not start your hike at the Mad Creek Trailhead, which is located at the north edge of the parking lot, near a USDA Forest Service kiosk.

THE HIKE

The first step is to find the trailhead. Park in the Mad Creek Trailhead parking lot, but keep in mind that the Hot Springs Trail doesn't actually begin at the Mad Creek Trailhead. Instead, begin at the large Routt National Forest sign alongside Elk River Road. From there, turn left out of the parking lot, and follow the narrow dirt path hugging the shoulder of the road. In 0.3 mile, immediately after passing several "Private Property"

signs, turn left onto a wide gravel drive. Walk slightly uphill toward a small Hot Springs Trail marker.

Bear left at a fork to continue hiking toward the Hot Springs Trail. After passing a cattle gate, the trail narrows before opening to bucolic views of the alpine countryside. The next mile is a hot walk through tall grass and thick shrubs. When you reach the fork at 0.7 mile, turn right onto the Hot Springs Trail (#1169). The trail passes a pond before dropping down to Hot Spring Creek.

The remaining 2.0 miles are a gradual ascent alongside the roaring creek. In addition to mountain vistas, there are steep drops and sheer ledges, so keep an eye on young hikers. Lodgepole pines dominate the landscape, offering intermittent shade and creating a cooler environment for patches of ferns and trailside wildflowers.

FUN FACTOR

IN STEAMBOAT SPRINGS, IT'S ALL ABOUT THE WATER.

The scenic mountain town of Steamboat Springs has a lot going for it, from alpenglow sunsets to its light-as-a-feather powder. And yet all my children's favorite things to do revolve around water.

Fish Creek Falls is a must. A super-short, 0.25-mile walk along a paved path takes visitors to an overlook offering a bird's-eye view of a 280-foot waterfall. After snapping aerial photos, hike downhill on a primitive trail to reach a bridge at the base of the falls. Bring cash for parking.

Playing in the sand, rocks, and water at Burgess Creek Beach is another quintessential family experience. Located at the base of Steamboat Ski Resort, the man-made beach offers hours of free, nature-based fun as children build sandcastles, hop on rocks, and splash in the ice-cold water.

If you want to enjoy the water like a local, rent fishing equipment from one of the many in-town outfitters, and sink a line in the Yampa River. Later, take a sunset stroll around the pond anchoring Yampa River Botanic Park, a charming donation-based arboretum featuring fifty different gardens as well as sculptures and a children's garden, accessible from downtown Steamboat Springs via the Yampa River Core Trail.

HOT SPRINGS TRAIL

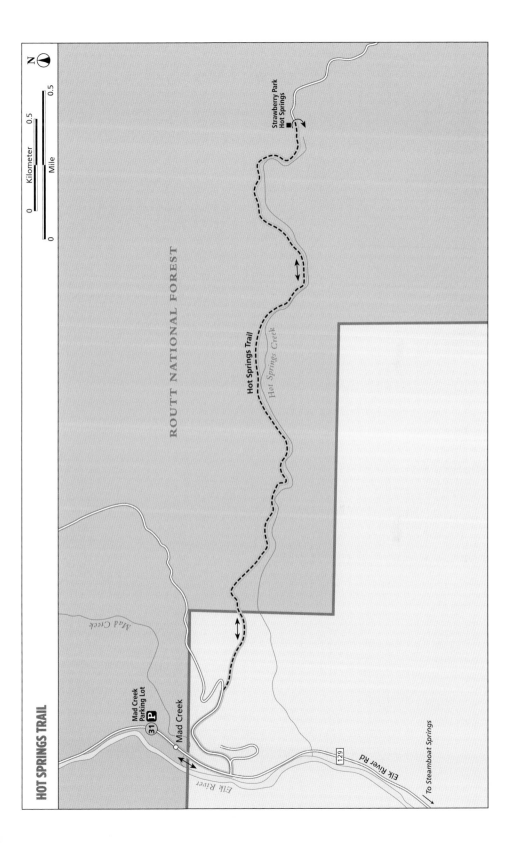

The Hot Springs Trail ends at Strawberry Park Hot Springs. At 2.8 miles, a wooden welcome sign steers guests straight toward the bare-bones resort. You're not quite there yet! It's another 0.3 mile to the water.

After passing a few campsites, you come to a large building with a slanted roof. Continue walking uphill to reach the welcome station. Make reservations online prior to arriving at Strawberry Park Hot Springs, and check in at the welcome station before soaking. Have cash handy to purchase drinks.

Mineral pool temperatures range from 101°F to 106°F. If your kids aren't crazy about the heat, they can take a dip in Hot Spring Creek instead. There's an access point beyond the pools.

Strawberry Park Hot Springs offers limited overnight lodging. The resort's off-grid camping is not recommended for families, though, since the site is clothing optional after dark.

Eventually you'll have to call it a day. Thankfully, the hike back is entirely downhill. Simply retrace your steps to the Mad Creek Trailhead.

Two Steamboat Springs–based shuttle services—Sweet Pea Tours and the Hot Springs Shuttle—transport guests to and from Strawberry Park Hot Springs. If you don't want to hike back, it's possible to hitch a ride home in one of their vans. But you must make arrangements in advance to ensure that the company you choose is operating on the day of your adventure.

MILES AND DIRECTIONS

0.0   Start from the large Routt National Forest Trailhead sign, and turn left onto Elk River Road. Carefully walk south down the narrow dirt trail beside the road. Elevation: 6,770 feet.

0.1   Cross Mad Creek on a metal bridge.

0.3   Turn left onto a wide dirt-and-gravel drive.

0.35   Bear left at the fork in the trail. Below a large "No Parking" sign is a smaller sign for the Hot Springs Trail.

0.7   Turn right at the trail marker to merge onto the Hot Springs Trail.

2.05   See if your kids can find the "secret hideout" created by a giant evergreen's expansive branches. *Hint:* It's on the left side of the trail.

2.8   Pass a Strawberry Park Hot Springs welcome sign.

3.1   After passing several streamside campsites, come to the restrooms. Walk uphill to reach the Strawberry Park Hot Springs entrance station. After soaking in the springs, hike back the way you came.

5.5   Don't forget to turn left when the Hot Springs Trail ends at the dirt-and-gravel road.

5.9   Turn right onto the dirt path paralleling Elk River Road.

6.2   Arrive back at the trailhead.

32 KRUGER ROCK TRAIL

Located in the Estes Valley, southeast of Estes Park, Hermit Park Open Space has a lot to offer, including wildlife viewing, secluded camping, beautiful picnic sites, and miles of hiking trails undulating between 7,880 and 8,964 feet. For the best views of Estes Park and the Roosevelt National Forest, climb to the top of Kruger Rock. By October, this quiet, hiker-only trail is prettier than ever as autumn colors reach their peak.

Start: Kruger Rock Trailhead
Distance: 3.4 miles out and back
Hiking time: 2–4 hours
Difficulty: Moderate to difficult
Elevation gain: 873 feet
Trail surface: Dirt and rock
Hours: Hiking trails inside the park open daily, sunrise to sunset
Best seasons: Apr through Oct
Water: None
Toilets: An outhouse at the trailhead
Nursing benches: The scenic overlook at 0.7 mile has several flat rocks on which breastfeeding moms can sit.
Stroller-friendly: No
Potential child hazards: Sheer cliffs, big drops at the top of Kruger Rock
Other trail users: None
Dogs: Must be on a leash no longer than 10 feet and cannot be left unattended

Land status: Larimer County
Nearest town: Estes Park
Fees and permits: Day-use permits available at the entrance and self-serve stations throughout the park; per-vehicle fee required for entry
Maps: Larimer County Department of Natural Resources Hermit Park Open Space
Trail contact: Larimer County Department of Natural Resources, 1800 South CR 31, Loveland 80537; (970) 619-4570; www.larimer.org/naturalresources/parks/hermit-park
Gear suggestions: Trail running shoes or hiking boots, shells or fleece, sunscreen, sunglasses, trekking poles, ample water, binoculars, a camera

FINDING THE TRAILHEAD

From downtown Estes Park, head east on North St. Vrain Avenue (US 36), and follow the road out of town. In 4.2 miles look for the entrance to Hermit Park Open Space on the right (south) side of the street. Hikers passing through Longmont should drive west on CO 66 to Lyons, turn right onto 5th Avenue (US 36), and drive for approximately 16.5 miles. Turn into Hermit Park Open Space. Check in at the ranger station, then continue driving through the park. Shortly after the turnoff for Bobcat Campground, look for the Kruger Rock parking lot, on your right. The trailhead takes off from this lot.

THE HIKE

I stumbled on the Kruger Rock Trail by accident, when an hour-long entrance line thwarted my planned trip to Cub Lake, a popular destination inside Rocky Mountain National Park. (See hike 7 for an alternative ROMO hike.)

A park ranger at ROMO's Beaver Meadows Visitor Center suggested Hermit Park Open Space as a less-crowded option. The beautiful, secluded property is a new addition to the Colorado hiking circuit.

Hermit Park opened as a cattle ranch. When the multinational IT company Hewlett-Packard purchased the property in 1967, it managed the area as a private retreat for its staff (and later, Agilent Technologies employees) until 2007. Through a community-supported partnership, Larimer County purchased the tract, opening it to the public in 2008.

Talk about a memorable fall foliage hike! From the kiosk at the Kruger Rock Trail-head, follow the rocky dirt trail straight toward electrifying stands of aspens. When you arrive at the four-way intersection, continue straight through it. The Kruger Rock Trail gets wider, and a little bit sandy, after the intersection. Watch for rocks and roots while ascending a series of switchbacks bordered by native shrubs.

At 0.5 mile into the route, the trail levels out before reaching a scenic overlook opening to spectacular views of downtown Estes Park. This rocky outcropping is the perfect place to snap a family photo. If you're hiking with young children, this viewpoint is a good target. Enjoy a picnic lunch, then turn around and retrace your steps for a 1.4-mile round-trip adventure.

Families with older kids should continue past the overlook. The trail winds away from town, and a moderate climb resumes. Watch for a sharp switch in the trail at 1.1 miles. The trail gets progressively steeper until reaching a massive boulder, at which point hikers enjoy a breather during a relaxing stroll through a sparse pine forest.

The massive rock at 1.6 miles is a false summit. Watch your children near the sheer ledge to the right, and continue uphill. You still have a little more terrain to cover before arriving at Kruger Rock. Follow rocky switchbacks up a ridge to the base of Kruger Rock.

FUN FACTOR

TAKE A DETOUR TO ESTES PARK.

Hermit Park Open Space is a stone's throw from the charming town of Estes Park. If you worked up an appetite hiking, stop for lunch and window-shopping along St. Vrain Avenue, the gateway to a bustling downtown district comprising more than 300 boutiques, shops, and restaurants.

From hiking in Rocky Mountain National Park to rock climbing at Lumpy Ridge, Estes Park is a haven for recreationists. Outdoorsy parents can sneak in a quick history lesson during a mellow stroll along the Knoll Willows Open Space Trail. Departing from downtown Estes Park, the mile-long path features the historic remains of early settlements.

Then check out the historic Stanley Hotel. Looming above Estes Park, the hotel is a popular stop for horror fans and history buffs alike. During a 75-minute Historic Stanley Day Tour, visitors learn all about how a resort for wealthy East Coasters with tuberculosis ultimately inspired Stephen King's novel *The Shining*. If it's fall and you're digging the spooky seasonal vibe, the Historic Stanley Night Tour takes visitors into a few darkened spaces while focusing on the hotel's spirit folklore.

Stay overnight, and wake up super early to drive into Rocky Mountain National Park. There won't be any lines at daybreak, and early-fall mornings are the best time to hear elk bugle in the clearing near the Moraine Park Campground.

Even if you stop here, you'll still get incredible views in every direction. But your kids will probably be curious about the crevice leading to the top of Kruger Rock. If you're up for it, squeeze through the narrow gap, and scramble to the breezy top of Kruger Rock for a bird's-eye view of Roosevelt National Forest, which wraps around Hermit Park Open Space. There are very big drops at the summit. Exercise extreme caution when hiking with children.

When you're ready, turn around and go back the way you came. At the switchbacks just shy of 3.1 miles, enjoy a glimpse of the towering rock you and your family just visited.

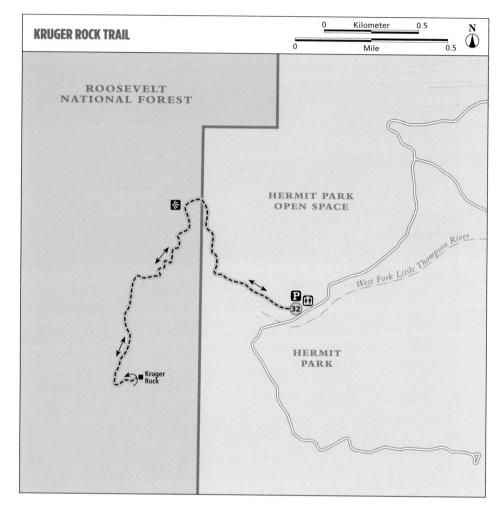

MILES AND DIRECTIONS

0.0 Start from the kiosk at the Kruger Rock Trailhead, and begin hiking uphill on a narrow dirt trail. Elevation: 8,490 feet.

0.4 Arrive at a four-way trail intersection for the Kruger Rock and Limber Pine Trails. Continue straight through the intersection.

0.7 Turn right to visit a scenic overlook.

1.0 Climb a stone staircase.

1.6 Reach a big rock, and be aware of the sheer drop to the right.

1.7 Arrive at the base of Kruger Rock. If you're hiking with older children, squeeze through the crevice, and climb to the top of the rock. After enjoying 360-degree views, turn around and hike back the way you came.

3.2 Back at the four-way intersection for the Kruger Rock and Limber Pine Trails, stay straight to continue on the Kruger Rock Trail.

3.4 Arrive back at the trailhead.

33 **ECHO CANYON TRAIL**

When fall colors are at their peak, savvy families bypass crowded national parks and explore the state's monuments instead. Measuring in at 32 square miles, Colorado National Monument packs a big punch with panoramic views of colossal sandstone monoliths towering above deep canyons.

Start: Devil's Kitchen Trailhead
Distance: 3.0 miles out and back
Hiking time: 1.5–3 hours
Difficulty: Moderate
Elevation gain: 478 feet
Trail surface: Dirt, rock, and shale
Hours: Colorado National Monument is open 24/7. Standard visitor center hours are 9 a.m. to 4:30 p.m., with extended hours during the summer.
Best seasons: Year-round; winter storms occasionally lead to temporary closures.
Water: None
Toilets: None
Nursing benches: 1 on the way to Echo Canyon
Stroller-friendly: No
Potential child hazards: Flash floods, heat exhaustion, dehydration, dangerous falls (**Note:** As with any canyon, exercise extreme caution with children near overlooks and viewpoints.)
Other trail users: None

Dogs: Not allowed on hiking trails inside the monument
Land status: National Park Service
Nearest towns: Grand Junction and Fruita
Fees and permits: Entrance fee per noncommercial vehicle or a federal recreation pass. Fourth grade students are eligible for the Every Kid Outdoors Pass, and entry into the monument is free on several fall days, including the National Park Service's birthday, National Public Lands Day, and Veterans Day.
Maps: NPS Colorado National Monument Map
Trail contact: National Park Service, Colorado National Monument, 1750 Rim Rock Dr., Fruita 81521; (970) 858-3617; www.nps.gov/colm/index.htm
Gear suggestions: Sunscreen, sun-protective clothing, brimmed hats, sunglasses, Nuun tablets, Dramamine for kids who get carsick

FINDING THE TRAILHEAD

From Grand Junction, take Broadway out of town. Travel northwest for 10.8 miles, then turn left onto Rim Rock Drive to enter the monument through its west (Fruita) entrance. It takes about an hour to drive across the park using Rim Rock Drive. To skip the scenic drive, enter the park through its east (Grand Junction) entrance.

THE HIKE

Colorado National Monument is the Centennial State's breathtaking version of the Grand Canyon. Start your adventure on the west side of the monument by entering through Fruita and driving up a winding road to the visitor center, offering dioramas, an informative video, and up-to-date information on park happenings. The visitor center is the only place inside the monument to buy snacks and drinks. Be sure to grab a Junior Ranger Activity Guide for hikers ages 12 and under.

Across the road, visit the Alcove Nature Trail. The easy, 0.5-mile path follows a wall of Entrada Sandstone from the mid- to late Jurassic period before ending at an interesting

alcove. It's a great place to stretch your legs before driving to the Devil's Kitchen Trailhead, and the first 0.25 mile is stroller and wheelchair accessible.

The 27-mile jaunt along Rim Rock Drive is incredible, with big views of dramatic canyons and sandstone towers and tunnels. Several trails depart from Rim Rock Road, and most lead to scenic overlooks. If you stop the car to take a look, exercise extreme caution. Many of the overlooks have steep ledges with significant drops.

During the drive, encourage children to look for wildlife. Colorado National Monument is home to one of the state's rare herds of desert bighorn sheep, scrappier cousin of our state animal, the Rocky Mountain bighorn sheep. Desert cottontail rabbits also live inside the monument. When hopping about, they leave tracks that look like the number 7, with the two hind feet planted first, then the two front feet set behind.

After descending Rim Rock Road, look for a small pullout parking lot on the right side of the street labeled "Devil's Kitchen Trailhead." If this lot's full, turn left at the intersection and park in the Devil's Kitchen Picnic Area.

Three trails depart from the Devil's Kitchen Trailhead. Merge onto the Old Gordon Trail, a primitive soft dirt pathway bordered by cactus, opening to spectacular views of Echo Canyon. After crossing a creek bed, you reach a shale hillside. This segment of the route may be slightly confusing. To stay on course, use the rock border on either side of the path.

When you reach the trail sign at 0.55 mile, stay straight to access the Echo Canyon Trail, which begins with a gentle descent. Avoid turning right onto the Old Gordon Trail, which extends for several additional miles but quickly becomes overgrown.

The last segment of the Echo Canyon Trail is primitive. A narrow dirt-and-sand trail takes you into a wide, dried-up creek bed with tons of rocks and boulders. In addition to tall native grasses, vegetation within the monument is primarily piñon-juniper woodland, receiving less than 12 inches average annual precipitation. Poison ivy grows in this area, providing a good reason to stay on-trail.

FUN FACTOR

LIVE IT UP DURING FALL FESTIVAL SEASON.

Autumn is a magical time in Grand Junction! The mornings are crisp, the days are sunny, and the streets are usually bustling with a fun-filled lineup of seasonal events. Whether your family is into high-flying airplanes, vintage cars, cowboy heritage, or spectacular art, the Grand Valley is home to some of the region's most intriguing fall festivals. Visit grandjunction.com is the best place to find up-to-date information on all of the town's yearly festivals.

For families, the town's annual Two Rivers Chautauqua is a low-cost living history jubilee hosted by the Museum of Western Colorado. The past truly comes to life as actors portray historical figures such as P. T. Barnum, Mark Twain, and Molly Brown. Don't miss the kickoff dance preceding a robust schedule of presentations and performances.

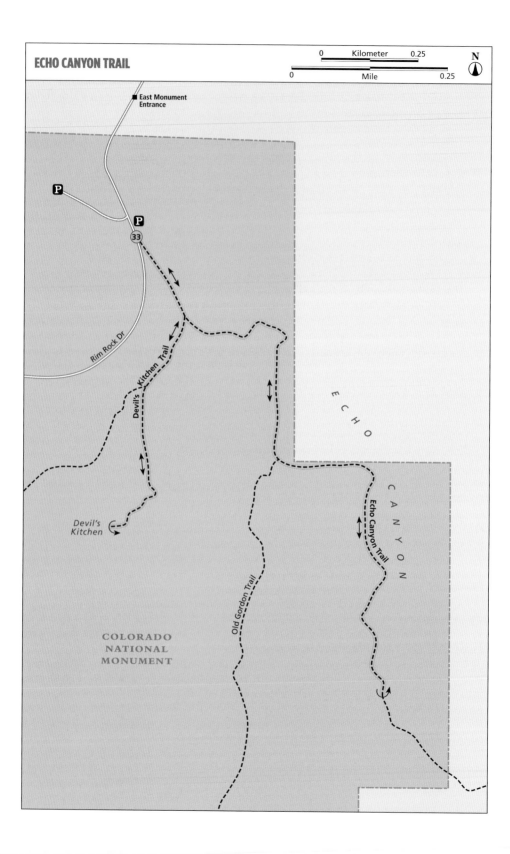

ECHO CANYON TRAIL

0   Kilometer   0.25

0   Mile   0.25

N

■ East Monument
  Entrance

P

P

33

Rim Rock Dr

Devil's Kitchen Trail

Devil's
Kitchen

Old Gordon Trail

Echo Canyon Trail

E C H O

C A N Y O N

COLORADO
NATIONAL
MONUMENT

Echo Canyon Trail ends abruptly at 1.1 miles at a giant rock formation. Turn around and retrace your steps to where the Old Gordon and Devil's Kitchen Trails meet. Turn left at the fork at 2.05 miles to visit a rock grotto known as the Devil's Kitchen. This out-and-back route adds an additional 1.0 mile round-trip to the hike and is included in the directions below.

Initially, the Devil's Kitchen Trail is a wide, flat dirt trail bordered by shrubs including rabbitbrush, broom snakeweed, Mormon tea, and mountain mahogany.

Walk straight through the intersection at 2.2 miles, and cross the creek. In another 0.1 mile, the dirt trail ends, and you'll begin a rocky ascent to the balanced rock visible in the distance.

In the last 0.2 mile, the trail becomes increasingly difficult to follow as it crosses a slope with a fair amount of slickrock. Steps are cut into the rock in two places to help hikers along.

This unique formation is a natural rock grotto bordered by giant boulders. The enclosure creates an arena that's just begging to be explored. Families are welcome to go into the grotto and climb up the wall on the east side to a window overlooking No Thoroughfare Canyon. You'll get top-of-the-world views from this vantage point—just keep in mind that if you climb up to the window, you must have an exit plan for getting your kids safely back down. When you're satisfied with the view—or can't take the heat anymore—get out of the kitchen by retracing your steps to the trailhead.

MILES AND DIRECTIONS

0.0   Start from the Devil's Kitchen Trailhead, and walk straight ahead onto a wide dirt path. Elevation: 5,064 feet.

0.15 Arrive at a fork in the trail. Bear left, and follow the arrow on the trail marker to Echo Canyon.

0.3   Cross a creek bed.

0.35 Traverse a shale slope.

0.55 Arrive at a fork in the trail. Keep straight to hike the Echo Canyon Trail.

0.65 After descending several wooden stairs, you're back on a narrow dirt trail.

0.7   Pass a sign for the Echo Canyon Trail.

0.9   Bear left at the fork, and follow a series of steps downhill.

1.1   The trail ends abruptly at a giant rock. Turn around and begin retracing your steps.

2.05 You're back where the Old Gordon and Devil's Kitchen Trails intersect. Make a sharp left.

2.2   Arrive at a trail intersection. Stay straight to merge onto the Devil's Kitchen Trail.

2.3   From the base of Devil's Kitchen, begin a challenging ascent up stone steps and rocks.

2.45 Reach Devil's Kitchen. Explore the grotto before hiking back the way you came.

2.7   This time, keep straight at the fork. Do not turn left onto the No Name Trail.

2.85 At the intersection of the No Thoroughfare and Old Gordon Trails, stay straight. Follow the dirt path back to the trailhead.

3.0   Arrive back at the trailhead.

34 MALLORY CAVE TRAIL

On those days when your kids need an incentive to hike, whip out Mallory Cave, a real-life bat cave that's guaranteed to thrill everyone in the group. The cave itself has been permanently closed to human use to protect its inhabitants, Townsend's big-eared bats. You can still get an up-close look if you're willing to attempt a free climb at the end of the route.

Start: NCAR Trailhead, behind the Mesa Laboratory
Distance: 2.6 miles out and back
Hiking time: 2–3 hours
Difficulty: Difficult
Elevation gain: 713 feet
Trail surface: Dirt and rock
Hours: Boulder OSMP trails open 24/7
Best seasons: Oct 2 through Mar 31. A buffer zone surrounding Mallory Cave is closed from Apr 1 until Oct 1 to protect the Townsend's big-eared bats. Due to potentially icy conditions, Mallory Cave Trail is not recommended as a winter hike for families.
Water: Water fountains inside Mesa Laboratory
Toilets: Flush toilets inside Mesa Laboratory
Nursing benches: On the Walter Orr Roberts Interpretive Trail and at the base of the notch
Stroller-friendly: The Walter Orr Roberts Trail is stroller and wheelchair accessible.

Potential child hazards: Rattlesnakes, very rocky terrain, a free climb
Other trail users: None
Dogs: Must be on hand-held leashes on NCAR property, including the Walter Orr Roberts Interpretive Trail. Beyond NCAR property, dog control requirements vary from trail to trail.
Land status: Boulder Open Space and Mountain Parks
Nearest town: Boulder
Fees and permits: None
Maps: Boulder OSMP NCAR Trail Map
Trail contact: Boulder Open Space and Mountain Parks, 1777 Broadway, Boulder 80302; (303) 441-3440; bouldercolorado.gov/osmp/national-center-for-atmospheric-research-trailhead
Gear suggestions: Trail running shoes or hiking boots, sunscreen, sun-protective clothing, windbreakers, trekking poles, Nuun tablets, high-energy snacks, binoculars

FINDING THE TRAILHEAD

From downtown Boulder's Pearl Street Mall, take Broadway (CO 93) south for 2.8 miles. Turn right (west) onto Table Mesa Drive, which eventually becomes NCAR Road. Continue driving uphill on NCAR Road for another 1.1 miles to reach the NCAR Mesa Laboratory. There is a large parking lot just past the laboratory, on the building's northwest side.

THE HIKE

Colorado's waterfalls and alpine lakes are stunning targets for family hikes, but if you ever have the option of (a) hiking to a bat cave, or (b) not hiking to a bat cave, you should always choose the bat cave!

Fixed on the eastern flank of Dinosaur Mountain (a subpeak of the better-known Green Mountain), Mallory Cave was originally discovered by loggers, and then rediscovered in 1932 by E. C. Mallory, a University of Colorado Boulder student.

The cave is special because it's one of eleven roosting sites for Townsend's big-eared bats in Colorado. Known for their long ears, which can grow to 38 millimeters (1.5 inches), the winged mammals hibernate at high elevations throughout the winter. Come summer, female Townsend's big-eared bats congregate in maternity colonies like the one established inside Mallory Cave.

Let your children know they won't be able to enter the bat cave. Even under normal conditions, Townsend's big-eared bat pups suffer high mortality rates. Mallory Cave was gated in 2011, and the trail leading to it is closed seasonally, April 1 to October 1, to create a buffer that protects the bats from white-nose syndrome during roosting season.

Start on the NCAR Trail, departing from a trailhead near the Mesa Laboratory. Hikers can park in the laboratory's large lot and use the restrooms before walking behind the building to a wooden kiosk marking the trailhead.

Walk uphill on a wide dirt-and-gravel trail to reach a welcome sign and five-way trail intersection. The first segment of the NCAR Trail is also called the Walter Orr Roberts Trail. The interpretive path contains several signs filled with science-themed tidbits. Families with toddlers can explore this short trail then visit the free museum inside Mesa Laboratory.

Walter Orr Roberts Trail is a loop, so go either way at the first fork. Then follow the trail as it tracks west on the mesa before dropping to a broad saddle. Watch for rattlesnakes sunbathing along the trail on warm days. To deter predators, they vibrate their tails, clicking segments together, producing an unmistakable buzz. Amazingly, nonvenomous bull snakes can mimic rattlesnakes by making the same noise.

Continue following the trail past a wooden barricade to begin a steep climb with switchbacks. At the top of the ridge, look for a giant water tank. Turn left at the tank, and follow the NCAR Trail as it dips into a valley before ending at the Mesa Trail. Walk straight through the four-way intersection. After passing a welcome kiosk, you've merged onto Mallory Cave Trail.

The trail is bumpy and can be very muddy. Eventually you'll come to a dark, forested area, and it actually feels like you're approaching a bat cave. It's a little eerie. From here, hikers must scramble up rocky terrain. Do your best to follow the obvious trail of switchbacks, and avoid climbing access passages. Metal posts help with guidance.

Look for a post at 1.2 miles. A few feet later, the trail cuts through two giant boulders and winds around to a notch with a plaque. The bat cave is at the top.

See the rope tethered to the rock? If you want to see the cave, you'll use it to free-climb up the notch. Even though the cave is sealed with an artful gate, it's still a worthwhile spectacle to behold. But don't attempt to free-climb with your kids unless you're absolutely sure everyone in the group can make it back down. You're ascending at your own risk, and the descent can be scary.

FUN FACTOR

TOUCH A CLOUD AT THE NATIONAL CENTER FOR ATMOSPHERIC RESEARCH.

The hike to Mallory Cave takes off from behind the NCAR Mesa Laboratory. Architect I. M. Pei designed this fortresslike facility to resemble the ancient Indian cliff dwellings in southwest Colorado (see hike 17). The lab functions as the headquarters for NCAR, a nonprofit organization providing national science communities with an array of resources.

Young hikers will care less about the building's design and more about what's inside: a hands-on visitor center packed with an impressive collection of free exhibits built to inspire budding scientists.

Start with an educational film in the theater tucked behind the Weather Gallery. Then chase your kids around the first-floor gallery while they touch clouds, view a tornado created by crosswinds, steer a hurricane, and tackle a science-themed game of memory on a giant touch-screen computer. There are several areas where children can make STEAM-inspired artwork.

The Mesa Lab Visitor Center is open to the public 363 days a year. Free hour-long tours of the facility are offered on select weekdays. Reservations are not required.

MALLORY CAVE TRAIL

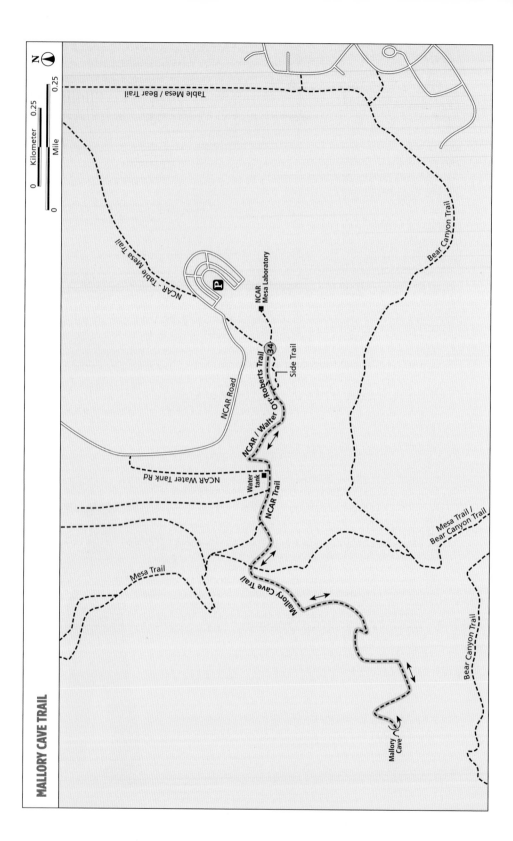

When you're done exploring, turn around and follow the route you came in on. At the four-way trail intersection that reappears at 1.9 miles, remember to stay straight to merge back onto the NCAR Trail. Keep straight at the next intersection a few feet later, or you'll end up on the Mesa Trail, which weaves into Chautauqua Park (see hike 12).

MILES AND DIRECTIONS

0.0 Start at a wooden kiosk on the northeast side of the NCAR Mesa Laboratory, and follow the wide dirt and gravel trail uphill. Elevation: 6,125 feet.

0.1 Arrive at a welcome sign and five-way intersection. Continue hiking uphill; follow the signs to the Mesa and Walter Orr Roberts Trails.

0.2 Reach a trail marker for the Mesa Trail. Bear left to follow the Mesa Trail downhill.

0.4 After a moderate ascent, come to a water tank. Turn left.

0.65 Walk straight through a four-way trail intersection to hike the Mallory Cave Trail. Do not turn onto the Mesa Trail.

1.0 Reach two massive boulders. Turn right to stay on the Mallory Cave Trail. This last segment gets dicey. Metal trail posts will help you stay on course. Ask other hikers for directions, if needed.

1.3 Arrive at a solid rock notch with a metal plaque. Stop here, or use the rope to ascend to the bat cave. When you're ready, turn around and follow the same route back to the Mesa Laboratory.

1.9 Merge onto the NCAR Trail by hiking straight through the four-way trail intersection.

2.6 Arrive back at the laboratory.

35 EAGLE AND SAGE LOOP TRAIL

This mellow stroll through North Boulder's rolling farmland is a pleasant experience for all hikers, but it's an especially approachable route for groups with young kids and newbies. The surrounding land—Boulder Valley Ranch—is both a currently working and historic ranch. Animal lovers will adore the site's grazing cattle and majestic horses, which live among a variety of wild species.

Start: Eagle Trail welcome sign
Distance: 3.75-mile lollipop
Hiking time: 1.5–3 hours
Difficulty: Easy
Elevation gain: 114 feet
Trail surface: Dirt and gravel
Hours: Boulder OSMP trails open 24/7; Eagle Trailhead parking lot open 5 a.m. to 11 p.m.
Best seasons: Year-round
Water: None
Toilets: An outhouse at the Boulder Valley Ranch Trailhead
Nursing benches: Several stationed throughout the route
Stroller-friendly: Yes
Potential child hazards: None
Other trail users: Equestrians, mountain bikers

Dogs: Must be on a hand-held leash at all times unless they meet the voice and sight control standard and display a City of Boulder voice/sight tag
Land status: Boulder Open Space and Mountain Parks
Nearest town: Boulder
Fees and permits: None
Maps: Boulder OSMP Boulder Valley Ranch / Lefthand / Eagle Trail Map
Trail contact: Boulder Open Space and Mountain Parks, 1777 Broadway, Boulder 80302; (303) 441-3440; bouldercolorado.gov/osmp/boulder-valley-ranch-trailhead
Gear suggestions: Sunscreen, brimmed hats, snacks, binoculars

FINDING THE TRAILHEAD

From downtown Boulder, take 28th Street north; turn right (east) onto CO 119. Follow CO 119 to Jay Road and turn left. As you drive west, look for 51st Street, which comes up fast. Turn right (north) onto 51st Street, and follow it for approximately 2.3 miles, until the Eagle Trailhead parking lot appears after a bend.

THE HIKE

Small-scale agriculture and the wilderness collide at Boulder Valley Ranch. While hiking along the Eagle and Sage Trails, families will notice a mixture of livestock and undomesticated species, including cattle, horses, prairie dogs, mule deer, coyotes, raptors, and bull snakes. Ask your children to track the animals they spot, and encourage budding zoologists to think about the similarities and differences between farm animals and their wild counterparts.

Two trailheads (Eagle and Boulder Valley Ranch) provide access to the flat loop created by combining the Eagle and Sage Trails. We're starting on the eastern side, at the Eagle Trailhead.

Look for a livestock gate on the far edge of the parking lot. Walk through the gate, and make sure to close it behind you as you merge onto a wide dirt path.

Stellar views of Boulder's Flatirons appear just past the parking lot. After a 0.5-mile stroll, walk through another livestock gate (there are more to come), and bear left at the fork to take the Eagle Trail down an eroded slope toward a small damned pond.

Watch out for prairie dog holes: The burrows will trip you if you aren't careful! Ask young children to listen for the rodent's signature bark, and see who in your family can spot the most prairie dogs.

When you reach the pond, skip rocks and look for waterfowl lurking between cattails. Families with toddlers can turn around at this point to complete a 1.3-mile out-and-back excursion.

With older kids, continue along the Eagle Trail as it curves around the pond and narrows before crossing an open field with tall grasses and scattered cottonwood trees. Boulder Valley Ranch's black shale barren soils nourish a very rare yellow plant in the mustard family, Bell's twinpod. Worldwide, the low-lying perennial has only been found in Larimer and Boulder Counties. Bell's twinpod won't flower until April and May, but its eye-catching silvery hairs are visible year-round.

Past the pond, look left for a stellar view of Boulder Reservoir. When you come to a fork at 1.45 miles, turn right to begin hiking on the Sage Trail. (A left takes hikers up a ridge to Mesa Reservoir, which is often dried out.) Wedged between a small ridge and a farmer's irrigation ditch, the Sage Trail travels west on level ground until arriving at the Boulder Valley Ranch Trailhead. To the right is a private working ranch with horse and cattle.

A small parking lot with an outhouse abuts the Boulder Valley Ranch Trailhead. After crossing the lot, follow the arrow on the trail marker to merge onto the Sage Trail, avoiding a driveway that's clearly labeled as private.

The next segment of the trail is a gravel footpath bordered by yuccas. To the right, children will see barns, stables, and friendly horses. Then the grade increases as the trail climbs a small hill. At the top, take in additional views of the Flatirons and Boulder Reservoir.

The Sage Trail intersects the North Rim Trail at 2.75 miles. Do not turn left onto North Rim. Instead, bear slightly right, and continue hiking along the Sage Trail. Raptors flock to Boulder Valley Ranch. Now is the time to search for eagles, northern harriers, and red-tailed hawks overhead.

FUN FACTOR

TOUR A WORLD-FAMOUS TEA FACTORY.

From its original blends (Sleepytime and Red Zinger), the $100-million Celestial Seasonings brand has mushroomed to include ninety-plus varieties. The company sells 1.6 billion cups of tea annually in forty-plus countries. Amazingly, all of its products are still processed locally, at its manufacturing plant in North Boulder.

At the Celestial Seasonings Factory, families gain insight into tea production and manufacturing on a free Tea Tour, which includes a 10-minute video and 30-minute guided walk through the factory.

For young environmentalists, the biggest Tea Tour takeaways come from Celestial Seasoning's sustainability initiatives. Long before anybody talked about corporate responsibility, Celestial Seasonings established a practice whereby its individual tea bags weren't overwrapped in plastic. That simple process saves 3.5 million pounds of packaging material from going into landfills every year.

Tours leave on the hour, and are first-come, first-served for walk-in guests. Reservations are not required. Due to FDA requirements, children under 5 aren't allowed on the factory portion of the Tea Tour. But tea lovers of all ages are invited to swing by the Celestial Café, featuring an on-site teahouse with free samples.

EAGLE AND SAGE LOOP TRAIL

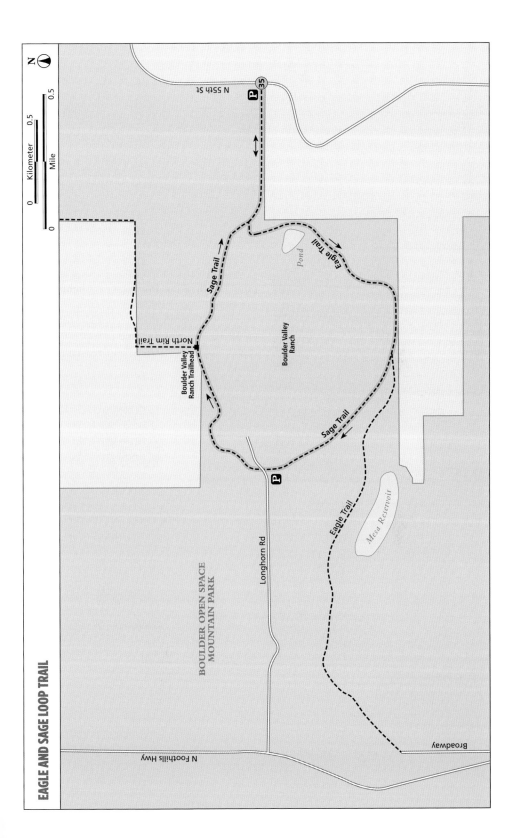

N 55th St

N

Kilometer

0   0.5

Mile

0   0.5

35

Sage Trail

North Rim Trail

Boulder Valley Ranch Trailhead

Eagle Trail

Pond

Boulder Valley Ranch

Sage Trail

Longhorn Rd

BOULDER OPEN SPACE MOUNTAIN PARK

Eagle Trail

Mesa Reservoir

N Foothills Hwy

Broadway

MILES AND DIRECTIONS

0.0   Start at the Eagle Trail welcome kiosk, and merge onto the Eagle Trail by walking through a livestock gate. Elevation: 5,239 feet.

0.5   Proceed to the wooden trail post with green blazes. Bear left at the fork to continue on the Eagle Trail.

0.65   Pass BVR Pond 1, a small dammed pond.

1.45   Go right at the fork to merge onto the Sage Trail.

2.1   Arrive at the Boulder Valley Ranch Trailhead. Walk through a small parking lot, then turn right onto the Sage Trail.

2.75   Bear right at the fork to continue on the Sage Trail.

3.28   Walk through a livestock gate. Stay straight at the fork to return to the Eagle Trailhead.

3.75   Arrive back at the trailhead kiosk.

36 SUNNY ASPEN AND LODGE POLE LOOP

Don't be fooled by this trail's proximity to Denver. The town of Conifer is 8,277 feet about sea level, about 200 feet higher than Aspen. Even if you don't feel the altitude while exploring Meyer Ranch Park, you'll experience the benefits that come with elevation—cooler temperatures, alpine wildlife viewing opportunities—during a pleasant ascent through tall lodgepole pines hovering up to 100 feet above ground. With three interwoven trails, there are lots of opportunities to vary the length of your hike.

Start: Meyer Ranch Park Trailhead
Distance: 2.4-mile loop with an optional 1.9-mile lollipop
Hiking time: 1–2 hours
Difficulty: Moderate
Elevation gain: 755 feet
Trail surface: Dirt and loose gravel; sometimes rocky
Hours: Open daily, 1 hour before sunrise to 1 hour after sunset
Best seasons: Spring through fall
Water: None
Toilets: Drop toilets 0.2 mile past the trailhead
Nursing benches: Spaced roughly every 0.5 mile throughout the route
Stroller-friendly: No
Potential child hazards: None

Other trail users: Mountain bikers, equestrians
Dogs: Allowed on-leash
Land status: Jefferson County Open Space
Nearest town: Conifer
Fees and permits: None
Maps: Jefferson County Open Space Meyer Ranch Park map
Trail contact: Jefferson County Open Space, 700 Jefferson County Pkwy., Golden 80401; (303) 271-5925; www.jeffco.us/1304/Meyer-Ranch-Park
Gear suggestions: Trail running shoes or hiking boots, fleece pullovers and/or windbreakers, sunscreen, high-energy snacks, Nuun tablets

FINDING THE TRAILHEAD

From Denver, take US 285 south toward Conifer. About 13 miles past the US 285/CO 470 junction, exit onto South Turkey Creek Road, and cross under the highway to park in the main lot on the south side of US 285. Overflow parking is available on the north side of the underpass. The South Turkey Creek exit can be tricky to spot. If you hit the "Welcome to Conifer" sign, you've gone too far.

THE HIKE

Winter draws snowshoers and sledders to Meyer Ranch Park, and shady trails offer hikers relief during the dog days of summer. But I recommend tackling this loop in the fall, when the aspens begin changing color and you're itching for a quick departure from after-school activities.

Fall is prime time to view wildlife as they prepare for winter. You might catch a chickadee hiding seeds in the forest or a nuthatch (red- or white-breasted) foraging on insects. Bonus points if your children spy the teeny-tiny northern pygmy owl, which hunts for songbirds during the day.

In dense pine forests, like those at Meyer Ranch, encourage children to listen as much as they look. Astute hikers can hear the giggle of the white-breasted nuthatch and the scolding *chick-a-dee-dee-dee* of the chickadee.

Although the initial views of US 285 aren't too impressive, don't second-guess this hike. By the time you hit the 0.5-mile mark, the highway fades as dirt singletrack gives way to a wider trail with switchbacks to ease the climb. Watch for tree stumps and large rocks during the ascent.

When you reach a large stone picnic shelter, you're roughly 1.0 mile into your journey. This is a great place to stop for lunch—or, at the very least, catch your breath after a solid uphill jaunt. If other hikers are also using the shelter, talk them up. Hikers are a friendly bunch, and meeting new people is all part of the experience.

At the picnic shelter, you have the option to extend your hike by making a sharp left turn onto the Old Ski Run trail, where a 1.9-mile lollipop takes families deeper into the forest. The climb up Old Ski Run is steep but totally doable, topping out at nearly 8,800 feet.

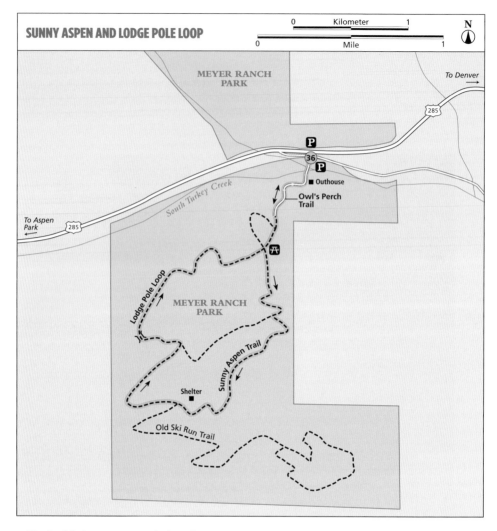

You're hitting some good altitude in Meyer Ranch Park. Make sure everyone stays hydrated, even on a cool day. Make sure everyone stays on the trail too; several game trails shoot out from the looped portion of Old Ski Run.

The second leg of this hike is a mellow stroll down Lodge Pole Loop featuring a generous dirt path, flatter terrain, and intermittent shade. If you're hiking with very young children, bypass Sunny Aspen Trail and stick to Lodge Pole Loop. This shortens your journey by 0.4 mile while forgoing the park's steepest segments.

MILES AND DIRECTIONS

0.0   Start from the trailhead on the southwest side of the parking lot, and follow a wide dirt road toward a large kiosk. Elevation: 7,850 feet.

0.05 Reach the kiosk. Continue slightly uphill on Owl's Perch.

FUN FACTOR

HAVE A BERRY GOOD TIME.

Hiking in September and October, you'll probably find chokecherries and other round, brightly colored treasures just begging to be picked by curious fingers. If your child asks to collect berries, take a moment to teach them about the importance of respecting the delicate ecosystem you're exploring. Natural foods should be left in place for wildlife to consume. That's why hikers in Jefferson County are prohibited from collecting berries, acorns, rose hips, etc. Intentionally feeding wildlife is also a big no-no.

This doesn't mean you can't have some fun. Consider purchasing a take-along guide such as FalconGuide's *Rocky Mountain Berry Book*. With a guidebook to reference, budding naturalists can learn all about the berries they see in Meyer Ranch Park.

0.2 Pass an outhouse. Multiple branches of Owl's Perch are confusing, but just for a moment. Take your second right and travel uphill, passing picnic benches at 0.3 mile.

0.38 Come to the intersection of the Owl's Perch Trail and Lodge Pole Loop. Take a sharp left at the marker to merge onto the Lodge Pole Loop.

0.45 Hit a series of switchbacks, and continue climbing.

0.52 Arrive at a trail marker. Make a sharp left turn onto the Sunny Aspen Trail.

0.67 Don't turn left at the trail marker. This unofficial path is not part of the JeffCo system.

1.05 Reach a stone picnic shelter. Continue straight on the Sunny Aspen Trail for a gradual descent. (**Option:** You can extend your hike by turning left onto Old Ski Run; mileage for this 1.9-mile add-on lollipop is not included here.)

1.32 Come to the junction of the Sunny Aspen Trail and Lodge Pole Loop. Turn left to merge onto the Lodge Pole Loop.

1.45 Pass a "Neighborhood Access" sign, and steer right at the bend.

1.85 Pass several shaded benches.

2.0 Turn left at the sign for Owl's Perch.

2.15 Bear left to continue moving toward your car. A right takes you slightly uphill to a shady picnic area with big boulders.

2.2 Pass the outhouse. Continue downhill toward the parking lot.

2.4 Arrive back at the trailhead.

37 LOOKOUT MOUNTAIN TRAIL

Through a dense ponderosa pine forest, past Buffalo Bill's stone grave, and straight into a nature preserve, the challenging hike up the Lookout Mountain Trail strikes a balance between outdoor adventure, touristy fun, and naturalist-approved learning. The summit is a 100-acre Jefferson County park offering an additional 2.6 miles of flat hiking trails.

Start: Lookout Mountain Trailhead
Distance: 3.5 miles out and back
Hiking time: 2–5 hours
Difficulty: Moderate
Elevation gain: 622 feet
Trail surface: Dirt and gravel
Hours: Open daily, 1 hour before sunrise to 1 hour after sunset
Best seasons: Summer and fall. The trail is often impassable in winter and during mud season.
Water: At the museum and nature center
Toilets: An outhouse at the trailhead, flush toilets at the museum and nature center
Nursing benches: Several along the trail and at the museum and nature center
Stroller-friendly: No, but the trails inside Lookout Mountain Nature Preserve can accommodate a jogging stroller or all-terrain wheelchair.
Potential child hazards: None
Other trail users: Mountain bikers
Dogs: Must be leashed
Land status: Jefferson County Open Space and Denver Parks and Recreation
Nearest town: Golden
Fees and permits: None
Maps: Jefferson County Open Space Windy Saddle Park map
Trail contact: Jefferson County Open Space, 700 Jefferson County Pkwy., Ste. 100, Golden 80401; (303) 271-5925; www.jeffco.us/1440/Windy-Saddle-Park
Gear suggestions: Windbreakers or light winter jackets, layers, Nuun tablets

FINDING THE TRAILHEAD

From downtown Golden, at the intersection of 6th Avenue and 19th Street, drive west on 19th Street, which becomes Lookout Mountain Road after passing Beverly Heights Park. Wind up the National Scenic Byway for 3 miles, until reaching a pullout parking area labeled "Windy Saddle." Cars may enter the lot immediately after passing the pedestrian crosswalk. Park along the road if the pullout is full. Lookout Mountain Road is a popular cycling destination: Watch out for bikers while driving.

THE HIKE

It's possible to start this hike in downtown Golden, at the base of the Chimney Gulch Trail, or even on the Clear Creek Trail. But that's a long haul. Families can begin at Windy Saddle Park and include kid-friendly stop-offs at Buffalo Bill's gravesite and Lookout Mountain Nature Preserve.

With hairpin turns, stunning vistas, and daredevil cyclists, the drive up Lookout Mountain Road is an experience in itself. Lookout Mountain Road is part of the Lariat Loop Byway, a 40-mile national historic driving route retracing the motoring adventures of the early 1920s.

Two trails depart in opposite directions from Windy Saddle Park. The one you're looking for is near the outhouse. Shaded by thick forest, the first segment of the Lookout Mountain Trail can be extremely treacherous in winter and early spring. Even with traction devices, novice hikers should not attempt this trail when there's ice.

Look right for sweeping views of the park's namesake saddle—that curved depression resting between Mount Zion and surrounding foothills peaks. Ask a passerby to snap a family photo before beginning a steep and breezy ascent. Renowned among hang gliders, this 755-acre park definitely lives up to its name, with strong drafts blowing down from the Continental Divide.

As you continue to climb, the soft dirt trail becomes rocky, and some passages might be slick. At 0.85 mile, take a detour to Buffalo Bill's famous gravesite. The site's visitor center and fee-based museum are touristy, but the grave itself is free to visit and lined with interpretive signs.

To get there, follow the Buffalo Bill Trail. When you reach the wooden barricades beginning at 1.05 miles, your children might be tempted to climb to the other side. Remind them to stay on designated trails, and look west across the Clear Creek watershed as it rises to the peaks of the Continental Divide. Can you see why the Ute and Arapahoe Indians used this area as a lookout point?

The trail continues to a stone staircase leading to a large parking lot. On the opposite end is a two-story gift shop with an assortment of sundries. Follow the signs to Buffalo Bill's gravesite, and read all about how William F. Cody fought in the Civil War, advocated for the rights of Native Americans and women, and hunted buffalo to feed railroad workers.

South of the gravestone, Denver maintains a herd of buffalo (actually, American bison)—direct descendants of the country's last wild herd.

FUN FACTOR

GET YOUR CULTURAL FIX IN GOLDEN.

From rock climbing at North Table Mountain to mountain biking in Apex Park, the former gold rush town of Golden is a favorite destination for outdoor enthusiasts. It's also a noteworthy historical site. Before Colorado was a state, Golden was the capital of the Territory of Colorado from 1862 to 1867. Today, the city's unique cultural offerings are especially appealing to active families.

The American Mountaineering Museum is the first and only museum in the country dedicated to preserving mountaineering history. To educate visitors on rock climbing culture, it features unique artifacts and a series of interactive exhibits. Nearby, kids will love the colorful Mines Museum (formerly the Colorado School of Mines Geology Museum), with a large collection of rocks, gems, and minerals, including a moon rock and the Miss Colorado jeweled crown.

If you're up for tackling additional mileage, Golden History Museum's self-guided walking tour is a 1.5-mile circuit with sixteen engaging stops. The tour is outlined in detail online at goldenhistory.org/learn-do/walkingtour.

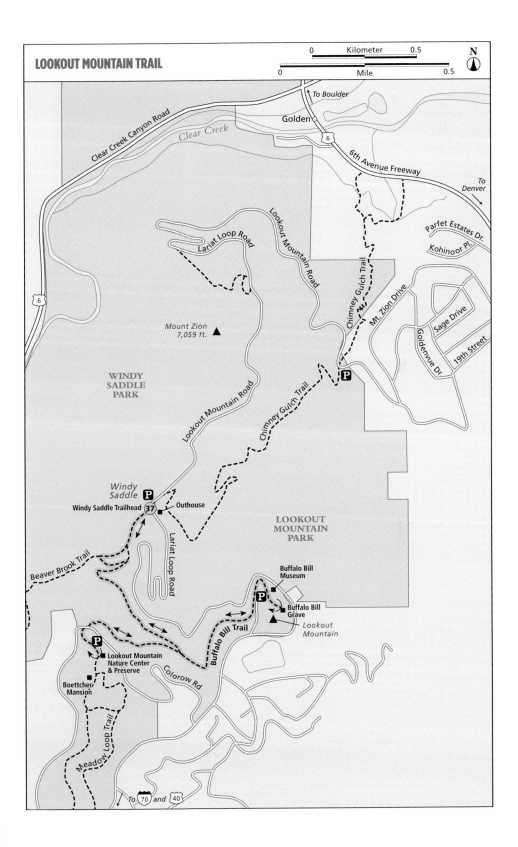

LOOKOUT MOUNTAIN TRAIL

0   Kilometer   0.5

0   Mile   0.5

N

To Boulder

Golden

6

Clear Creek Canyon Road

Clear Creek

6th Avenue Freeway

To Denver

6

Parfet Estates Dr.

Kohinoor Pl.

Lariat Loop Road

Lookout Mountain Road

Chimney Gulch Trail

Mt. Zion Drive

Sage Drive

Goldenvue Dr.

19th Street

Mount Zion
7,059 ft.

WINDY
SADDLE
PARK

Lookout Mountain Road

Chimney Gulch Trail

P

Windy
Saddle

P

Windy Saddle Trailhead

37

Outhouse

LOOKOUT
MOUNTAIN
PARK

Lariat Loop Road

Beaver Brook Trail

Buffalo Bill
Museum

P

Buffalo Bill
Grave

Lookout
Mountain

P

Lookout Mountain
Nature Center
& Preserve

Buffalo Bill Trail

Colorow Rd.

Boettcher
Mansion

Meadow Loop Trail

To 70 and 40

Back at the stone staircase, retrace your steps to the intersection of the Buffalo Bill and Lookout Mountain Trails. Go left at the fork to push to the summit. As the grade intensifies, remind children to watch for rocks and roots.

When you reach Colorow Road, carefully cross the street, enter Lookout Mountain Nature Preserve, and walk across the large parking lot to visit the nature center, where park rangers are on hand to answer questions. Behind the nature center, a beautiful preserve features miles of hiker-only trails, open from 8 a.m. to dusk year-round. The Meadow Loop Trail is a great place for families to survey the site, which provides habitat for a range of animals, including black bear, deer, mountain lions, skunks, raccoons—even elk.

All that's left is an easy descent to the car. If your child isn't ready for the climb up the Lookout Mountain Trail, drive to Lookout Mountain Nature Preserve, and explore the site's scenic trail system.

MILES AND DIRECTIONS

0.0   Start at the Windy Saddle Park kiosk (near the outhouse), and merge onto the narrow dirt trail extending from the south side of the pullout parking lot. Elevation: 6,920 feet.

0.25   Go left at a fork in the trail to continue on the Lookout Mountain Trail. Do not turn onto the Beaver Brook Trail.

0.5   Pass an overlook to the left.

0.85   Arrive at the intersection of the Buffalo Bill and Lookout Mountain Trails. Turn left at the fork to visit Buffalo Bill's grave via the Buffalo Bill Trail.

1.1   Pass an overlook and interpretive sign.

1.3   Follow the stone staircase to a parking lot. Cross the lot to reach a gift shop. From here, follow the signs to Buffalo Bill's grave. (**Note:** The mileage in this guide doesn't include the museum, gift shop, and gravesite.) When you're finished exploring the area, retrace your steps to the intersection of the Buffalo Bill and Lookout Mountain Trails.

1.8   You're back at the intersection of the Buffalo Bill and Lookout Mountain Trails. Once again, bear left at the fork, and begin walking uphill toward Lookout Mountain Nature Center and Preserve.

2.1   Pass a trail marker, and continue hiking uphill to reach the Windy Saddle Park Trailhead. Carefully cross Colorow Road. Walk through steel gates into Lookout Mountain Nature Center and Preserve.

2.2   Arrive at the nature center, and explore the premises. Families in need of additional mileage can hike around the preserve, which offers 2.6 miles of flat, interconnected trails (not included in this guide). When you're ready, retrace your steps to the intersection of the Buffalo Bill and Lookout Mountain Trails.

2.6   Turn left at the fork to continue following the Lookout Mountain Trail downhill.

3.5   Arrive back at the trailhead.

38 DOC HOLLIDAY GRAVE TRAIL

The life and times of John Henry "Doc" Holliday have become the stuff of American legend. The infamous dentist-turned-gunslinger is buried in Linwood Cemetery, overlooking the historic mountain town of Glenwood Springs. A steady climb to his grave marker is attainable for very young hikers, and older kids will also enjoy the Wild West folklore.

Start: Pioneer Cemetery Trailhead, on the corner of Bennett Avenue and 12th Street Ditch
Distance: 0.9 mile out and back
Hiking time: 1–2 hours
Difficulty: Easy to moderate
Elevation gain: 190 feet
Trail surface: Dirt
Hours: Open daily, dawn to dusk
Best seasons: Summer and fall
Water: None
Toilets: None
Nursing benches: Several alongside the trail and at the base of the route
Stroller-friendly: No
Potential child hazards: None

Other trail users: None
Dogs: Must be leashed
Land status: City of Glenwood Springs
Nearest town: Glenwood Springs
Fees and permits: None
Maps: National Geographic Trails Illustrated Flat Tops South map
Trail contact: City of Glenwood Springs Parks and Recreation, 100 Wulfsohn Rd., Glenwood Springs 81601; (970) 384-6301; www.glen woodrec.com/267/Hiking-Trails
Gear suggestions: Athletic shoes, sunscreen, brimmed hats, water

FINDING THE TRAILHEAD

From I-70, drive south on Grand Avenue toward 8th Street. Turn left (east) onto 13th Street, and head toward Bennett Avenue. The trailhead is located in downtown Glenwood Springs, at the corner of 12th Street Ditch and Bennett Avenue. Street parking is available in the residential neighborhood.

THE HIKE

Several excellent hiking trails extend from Glenwood Springs, a resort city surrounded by the White River National Forest. Originally I'd planned to include the trek to Hanging Lake in this book. The rigorous-but-doable trail ascends through travertine geological formations to a turquoise lake. But the route has become so popular in recent years that hikers are now required to buy a permit and reserve their spots on the trail in advance. It's worth the trouble, but the admission process makes the route too arduous to include in a book highlighting Colorado's most accessible trails.

Departing from a well-marked trailhead at the corner of Bennett Avenue and 12th Street Ditch, the Doc Holliday Grave Trail is a fun, in-town hike ending at Linwood Cemetery and containing the grave marker of Glenwood Springs' most famous outlaw. *Expert tip:* There aren't any secluded places along this moderately trafficked trail, so ask everyone in your group to use the restroom before heading to the trailhead.

From Bennett Avenue, walk up a few wooden steps to reach a welcome sign, where you can stop and read about the cemetery. Next, cross a paved path to merge onto a narrow dirt trail. This isn't a backcountry hiking experience, but there are several pleasant views over a moderately steep incline. The real appeal, though, is the folklore behind the trail.

Doc Holliday's fascinating life has been depicted in books, TV shows, and movies, and the outlaw has also been portrayed by several big-name actors, including Kirk Douglas, Val Kilmer, and Dennis Quaid. Holliday was a dentist turned gambler and gunslinger. Rumor had it that he killed dozens of men in his heyday, but modern researchers have determined that he wasn't actually that lethal. Either way, Holliday is best known for his role in the events leading up to the Gunfight at the O.K. Corral, a 30-second shootout between lawmen and members of a loosely organized group of outlaws that took place in Arizona Territory in 1881.

When he developed tuberculosis, Holliday hoped the mineral-rich waters in Glenwood Springs would cure him. They didn't, and he died from the disease in 1887, at the age of 36, in the ornate Hotel Glenwood.

After the trail rounds a bend, the cemetery comes into sight beyond a wooden barricade. Keep walking uphill to reach the gated entrance, and turn left to follow a series of

FUN FACTOR

LEARN MORE ABOUT THE GUNSLINGER OF GLENWOOD SPRINGS.

If the hike to Doc Holliday's grave marker piqued your child's interest, your next stop should be the Doc Holliday Museum, on the lower level of Bullock's Western Store on Grand Avenue. This satellite museum for the Glenwood Springs Historical Society recounts the story of Holliday's sordid life. In addition to a short film, visitors discover photos and drawings of the gunslinger, as well as other knickknacks and artifacts—his pocket watch, for example, and a small handgun known as a derringer.

Brush up on the town's Wild West history, then explore its modern attractions. Tourists come from far and wide to soak in the geothermally heated waters at Glenwood Hot Springs Lodge and the town's quieter resort, Iron Mountain Hot Springs.

Glenwood Caverns Adventure Park is a mountaintop theme park built around fairy caves that have been described as an "eighth world wonder." In addition to thrill rides and tamer attractions, a 40-minute guided cave tour leads parents and their kids on a 0.25-mile underground trek through winding passages and natural water features. Learn more about the caves you explored while watching "The Fairy Caves," an episode of Rocky Mountain PBS's show Colorado Experience.

DOC HOLLIDAY GRAVE TRAIL

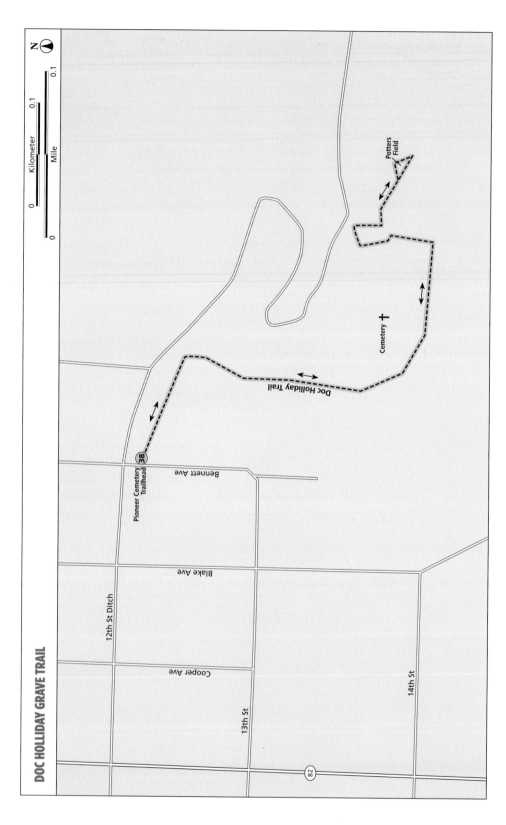

Potters Field

Cemetery

Doc Holliday Trail

Pioneer Cemetery
Trailhead

38

Bennett Ave

Blake Ave

12th St Ditch

Cooper Ave

13th St

14th St

82

N

Kilometer
0   0.1   0.1

Mile
0

hand-shaped arrows to Doc Holliday's grave marker. An interpretive sign near a prominent headstone provides biographical details.

View the main attraction, then walk through the burial ground and read old tombstones adorned with flowers, dolls, and stones. To incorporate STEAM education, pack paper and a few crayons, and make grave rubbings by placing the paper on a headstone and gently rubbing it with a crayon.

At the top of the cemetery, walk straight through the trail intersection to visit a potter's field—a graveyard containing the remains of unknown, unclaimed, or indigent people. A trail post with an arrow guides hikers to the place where Kid Curry was laid to rest. The outlaw rode with Butch Cassidy and the Sundance Kid's infamous Wild Bunch gang. Then follow the "Exit" sign downhill, and retrace your steps to the trailhead.

MILES AND DIRECTIONS

0.0 Start from the Pioneer Cemetery Trailhead, walk up a few wooden steps to a welcome sign, then merge onto the dirt Doc Holliday Trail. Elevation: 5,918 feet.

0.2 Pass a bench and scenic overlook.

0.3 After rounding a bend, climb several wood steps before arriving at the entrance to Linwood Cemetery.

0.4 Follow the signs to Doc Holliday's grave marker.

0.45 Return to the top of the cemetery. Walk straight through the trail intersection to visit Kid Curry's gravesite.

0.5 Arrive at Kid Curry's marble headstone. Turn around and retrace your steps to Linwood Cemetery.

0.55 Follow the "Exit" sign downhill, and hike back the way you came.

0.9 Arrive back at the trailhead.

39 CALHAN PAINT MINES TRAIL

Paint Mines Interpretive Park is a bucket-list destination for hikers and nonhikers alike. Between the windswept hoodoos and bright bands of colorful clay, this extraordinary 750-acre site contains some of Colorado's most distinctive geological features, offering a scenic departure from typical foothills terrain. The Paint Mines themselves are prehistorically significant.

Start: Paint Mines Interpretive Park Trailhead
Distance: 2.0 miles out and back
Hiking time: 1–3 hours
Difficulty: Easy
Elevation gain: 205 feet
Trail surface: Dirt and loose gravel
Hours: Open daily, dawn to dusk
Best seasons: Fall and spring
Water: None
Toilets: Vault toilets at the trailhead
Nursing benches: None
Stroller-friendly: Doable with a good jogging stroller
Potential child hazards: Rattlesnakes
Other trail users: None

Dogs: Not permitted inside this fragile park
Land status: El Paso County Parks
Nearest town: Colorado Springs
Fees and permits: None
Maps: El Paso County Parks Paint Mines Interpretive Park Trail Map
Trail contact: El Paso County Parks, 2002 Creek Crossing St., Colorado Springs 80905; (719) 520-7529; communityservices.elpasoco.com/parks-and-recreation
Gear suggestions: Sunscreen, sun-protective clothing, brimmed hats, Nuun tablets, more water than you think you'll need, a camera

FINDING THE TRAILHEAD

From Colorado Springs, take US 24 east to Calhan. After driving 25 miles, turn right (south) on Yoder Street, which becomes Calhan Highway. In 0.5 mile turn left on Paint Mine Road. Look for the designated parking area on the east side of the road. There are several signs guiding visitors toward the park. A second lot—the Paint Mine upper lot—is located 1 mile down the road, on the park's south side.

THE HIKE

For something totally out of the ordinary, take a day trip to Paint Mines Interpretive Park, a ruggedly beautiful refuge listed on the National Register of Historic Places. The big shebang is the Paint Mines, a basin filled with rainbow-tinged cliffs and hoodoos bordered by giant boulders and dazzling white quartzite crystal.

Oxidized iron compounds give the formations their spectacular colors. The chemical reaction that occurs when iron combines with oxygen is common in a special type of place known as a badland, where sedimentary rocks have been shaped into unusual formations by naturally occurring erosion from wind and water.

From short- and tallgrass prairie to shrublands and wetlands, there's more to this park than its vibrant mines. A low-grade trail takes hikers on a double loop around the badlands.

The first loop—the Bison Loop—has not been maintained. It's washed out, overgrown, and requires some mild bushwhacking to complete. For these reasons, the trail is not included in the detailed directions below. Adventurous families can explore the first

loop by going straight at the trail intersection at 0.1 mile. Over the next mile, you'll pass two interpretive signs while traversing a prairie community.

Marked with bison trail markers, the loop pays homage to the large game that roamed freely before Euro-American settlers arrived in the region. The buffalo are long gone, but plenty of wildlife still flock to Paint Mines Interpretive Park. Look for pronghorn, mule deer, and coyotes, as well as small animals such as raccoons, skunks, rabbits and other burrowing rodents, and the short-horned lizard, a member of the iguana family. Keep an eye out for snakes.

If this is your family's first time visiting the park, hike directly to the badland. From the trail intersection at 0.1 mile, signs and arrows direct hikers to a wide dirt trail leading to the Paint Mines.

After an easy 0.8-mile trek, families get an up-close view of the site's incredible rock formations by following the trail into the basin. Use a series of narrow footpaths to explore the area at your own pace, exercising caution and common sense around the fragile pinnacles, spires, and hoodoos.

Make sure to remind children that climbing on formations is prohibited. The plants, rocks, minerals, and artifacts found within park boundaries are protected by law—and for good reason. It takes decades for nature to restore damage to the eroded geologic outcrops, which are made from clay deposited 55 million years ago during the Tertiary period, when the region was a tropical forest.

Evidence of prehistoric human life in the area dates all the way back to 7,000 BCE. The site's earliest inhabitants, the Paleo-Indians, were most likely descendants of the first peoples to migrate over the Bering Land Bridge. Centuries later, Native Americans used colorful clay from the mines to make paint.

FUN FACTOR

TAKE YOUR BEST SHOT.

The trails inside Paint Mines Interpretive Park are fully exposed (read: blazing hot). On a warm fall day, it's best to explore them as close to dawn as possible. There's a bright side to getting your family mobilized before daybreak: Early-morning photography can result in seriously stunning images, no professional training required.

To integrate three of the five STEAM disciplines—science, technology, and art—into your hike, give your child a visual arts lesson before hitting the trail. In photography, the periods immediately after sunrise and before sunset are called golden hours because the natural light is redder and softer than usual. Pack a camera, or an iPhone with a good lens, and see what the youngest hikers in your group can create when the Paint Mines are glowing in natural, post-dawn light.

After you've explored the Paint Mines, retrace your steps to the trailhead. At the four-way trail intersection that reappears at 1.4 miles, there's an option to begin a second loop by turning right and hiking uphill on a wide dirt trail. Unlike the Bison Loop, this 1.9-mile option is easy to follow, with interpretive signs and several scenic overlooks. This additional mileage is not included in the directions below.

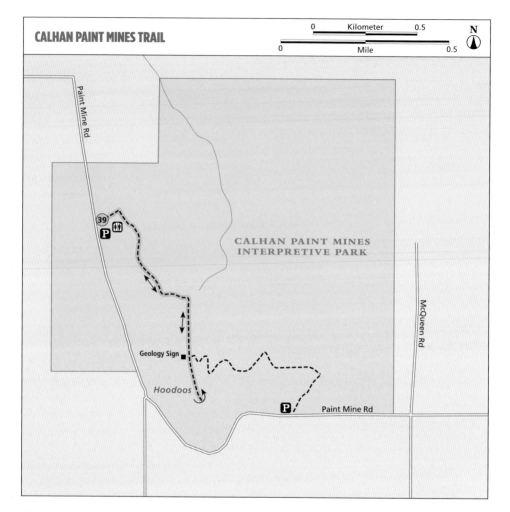

MILES AND DIRECTIONS

0.0   Start at the trailhead on the east side of the main parking lot. Elevation: 6,535 feet.

0.1   Come to a trail junction. Turn right to hike directly to the Paint Mines.

0.6   Arrive at a four-way trail intersection. Make a sharp right turn at the intersection, and continue hiking slightly downhill.

0.65 You'll see a few interesting formations to your right. These are not the Paint Mines. Continue hiking.

0.8   You've reached the Paint Mines. The trail forks at the mouth of a basin. Stay straight to follow a washed-out path through the site's colorful formations.

1.0   Reach the end of the trail; Turn around and hike back the way you came.

1.4   At the four-way trail intersection, turn left to return to the trailhead.

2.0   Arrive back at the trailhead.

WINTER

Hiking might not be the first activity that comes to mind when you think of winter pastimes in Colorado. You might be wondering if it's even possible to hike mid-January. Snowshoeing is always an option, but with the right gear and insider knowledge, regular hiking is also satisfying during the coldest months of the year. Winter is a peaceful time to explore trails along the Front Range, the easternmost section of the southern Rocky Mountains. As snow piles up in the state's mountain towns, it's not uncommon for Denver-area temperatures to rise into the 60s. Average highs are usually in the high 30s and 40s, though, so everyone in your group will need layers, as well as traction devices such as spikes or micro-spikes. The reward is worth the effort. Remember those summer crowds? Come winter, you and your kids might have the whole trail to yourselves.

40 PINES TO PEAKS LOOP

A great hike doesn't have to be long or strenuous. If you need convincing, check out the trek to the top of Bald Mountain. The route is easy enough for a preschooler to complete, and yet older children can also enjoy birding opportunities and sweeping views of the Great Plains and Continental Divide. The trail travels through Bald Mountain Scenic Area: Boulder County's very first open space property.

Start: Bulletin board on the south side of the parking lot
Distance: 1.1-mile lollipop
Hiking time: 1–2 hours
Difficulty: Easy
Elevation gain: 233 feet
Trail surface: Dirt
Hours: Open daily, sunrise to sunset
Best seasons: Year-round
Water: None
Toilets: Portable toilets in the parking lot
Nursing benches: Near the trailhead and at the summit
Stroller-friendly: No
Potential child hazards: None
Other trail users: Equestrians

Dogs: Must be leashed
Land status: Boulder County Parks & Open Space
Nearest town: Boulder
Fees and permits: None
Maps: Boulder County Open Space, Bald Mountain Scenic Area
Trail contact: Boulder County Parks & Open Space, 5201 St. Vrain Rd., Longmont 80503; (303) 678-6200; bouldercounty.org/open-space/parks-and-trails/bald-mountain
Gear suggestions: Snow boots or waterproof footwear, layers, waterproof gloves, wool or fleece hats, micro-spikes, warm herbal tea, binoculars, a pen

FINDING THE TRAILHEAD

From downtown Boulder, take Broadway (CO 93) north toward Mapleton Avenue. Turn left (west) onto Mapleton Avenue. In 0.6 mile, Mapleton Avenue becomes Sunshine Canyon Drive. Follow this road as it winds north for 4.2 miles. Shortly after rounding a bend, you'll see the entrance into Bald Mountain Scenic Area on the left side of the road. The trailhead is on the south end of a small parking lot.

THE HIKE

The site's one and only trail, the Pines to Peak Loop, crosses three distinct ecosystems: meadow, ponderosa pine parkland, and ponderosa forest. Gold mines were established in the area in the late 1860s, and evidence of mining can be seen on the south, west, and eastern slopes of Bald Mountain.

As early as 1886, pioneers began grazing their livestock in the meadows surrounding Bald Mountain. An old livestock-loading corral and chute still stand near the park entrance. Cheatgrass is another remnant from the homesteading days. The exotic weed was likely introduced with grazing.

A few hundred feet past the parking lot, look for a "Nature Detectives Club" mailbox. Open the box, and grab a mystery guide. In addition to a park map designed just for kids, the booklet contains several activities for children to complete while exploring Bald Mountain Scenic Area.

When you come to a fork in the trail at 0.15 mile, you have arrived at the Pines to Peak Loop. It's fine to go either way, but we'll travel clockwise through Boulder County's first open space property.

In land-use planning, an open space is usually an undeveloped parcel of land accessible to the public. In 1973, Boulder County Parks & Open Space leased the 108-acre area surrounding Bald Mountain from the Colorado State Board of Land Commissioners. The nature trail you're using was developed soon after, and the original lease is still active today.

As you curve around Bald Mountain, you might pass a few mule deer and chipmunks, but due to the park's relatively small size and scarcity of water, animal diversity is low. If you're hiking with an animal lover, your best bet is to look up! See if you can spot ravens, downy and hairy woodpeckers, or the bright blue Steller's jay.

After a quick 0.35-mile climb, you've reached Bald Mountain's barren, 7,160-foot summit. You're standing on the highest peak within a physiographic province known as the Southern Rocky Mountain Province. From this vantage point, you'll gain bird's-eye views of the Great Plains and Continental Divide.

This really is the perfect place for a picnic! If the forecast is mild, let your children help you prepare a picnic lunch to enjoy mid-hike. Kids love playing chef, and older children can plan the entire meal by creating an itemized shopping list (spelling and handwriting practice) and joining parents on a trip to the store (a great economics lesson).

After taking in sweeping views, continue past the bench to begin your descent. The southwest portion of the Pines to Peaks Loop is rugged, with steep slopes and exposed rock outcrops. Initially, you might wonder if you're on the trail. Keep heading downhill; before long, a clear path resumes as the trail tracks west.

As you round a bend, look for the charred trees on the hillsides to the west. In 2010, the destructive Fourmile Canyon Wildfire blazed through the area for eleven days, causing $220 million in property damage. Park rangers are still working to restore the forest.

FUN FACTOR

PLAY LIKE A LOCAL.

Boulder began as an 1800s supply town for gold miners, and Pearl Street has been the city's commercial core ever since—although it wasn't until the 1970s that local activists paved the way for today's bustling pedestrian mall.

Pearl Street Mall is a 4-block cluster of retailers stretched out along Pearl Street between 11th and 15th Streets. Most businesses on the mall are local, and there are nearly a dozen coffee shops in and around the main strip—making it the perfect place to stop for hot cocoa post-hike.

On the 1400 block, look for marble and brass animal statues. Children are encouraged to climb on the figures and can also scale the bricks between 13th Street and Broadway.

Winter is a magical time on Pearl Street. On the first Saturday in December, check out the yearly Lights of December Parade, with handmade floats, high school marching bands, and more. Boulder's holiday mascot, Freezie the Snowman, has his own special day in December. During Freezie Fest, the mall is jam-packed with free children's activities, including a scavenger hunt, train rides, and crafts.

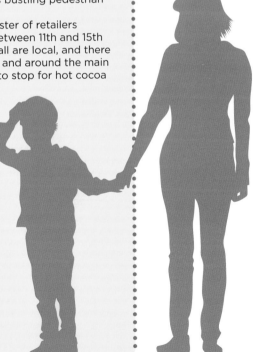

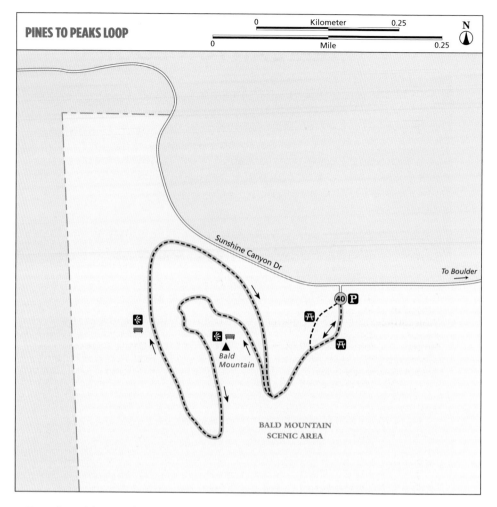

From here, it's a gentle descent across the back side of the mountain. In addition to passing a series of benches, hikers will also go by several scenic overlooks and some interesting rock formations.

MILES AND DIRECTIONS

0.0   Start at the bulletin board on the south side of the parking lot, and begin hiking along the narrow dirt trail. Elevation: 6,400 feet.

0.15   The trail forks after rounding a sharp bend. Look for the Pines to Peaks Loop trail sign. Bear left to complete a clockwise loop around Bald Mountain.

0.35   Reach the top of Bald Mountain. Continue straight past the bench, and begin descending across a rocky slope.

0.95   You're back at the Pines to Peaks Loop trail sign. Keep straight, then hike downhill to the trailhead.

1.1   Arrive back the trailhead.

41 LAKE GULCH AND INNER CANYON LOOP

Remember the time Denver was submerged by 4 feet of standing water? The second-worst flood in the city's history started in 1933, at Castlewood Dam. The ruins of the dam are located inside Castlewood Canyon State Park, a 2,636-acre space preserving an ecologically unique area known as the Black Forest. In addition to its unusual history, Castlewood Canyon contains several hiking trails that wind past a waterfall, homesteading ruins, and spectacular geological formations.

Start: Lake Gulch Trailhead bulletin board
Distance: 2.2-mile lollipop
Hiking time: 1–3 hours
Difficulty: Easy to moderate
Elevation gain: 173 feet
Trail surface: Dirt, crushed gravel, rock, sand, sidewalk
Hours: Sunrise to sunset (Park gates are locked promptly at sunset.)
Best seasons: Year-round
Water: Drinking fountains inside the visitor center
Toilets: Near the trailhead and at the visitor center
Nursing benches: Plentiful along this route
Stroller-friendly: No, but the nearby paved Canyon View Nature Trail is stroller and wheelchair accessible.
Potential child hazards: Steep ledges, poison ivy. Flash floods are always possible in a canyon, but they are very rare in winter.
Other trail users: None
Dogs: Permitted on a leash no longer than 6 feet everywhere except the East Canyon Trail
Land status: Colorado Parks & Wildlife
Nearest town: Castle Rock
Fees and permits: Per-vehicle day-use fee or Colorado Parks & Wildlife Annual Pass
Maps: Colorado Parks & Wildlife Castlewood Canyon State Park
Trail contact: Colorado Parks & Wildlife, 2989 South State Hwy. 83, Franktown 80166; (303) 688-5242; cpw.state.co.us/placestogo/parks/CastlewoodCanyon
Gear suggestions: Waterproof footwear, layers, waterproof gloves, wool or fleece hats, Smartwool socks, micro-spikes, warm herbal tea

FINDING THE TRAILHEAD

To reach the main (east) entrance of Castlewood Canyon State Park, take I-25 to Castle Rock, and exit eastbound onto Founders Parkway. Take Founders Parkway to CO 86 / 5th Street. Turn left (east). In just under 5 miles you'll come to Franktown. Turn right (south) onto CO 83 / South Parker Road, and follow the road for another 5 miles to the park's main entrance, on the right side of the road. To reach the Lake Gulch Trailhead, enter the park, and drive past the visitor center to the Canyon Point parking lot. The trailhead is near the outhouse.

THE HIKE

There are two entrances into Castlewood Canyon State Park. Both have trails leading to the dam ruins. In this guide, we'll use the park's main (east) entrance, where facilities include a visitor center, flush toilets, and picnic areas.

Because it is hidden in the plains—away from the foothills and mountains—outdoors enthusiasts sometimes overlook Castlewood Canyon State Park. As a result, hikers are typically greeted with a quiet network of easy and moderate trails. In winter, the Lake Gulch and Inner Canyon Trails can be combined to create a flat, sunny loop.

This hike starts on a paved sidewalk that quickly becomes a dirt and crushed gravel trail. Look left to see Pikes Peak Amphitheater, a year-round concert venue, before winding downhill into the canyon. The Lake Gulch Trail is easy to follow, but things get a little hairy at the rocky clearing at 0.3 mile. Keep going downhill until a clear trail reappears.

At the first overlook, look for Pikes Peak in the distance, and read an interpretive sign about the clearing ahead, which used to be a lake. Ask children to search for signs that the area was previously waterlogged. (**Hint:** Look at the rock patterns! They imitate patterns the surf makes on sand, because stones were tossed and turned in the water as they traveled from mountains to the plains.)

Past the overlook, the Lake Gulch Trail follows a ledge through strands of ponderosa pine and shrubs such as Gambel oak, mountain mahogany, and snowberry. Castlewood Canyon State Park supports several threatened plants, including Richardson's alumroot, American currant, and carrion flower. The park is also home to Preble's meadow jumping mouse, a threatened species. If you have binoculars, use them to view some of the one hundred-plus bird species nesting inside Castlewood Canyon. Turkey vultures roost along the canyon rim.

Past the trail marker at 0.7 mile, kids will love squeezing between a couple of boulders before crossing Cherry Creek, a tributary of the South Platte River. Follow sandy single-track uphill, toward a three-way trail intersection.

To visit the dam ruins, turn left onto the Inner Canyon Trail and hike about 0.3 mile to the Creek Bottom and Rim Rock Trail marker, where you'll have a clear view of the dam that devastated Denver.

Castlewood Dam was built in 1890 to provide irrigation for the agricultural development of Douglas County. Its foundation was poor, and in August 1933 the dam collapsed—sending a massive, 15-foot-high wall of water through Denver. This disaster ultimately led to the construction of the Cherry Creek Dam and Reservoir.

Hikers can combine the Creek Bottom and Rim Rock Trails to create another loop, adding an additional 4.2 miles of difficult hiking to the miles and directions below.

In this guide, we'll turn around and hike back to the three-way trail juncture. Keep straight at the intersection to stay on Inner Canyon Trail. In a few hundred feet, look for a fantastic boulder garden. Barren rock outcrops and cliffs support lichen and moss communities.

LAKE GULCH AND INNER CANYON LOOP

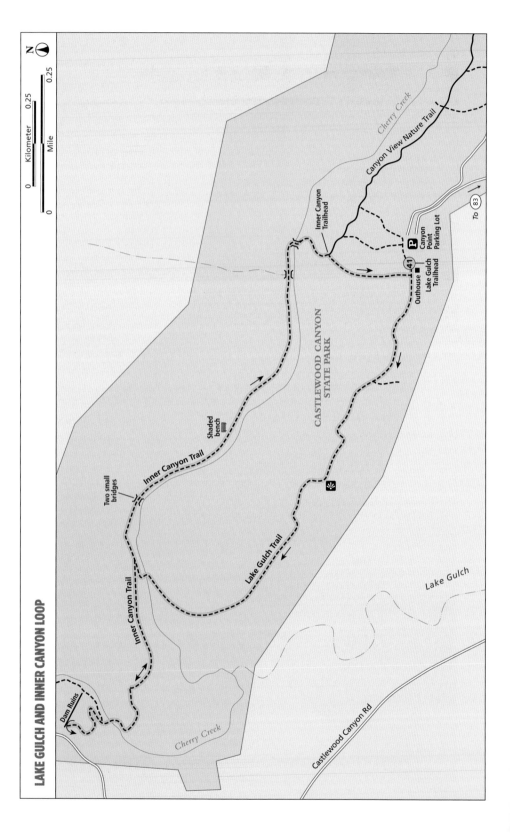

N

Kilometer
0   0.25

0   0.25
Mile

Cherry Creek

Canyon View Nature Trail

Inner Canyon
Trailhead

Canyon Point
Parking Lot

P

41

Outhouse
Lake Gulch
Trailhead

To 83

CASTLEWOOD CANYON
STATE PARK

Shaded
bench

Inner Canyon Trail

Two small
bridges

Lake Gulch Trail

Inner Canyon Trail

Lake Gulch

Dam Ruins

Cherry Creek

Castlewood Canyon Rd

Over the next 0.5 mile, you'll cross several wooden bridges, climb stairs, and pass interesting rock formations. There's a fork in the trail at 1.55 miles. Go either way, since the paths link back up, and avoid any unofficial trails leading to the creek.

After the trail crosses a rickety bridge, a short but steep climb takes hikers to the Inner Canyon Trailhead. When the dirt trail becomes a sidewalk, you're on the Canyon View Nature Trail, a stroller-friendly and wheelchair-accessible pathway leading to a scenic overlook.

MILES AND DIRECTIONS

0.0 Start at the Lake Gulch Trailhead, located on the far end of the Canyon Point parking lot. From the bulletin board, use a sidewalk to access the trail. Elevation: 6,630 feet.

0.1 Pass Pike's Peak Amphitheater.

0.35 Arrive at an overlook and interpretive sign.

0.7 Pass a trail marker. Continue downhill before squeezing between two boulders.

0.8 Cross Cherry Creek.

0.83 Reach a three-way trail intersection. Turn left onto the Inner Canyon Trail, and follow the sign toward Castlewood Dam.

1.0 Arrive at the Creek Bottom / Rim Rock Trail marker. Look straight ahead to view the remains of dam that flooded Denver, then turn around and retrace your steps to the three-way intersection.

1.3 Back at the three-way intersection, hike straight through to return to the parking lot via the Inner Canyon Trail.

1.5 Climb two dozen wooden steps and turn right.

1.85 Pass an informative sign about poison ivy. Although poison ivy plants die down in winter, they can still cause an itchy rash. Be sure to stay on the trail.

1.9   Bear right at the fork, and cross a wooden bridge.

1.95   Use a rickety bridge to cross the creek.

2.05   The dirt trail becomes a paved sidewalk when you reach the Inner Canyon Trailhead sign. Turn right at the fork.

2.2   Arrive back at the parking lot.

FUN FACTOR

STUDY DAMS WITH YOUR KIDS.

Dams are impressive man-made structures that serve as barriers on rivers. While they were originally constructed to control the flow of water, modern engineers also build them to produce electricity. Post-hike, check out Castlewood Canyon Visitor Center. The building houses a small museum with exhibits and a slideshow re-creating the dramatic events of August 3, 1933.

Back home, watch the PBS *Science Trek* episode on dams, then ask children to create their own backyard dams using a garden hose, water containers (buckets, bottles, cups), digging tools, sticks, rocks, bricks, and other objects that block water.

When constructing dams, civil engineers and planners need to know exactly how much water demand their design must meet. Round out your dam curriculum by learning more about Colorado's per capita water usage. History Colorado has a fascinating Water Footprint Calculator, plus several accompanying exhibits on the important role water has played in the state's history. If you're feeling inspired, National Geographic's website has facts and tips on water conservation.

42 COYOTE SONG AND SWALLOW TRAIL LOOP

Wedged between Littleton and the Arapaho-Roosevelt National Forest, South Valley Park is a 995-acre haven abutting the suburban community of Ken Caryl. Between the flat terrain and Front Range elevation, the site's scenic hiking trails are an excellent option on a cold winter day. If your children are brand new to hiking, visit South Valley Park when it's warm for an entry-level experience.

Start: South Valley Park North Trailhead
Distance: 2.1-mile loop
Hiking time: 1–3 hours
Difficulty: Easy
Elevation gain: 192 feet
Trail surface: Dirt, sand, and gravel
Hours: Open daily, 1 hour before sunrise to 1 hour after sunset
Best seasons: Year-round
Water: None
Toilets: On the north side of the parking lot
Nursing benches: Near the trailhead and stationed along both trails
Stroller-friendly: Doable with a jogging stroller on a snow-free day
Potential child hazards: None

Other trail users: Equestrians, mountain bikers
Dogs: Must be leashed
Land status: Jefferson County Open Space
Nearest town: Ken Caryl
Fees and permits: None
Maps: Jefferson County Open Space, South Valley Park
Trail contact: Jefferson County Open Space, 700 Jefferson County Pkwy., Ste. 100, Golden 80401; (303) 271-5925; www.jeffco.us/1431/South-Valley-Park
Gear suggestions: Sunscreen, sunglasses, snow boots, layers, waterproof gloves, wool or fleece hats, Smartwool socks, micro-spikes, warm herbal tea

FINDING THE TRAILHEAD

From I-70, merge onto CO 470. Follow CO 470 past Red Rocks Amphitheater and the town of Morrison. In 10 miles, take the Ken Caryl Avenue exit. Turn right onto West Ken Caryl Avenue then left onto South Valley Road (use any lane). In 1 mile, make a left into South Valley Park's north parking lot. The South Valley Park North Trailhead is located at the southeast corner of the lot. Overflow parking is available down the road, at a smaller south parking lot. To access it, go down South Valley Road and make a right turn onto Deer Creek Canyon Road.

THE HIKE

Two trails depart from South Valley Park's North Trailhead. Hikers can go either way to make a loop. We'll travel clockwise, starting on the Coyote Song Trail, a wide dirt path beginning on a gentle incline.

South Valley Park's trails are well marked, well maintained, and incredibly easy to follow. Be sure to stay on them at all times. The northwest section of the park has been designated as a sensitive area and is closed to public use to protect nesting sites.

Right away, take in big views of dramatic red sandstone spires and craggy outcroppings. Turn right at the trail marker at 0.15 mile, and you're heading straight toward

FUN FACTOR

DON'T FORGET YOUR TOBOGGAN.

When the trails are dry, South Valley Park is the perfect place for beginner mountain bikers to shred. In the middle of winter, trade those wheels for a sled, and make tracks at the nearby Sledding Hill Park, an undeveloped green space at the intersection of South Kipling Parkway and West Ken Caryl Avenue in Littleton. Dropping toward a snowy bank, the site's north-facing hill is fast and thrilling. Benches are available for parent chaperones.

To access the Sledding Hill Park from South Valley Park, drive north along South Valley Road. Turn right when the road intersects West Ken Caryl Avenue, and head west. In 2 miles you'll see the sledding hill on the left side of the road, past Meadows Sanctuary. Parking is limited along Ken Caryl Avenue. If the road is full, sledders can park in Meadows Sanctuary.

these geological features. Most kids will want to climb on the rocks. It's tempting! Remind young hikers that climbing isn't allowed on South Valley Park's delicate sandstone formations.

When you reach the next trail marker, do not turn left onto Lyons Back Trail—unless you'd like to use the short spur to access South Hogback Open Space, a larger trail network maintained by Ken Caryl.

Continue down the Coyote Song Trail. After rounding two bends, the path winds downhill. In summer, when the trail's dry, there's sparkling rock dust everywhere. It looks like "fairy glitter"; if you're hiking with a preschooler, keep an eye out for fairies, gnomes, and other woodland creatures.

After 1.0 mile, the Coyote Song Trail links up with the Prairie Falcon Trail. Turn right to complete a loop. But if you'd like to see the entire park, continue hiking along the Coyote Song Trail until you reach the south parking lot. Then turn around and hike back to this junction. This option adds 0.8 mile to the route below and is not included in the detailed directions.

You'll be on the Prairie Falcon Trail for only a moment. At the three-way trail intersection, turn right onto the Swallow Trail, a hiker-only footpath. The last segment of the prescribed loop is a peaceful stroll through a pastoral valley. After rounding a private reservoir, the trail returns to the north parking lot.

For a longer hike, families can go left at the three-way intersection and follow the Prairie Falcon Trail across South Valley Road. South Valley Park resumes on the other side of the street, offering an additional 2.8 miles of hiking on the Gazing Elk Trail.

COYOTE SONG AND SWALLOW TRAIL LOOP

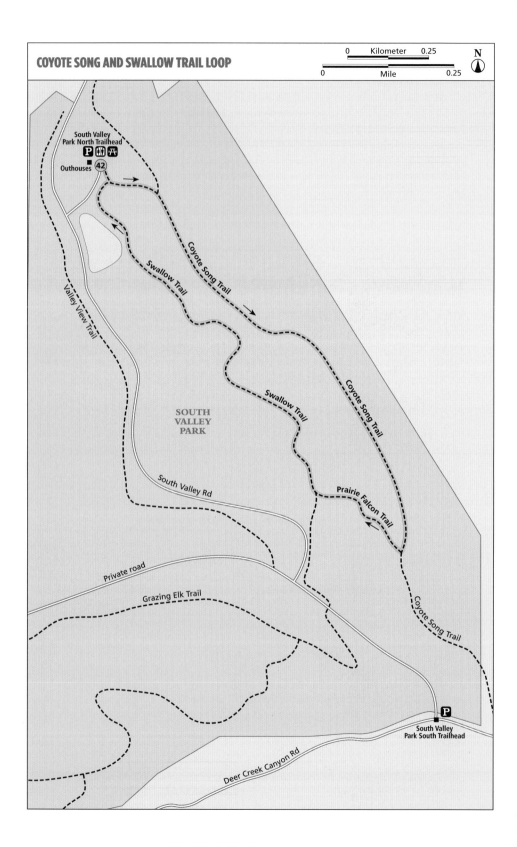

MILES AND DIRECTIONS

0.0 Start from the South Valley Park North Trailhead, and follow the dirt and gravel trail uphill. Go left at the fork to begin hiking on the Coyote Song Trail. Stay on designated trails to protect sensitive areas inside the park. Elevation: 5,760 feet.

0.15 Arrive at a junction. Following the signs, turn right to continue downhill on the Coyote Song Trail.

1.05 The Coyote Song Trail intersects the Prairie Falcon Trail. Turn right to complete a loop.

1.25 Reach a trail marker and three-way intersection. Turn right onto the Swallow Trail.

1.95 Pass a private reservoir.

2.1 After descending several steps, arrive back at the parking lot.

43 RIM TRAIL SOUTH TO SPIRAL POINT

Snowmass Mountain claims the most kid-friendly alpine slopes in Pitkin County. But you don't have to ski to enjoy the resort. Try a winter hike to one of the town's most iconic vistas, Spiral Point (9,210'), nicknamed the Yin-Yang for the marble platform at its summit. From this lookout, families have aerial views of Mount Daly, Capital Peak (14,137'), and the Snowmass ski area—plus Ziegler Reservoir, the site of an ice age discovery. Every summer, the winter wonderland melts into a colorful wildflower hike.

Start: Rim Trail South Trailhead
Distance: 2.6 miles out and back
Hiking time: 1.5–3 hours
Difficulty: Moderate
Elevation gain: 636 feet
Trail surface: Dirt
Hours: None posted
Best seasons: Year-round
Water: None
Toilets: None
Nursing benches: A secluded picnic table at 0.5 mile
Stroller-friendly: No
Potential child hazards: Steep ledges, black bears, disorientation (winter only)
Other trail users: Mountain bikers, equestrians
Dogs: Must be leashed on all trails
Land status: Snowmass Village Parks, Recreation & Trails

Nearest town: Snowmass Village
Fees and permits: None
Maps: Snowmass Village Parks, Recreation & Trails Village Core insert
Trail contact: Snowmass Village Parks, Recreation & Trails, 2835 Brush Creek Rd., Snowmass Village 81615; (970) 922-2240; www.snowmassrecreation.com/149/Parks-Trails
Gear suggestions: Sunscreen, sunglasses, snow boots, snowshoes (available to rent in town), layers, waterproof snow pants, waterproof gloves, wool or fleece hats, Smartwool socks, balaclavas, chemical hand warmers, high-energy snacks that won't freeze, warm herbal tea

SARA STOOKEY SANCHEZ

SARA STOOKEY SANCHEZ

FINDING THE TRAILHEAD

From Snowmass Village, drive west on Brush Creek Road. After bypassing the Snowmass ski resort, Brush Creek Road splits. Turn right (north) onto Divide Road. (If you get to the Snowmass Village Mall, you've gone too far.) Pass Deerfield Drive. Almost immediately, a paved parking lot appears on the right (north) side of the road. Continue up Divide Road to reach the Rim Trail Angle parking lot (to the left), with six spaces. The Rim Trail South Trailhead is across the street. If this lot is full, backtrack to the paved lot near Deerfield Drive. Or if you're staying in Snowmass, park in one of the numbered lots near the Snowmass Mall, and start your hike at the Nature Trailhead, located in parking lot 7. Walk along the Nature Trail until you come to the South Rim Connector Trail (on the right). The South Rim Connector Trail merges with the Rim Trail South.

THE HIKE

Twenty minutes from Aspen, Snowmass Village is a four-season destination for adventurous hikers. Whether you're exploring alpine meadows or dense forests, the scenery is always epic.

Rim Trail South is particularly memorable. Eventually it runs into Rim Trail North, but completing the entire trek end to end is a daylong undertaking. Many hikers opt for a quicker out-and-back trip to Spiral Point. Most locals refer to the 9,210-foot peak by its nickname, the Yin-Yang, and you'll see why when you get there.

From the trailhead, hike west through a sparse grove of aspens. Rim Trail South is such a popular snowshoeing route that the trail is almost always packed down, making it easy to follow. To reduce the risk of getting lost, don't hike this route immediately after a big snowstorm.

Before long, the trail tracks north through thick brush. Between mid-June and August, wildflowers bloom everywhere, and keen observers might spot the elusive state flower, the Rocky Mountain columbine, with cream and lavender petals surrounding a yellow center.

SARA STOOKEY SANCHEZ

You're headed straight uphill for the first 1.3 miles. The trail switches back and forth across the slope so much, it looks like a zigzag on the map. The views only get better the higher you go.

After passing a bench at 0.5 mile, the trail rounds a corner, and the Snowmass ski area comes into sight. Rim Trail South is a great place to get your bearings, since the route to Spiral Point overlooks Snowmass Village and its two nodes (Snowmass Mall and Base Village). Continue across the ridge until you reach the turnoff for Spiral Point. If you miss the turnoff, there's another chance to bear left a few feet farther down the trail, at a second marker.

After a few moments of low-grade walking, prepare for a short but steep push to the top. In a clearing bordered by sage and scrub oak, hikers stumble upon a massive marble platform depicting a labyrinth with a yin–yang symbol at its center.

See if your children can find a poem etched into a nearby rock. The poem and yin-yang memorialize a local lawyer and poet, Stark King, who came up with the idea of enhancing extraordinary locations on existing Snowmass trails. Before King's vision came to fruition, he died of cancer, and a group of community members completed the project.

The yin-yang really does enhance an extraordinary place! From the platform, you'll have 360-degree views of Mount Daly (13,300'), with its telltale white stripe, and two 14ers, Capitol Peak (14,131') and Pyramid Peak (14,026').

The yin-yang overlooks the Ziegler Reservoir fossil site. This privately owned, 5-hectare (12.4-acre) reservoir supplies Snowmass Village with water. In 2010, during route construction, a bulldozer operator turned over a giant tusk, setting off a full-on excavation. Scientists from the Denver Museum of Nature & Science discovered more than 50,000 ice age bones, including the remains of a juvenile Columbian mammoth.

Hiking back to the trailhead is another 1.3 miles of course, but going down is much easier than coming up.

SARA STOOKEY SANCHEZ

SARA STOOKEY SANCHEZ

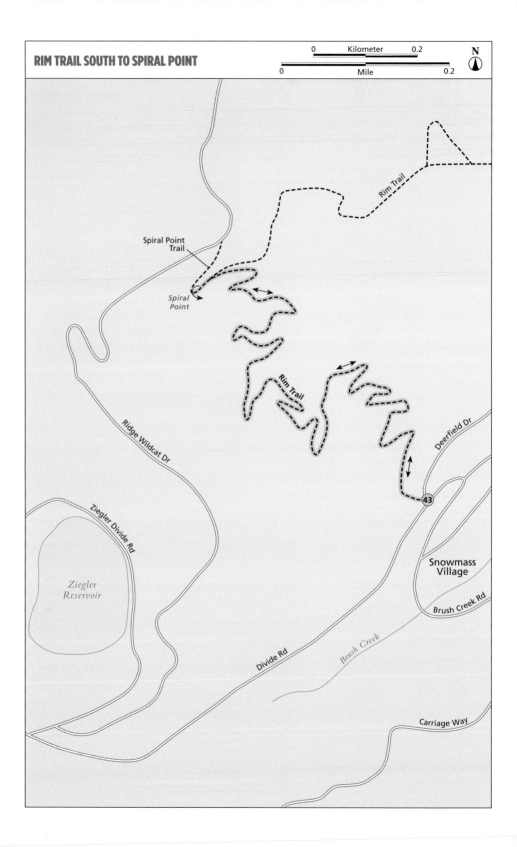

RIM TRAIL SOUTH TO SPIRAL POINT

0   Kilometer   0.2

0   Mile   0.2

N

Rim Trail

Spiral Point
Trail

Spiral
Point

Rim Trail

Ridge Wildcat Dr

Deerfield Dr

43

Snowmass
Village

Brush Creek Rd

Ziegler Divide Rd

Ziegler
Reservoir

Divide Rd

Brush Creek

Carriage Way

SARA STOOKEY SANCHEZ

MILES AND DIRECTIONS

0.0 Start from the welcome sign at the Rim Trail South Trailhead, and begin hiking uphill on a narrow trail. Elevation: 8,574 feet.

0.2 Come to a fork, and bear slightly left to stay on Rim Trail South. A connector trail, Hawk Ridge, juts off to the right.

0.5 Pass a secluded picnic table.

0.8 An unofficial trail branches off from Rim Trail South. Put Leave No Trace principles into practice by staying on the main route.

1.2 Reach a fork in the trail. Bear left onto the Spiral Point Trail.

1.3 Arrive at Spiral Point and the yin-yang symbol. When you're ready, turn around and retrace your steps to the trailhead.

2.6 Arrive back at the trailhead.

FUN FACTOR

GIVE YOUR KIDS THE V.I.P. TREATMENT.

Snowmass Village caters to families. If you're visiting during ski season, don't miss V.I.K. Snowmass. Short for "Very Important Kids," V.I.K. is a hub of kid-friendly activities designed to keep children busy after the skiing or hiking day ends.

In addition to toasting s'mores (free every afternoon), Snowmass's youngest visitors can try ice-skating at The Rink in Snowmass Base Village, swimming at the Snowmass Rec Center, or visiting the Breathtaker Alpine Coaster on select Friday nights.

But the best way to reward young hikers is with a trip to the Game Lounge, a kid-approved gathering space located inside The Collective at Snowmass Base Village. The Game Lounge has it all: foosball, tube table tennis, a ball pit, interactive touch-screen wall mural, board games, video games, full-size pin art, and air hockey. Everything's free, and most offerings are amplified versions of the traditional games. Above the game lounge, parents can grab a drink at the on-site bar.

44 ELDORADO CANYON TRAIL

With more than 500 technical climbing routes, Eldorado Canyon State Park's sheer golden cliffs are a mecca for rock climbers. Families don't need a belayer and chalk bag to enjoy breathtaking views. The site's wooded trails draw mountain bikers and photographers. On summer weekends, the park often reaches capacity, prompting long waits at the entrance gate. Winter is a quieter time to enjoy Eldo's trails—just make sure to come prepared with traction, snowshoes, or cross-country skis.

Start: Eldorado Canyon Trailhead
Distance: 3.8 miles out and back
Hiking time: 2–4 hours
Difficulty: Moderate to difficult
Elevation gain: 1,056 feet
Trail surface: Dirt and rock
Hours: Open daily, dawn to dusk
Best seasons: Year-round
Water: Drinking fountains inside the visitor center
Toilets: Flush toilets inside the visitor center
Nursing benches: Several along the Eldorado Canyon Trail
Stroller-friendly: No
Potential child hazards: Sheer ledges, talus fields
Other trail users: Equestrians, mountain bikers. Labor Day through Mar 31, hunters are allowed in the Crescent Meadows portion of the park only.

Dogs: Permitted on a 6-foot or shorter leash
Land status: Colorado Parks & Wildlife
Nearest towns: Superior and Boulder
Fees and permits: Per-vehicle day-use fee or Colorado Parks and Wildlife Pass.
Maps: Colorado Parks & Wildlife Eldorado Canyon State Park brochure
Trail contact: Colorado Parks & Wildlife, Eldorado Canyon Office, 9 Kneale Rd., Eldorado Springs 80025; (303) 494-3943; cpw.state.co.us/placestogo/parks/EldoradoCanyon
Gear suggestions: Snowshoes or traction devices, waterproof boots, layers, waterproof gloves, wool or fleece hats, Smartwool socks, balaclavas, chemical hand warmers, high-energy snacks that won't freeze, warm herbal tea

FINDING THE TRAILHEAD

From CO 36, take the Louisville-Superior exit and go left (south) on McCaslin Boulevard. Almost immediately, turn right (west) onto Marshall Road and wind through Superior Marketplace. Continue driving west for about 6 miles. The road becomes dirt as it passes through the offbeat town of Eldorado Springs. Do not park in town. Continue following CO 170 to Eldorado State Park's main entrance. From here, drive through Eldorado Canyon State Park, cross a small bridge, and steer left to follow signs to the visitor center. The road is bumpy but doesn't require high clearance. The Eldorado Canyon Trailhead is on the east side of the visitor center.

THE HIKE

It's no wonder Eldorado Canyon State Park has been the backdrop for commercials and documentaries. Even from the parking lot, the views are spectacular!

Eldorado Canyon is divided into two main sections: the Inner Canyon and Crescent Meadows. The park's three major trails—Fowler, Rattlesnake Gulch, and Eldorado Canyon—depart from the Inner Canyon.

In mild weather, Fowler Trail is an easy, stroller-friendly option for families with young children. The 1.4-mile out-and-back route contains a series of interpretive signs about local wildlife, and it's the best place, by far, to view the canyon's lichen-covered walls while watching rock climbers in action.

The Fowler Trail runs into the Rattlesnake Gulch Trail, another kid-approved trek leading to the historic Crags Hotel ruins, hovering 800 feet above the trailhead. The Crags Hotel was built in 1908 but burned down a few years later, during the original

heyday of nature-based tourism. Before it was set aside as a state park, Eldorado Canyon was the Eldorado Springs Resort, with two hotels, three swimming pools, ballrooms, roller- and ice-skating rinks, cabins, and stables. Nicknamed the "Coney Island of the West," the resort welcomed celebrities, including Dwight and Mamie Eisenhower, who honeymooned there in 1916.

Rock climbers didn't come to the canyon until the 1950s. When the canyon's owner threatened to sell the area for a rock quarry, public outcry prompted Colorado to purchase the site in 1978.

The Fowler and Rattlesnake Gulch Trails can be extremely icy in winter and early spring. Farther down the road, on the west end of the Inner Canyon, the Eldorado Canyon Trail is a sunny route that dries quickly between storms.

The trail takes off from a kiosk outside the visitor center. After climbing stone and wood stairs and crossing a road, the first section of the hike is a challenging 1,000-foot ascent with excellent views. Switchbacks ease the climb, and benches offer break points at 0.2 and 0.35 mile. Past the second bench, after a big bend, pass the turnoff for Rincon Wall. Don't turn right onto this climbing-access trail. Instead, continue along the main trail, which is much wider.

The hardest part of the hike is behind you. Even so, families hiking with young children can use the Rincon Wall junction and the nearby overlook as a "summit." If you're up for more, continue following the Eldorado Canyon Trail as it dips into a forest of ponderosa pine and Rocky Mountain juniper.

Large populations of bats breed in the caves in the Inner Canyon. In fact, seven out of the ten bat species recorded in Boulder County can be found in Eldorado Canyon. Since bats are nocturnal, hikers have a better chance of observing some of the canyon's eighty species of migratory and resident birds. South Boulder Creek supports cold-water fish species such as white and longnose suckers and trout. Mule deer, elk, black bear, bobcat, red fox, and coyote inhabit the land too.

Cross through a field of boulders, and beware of talus fields nearby. Talus fields occur when rocks accumulate on scree. The rocks are extremely unstable. When they're disturbed, they'll roll down until they find a stopping point, creating a potentially dangerous situation for hikers. Supervise children, and don't go off-trail.

ELDORADO CANYON TRAIL

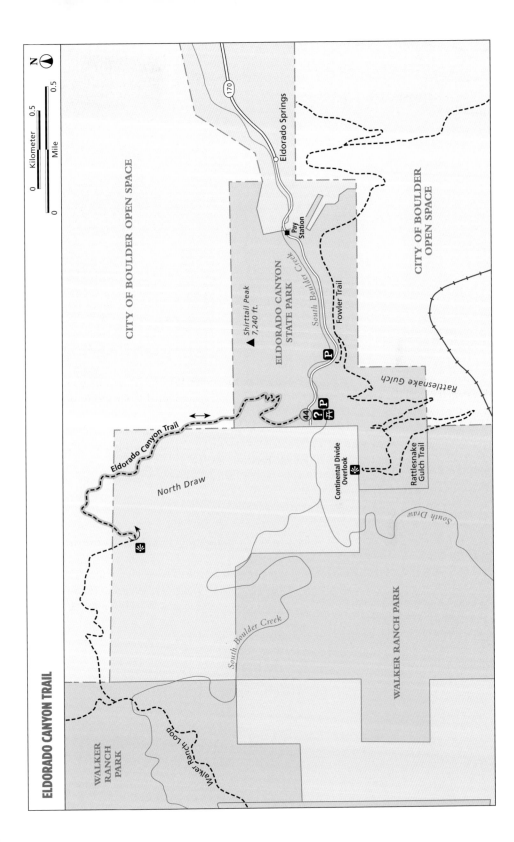

FUN FACTOR

SKATE THROUGH THE SEASON.

Eleven miles west of Eldorado Canyon, across the Denver-Boulder Turnpike, the town of Louisville has been ranked a top place to raise a family. It's also a fun place to visit with a family.

On a warm day, it's always fun to explore Louisville's compact shopping district. Many of the charming, hundred-year-old storefronts house family-owned and -operated businesses, and there's no shortage of excellent restaurants along the main strip.

When it's too cold to window-shop, head to Steinbaugh Pavilion instead for some good old-fashioned skating. WinterSkate is a seasonal, family-friendly offering that typically operates November through February. Skate rentals are included with admission to the outdoor ice arena.

After crossing a small bridge, you're almost to the top of the hill. In another 0.3 mile, the trail weaves out of the forest, opening to sensational views of the Continental Divide. Eldorado Canyon Trail continues on for another 1.4 miles, until terminating at the Walker Ranch Loop Trail. It's possible to complete a 14-mile lollipop by combining these two trails, but that's ambitious with children.

We'll stop at the scenic overlook at 1.85 miles (GPS coordinates: 39.94136 / –105.30329). Turn around and retrace your steps to the trailhead. It's all downhill from here!

MILES AND DIRECTIONS

0.0 Start from the Eldorado Canyon Trailhead, and begin climbing the steps behind the kiosk. Elevation: 6,000 feet.

0.2 Bear right at the trail marker.

0.38 Pass a bench and scenic overlook.

0.63 Arrive at the turnoff for Rincon Wall, a technical rock climbing access point. Continue hiking along the Eldorado Canyon Trail.

0.75 Pass a trail marker.

1.55 Cross a bridge.

1.85 Reach a scenic overlook at the top of a hill (GPS coordinates: 39.94136 / –105.30329). After enjoying the views, turn around and retrace your steps to the trailhead.

3.8 Arrive back at the trailhead.

45 **WETLAND LOOP**

Cherry Creek State Park is one of the most convenient hiking destinations for Denver families. Summers are action-packed as locals flock to the park's sandy beaches, marina, and campground. When snow hits the Front Range, anglers ice fish on Cherry Creek Reservoir, while cross-country skiers take to the trails. For families, the Wetland Loop is an ideal spot for a mellow, midwinter stroll.

Start: Cottonwood Creek Trailhead
Distance: 1.7-mile lollipop
Hiking time: 1–2 hours
Difficulty: Easy
Elevation gain: 73 feet
Trail surface: Natural surface
Hours: Open daily, sunrise to sunset; check ahead for any modified winter day-use hours.
Best seasons: Year-round
Water: None
Toilets: Drop toilets near the trailhead
Nursing benches: None
Stroller-friendly: Yes, when the trail is clear of snow and ice; the park also has wheelchair-accessible routes.
Potential child hazards: None
Other trail users: None

Dogs: Welcome on some trails at Cherry Creek State Park, but not permitted in the wetlands
Land status: Colorado Parks & Wildlife
Nearest towns: Denver and Centennial
Fees and permits: Per-vehicle day-use fee or Colorado Parks and Wildlife Annual Pass
Maps: Colorado Parks & Wildlife, Cherry Creek State Park trails map
Trail contact: Colorado Parks & Wildlife, Cherry Creek State Park, 4201 South Parker Rd., Aurora 80014; (303) 690-1166; cpw.state.co.us/placestogo/parks/CherryCreek
Gear suggestions: Insulated/waterproof boots, layers, waterproof gloves, wool or fleece hats, Smartwool socks, high-energy snacks that won't freeze, herbal tea

FINDING THE TRAILHEAD

From I-25 in Denver use exit 200 to merge onto DTC Boulevard. Turn left (east) onto Temple Drive, which becomes East Union Avenue. Drive past Cherry Creek High School, and turn right onto South Dayton Street. Immediately after turning onto South Dayton Street, make a left into Cherry Creek State Park via West Lake View Road. Check in at the entrance station, then follow West Lake View Road around the reservoir. The Cottonwood Creek parking lot is on the left, past the model airfield. Look for a trailhead on the east side of the lot. There are only eight spots in this pullout, but parking is rarely an issue. If the Cottonwood Creek parking lot is full, backtrack to one of the many lots you passed on your way in.

THE HIKE

Cherry Creek State Park is an urban haven with 12 miles of multiuse trails laid out across a rolling prairie. When early wagon train travelers on the Smoky Hill Trail cut through the area in the mid-1800s, they surely gawked at the yucca-studded, mountain-framed landscape.

For hikers, the park's wetlands offer several miles of foot–only trails traversing a protected aquatic ecosystem on the south edge of the reservoir. This waterlogged area is a prime destination for avid birders with its wide variety of rare songbirds, waterfowl, and shorebirds.

There are several ways to access the wetlands. We'll start at the Cottonwood Creek Trailhead, near the park's west entrance. From the outhouse and welcome sign, follow the Cherry Creek Trail for a few hundred feet. Before long, this paved sidewalk intersects the Pipeline Trail, a natural-surface path marked by two metal posts. The Pipeline Trail leads hikers straight into the Wetlands Preserve.

This isn't your typical foothills hike. From wide-open grasslands, hikers enter a marshy area shaded by tall cottonwoods. Turn left onto the Wetland Loop, and the scenery really changes as the flat trail winds past aquatic plants.

Around 0.85 mile, a narrow dirt path juts out to the left. The North Connector Trail is a 0.27-mile (one way) trail ending at the Parker Road Trail. When it's open, it's a fun add-on, but additional miles are not included in the detailed directions below.

Continue along the Wetland Loop. Turn right when the Wetland Loop ends at a second set of wooden barricades, and follow the Pipeline Trail back to the parking lot where you started.

Alternatively, families looking for additional mileage should turn left onto the Pipeline Trail and walk to Cherry Creek, which flows into the reservoir. A bridge crosses over the creek. Most kids will love throwing sticks into the water and watching them sail away. Turn right before the bridge, and walk against the flow of water to discover several beaver dams visible from the shore.

For a much longer route, take the Pipeline Trail all the way to East Lake View Road. Across the street is the 12 Mile Trail, providing access to the park's off-leash dog area,

FUN FACTOR

TOUCH THE ART AT MARJORIE PARK.

A few miles west of Cherry Creek State Park, the Denver Technological Center is a metropolitan business district straddling the cities of Denver and Greenwood Village. Often referred to as "the DTC," the city suburb is a great place for active kids. Eat at one of the restaurants along South Newport Street then let children run amuck at the massive playground inside Westlands Park—one of the best in the metro area.

Better yet, head over to Marjorie Park (6331 South Fiddler's Green Circle), a free, open-air sculpture garden curated by the Museum of Outdoor Arts. Behind the gates, *Alice's Adventures in Wonderland* meets *The Secret Garden* as a winding path weaves through a fantastical series of bronze statues inspired by Alice's adventures. Interspersed between beloved Lewis Carroll characters, you'll find Italian lions too, dating back to the 1500s.

Go ahead, and touch the art! Marjorie Park is a magical, hands-on place where kids can run around—and crawl inside *Weidenblume*, a dome-shaped conceptual work overlooking a pond, built from live willow trees by German artist Sanfte Strukturen. The museum is open during daylight hours.

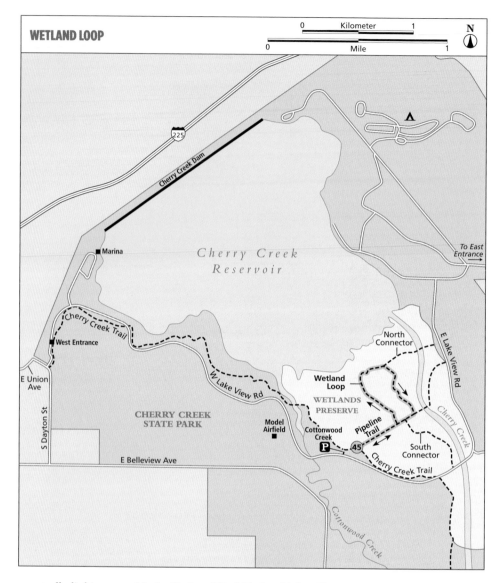

eventually linking up with the Railroad Bed Trail, which will get you back to the Cottonwood Creek Trailhead, where you started. This loop adds approximately 5 miles to the prescribed route.

You can't see it from the Wetland Loop, but Cherry Creek State Park is anchored by an 850-acre reservoir attracting boaters, stand-up paddleboarders, anglers, and picnickers. Parallel to I-225, the reservoir's dam was built in 1950 by the US Army Corps of Engineers to prevent flooding in Denver.

Due to its convenient location and water feature, the park often fills to capacity on summer weekends and holidays. If you visit during peak season, arrive early to avoid waiting in line at the entrance gates.

MILES AND DIRECTIONS

0.0 Start from the Cottonwood Creek Trailhead, follow the Cherry Creek Trail toward a dirt path, keeping right at the fork in the sidewalk. Elevation: 5,550 feet.

0.1 Arrive at the Pipeline Trail. Turn left at the metal sign.

0.25 Pass a large Wetlands Preserve welcome sign.

0.35 Come to an intersection. Turn left onto the narrow dirt trail, and walk through two wooden barricades to begin the Wetland Loop. The trail is not marked.

1.2 After making a broad U-turn through the Wetlands Preserve, you're at the end of the loop. Walk through the wooden barricades then turn right to merge onto the Pipeline Trail.

1.25 Pass a turnoff for the South Connector Trail.

1.55 The Pipeline Trail dead-ends. Turn right onto the Cherry Creek Trail.

1.7 Arrive back at the trailhead.

46 TILTING MESA AND MESA TOP TRAILS

Snow melts lightning-quick on the sunny trails inside North Table Mountain Park, making this fully exposed mesa an optimum destination for winter hiking. The North Table Loop is a 7.0-mile route circumnavigating the open space. Parents can shorten the journey by connecting the Tilting Mesa and Mesa Top Trails. The abbreviated loop includes stops at noteworthy landmarks: an old rock quarry and a lichen-covered peak.

Start: West Trailhead
Distance: 3.6-mile loop
Hiking time: 2–4 hours
Difficulty: Moderate
Elevation gain: 506 feet
Trail surface: Dirt, asphalt, gravel, and rock
Hours: Open daily, 1 hour before sunrise to 1 hour after sunset
Best seasons: Year-round
Water: None
Toilets: Flush toilets near the West Trailhead
Nursing benches: Several spaced out along the route
Stroller-friendly: No
Potential child hazards: Rattlesnakes, high winds

Other trail users: Equestrians, mountain bikers
Dogs: Must be leashed
Land status: Jefferson County Open Space South
Nearest town: Golden
Fees and permits: None
Maps: Jefferson County Open Space South Table Mountain Park
Trail contact: Jefferson County Open Space, 700 Jefferson County Pkwy., Ste. 100, Golden 80401; (303) 271-5925; www.jeffco.us/1427/North-Table-Mountain-Park
Gear suggestions: Layers, windproof jackets, waterproof gloves, Smartwool socks, high-energy snacks that won't freeze, binoculars

FINDING THE TRAILHEAD

From the intersection of I-25 and 6th Avenue, drive west on 6th Avenue toward Golden. Pass the I-70 exchange, and continue driving straight along 6th Avenue. In about 4 miles you'll come to a stoplight and intersection. Drive through the intersection, at which point the road becomes CO 93. In 2 miles, turn right into North Table Mountain Park's west entrance. The road ends at a large parking lot. Look for the trailhead on the south edge of the lot.

THE HIKE

North Table Mountain Park's trail network was built for families. The hike detailed here is a shortcut that tours a small portion of the mesa. Ambitious families can complete a longer route by following the North Table Loop around the entire mesa, while families with young children can turn back at Lichen Peak. Whatever your preference, the park is a popular destination for winter hiking because its fully exposed trails dry quickly after snowstorms.

Use the restroom in the parking lot before starting this hike. There aren't many private places alongside these heavily trafficked trails, and the mesa is almost completely barren.

The adventure begins with a glute-burning, 0.5-mile climb up a wide dirt and asphalt road. After the initial ascent, the rest of the hike is mostly flat or downhill.

At the top of the mesa, look for a ridge to the right. The ridge makes a crescent-shaped arc around the North Quarry Climbing Area. Children are welcome to explore the rocks in the quarry. When it isn't snow-packed or icy, it's easy to follow the unnamed trail across the ridge. This option adds 0.5 mile to the prescribed route.

Continue hiking on the North Table Loop to reach a large boulder with a plaque. Walk past it, and turn left at the fork to begin hiking on the Tilting Mesa Trail.

Hovering above the plains, bounded on all sides by steep escarpments, North Table Mountain's flat-topped mesa looks like a lost world. Lava flows shaped the landform 60 million years ago, and the barren scenery retains an otherworldly feel.

Turn left onto the Lichen Peak Trail at 0.6 mile to take a quick detour to the site's craggy summit. The higher you go, the windier and rockier the trail gets. Push on for sweeping views of downtown Denver and the plains. When you get to the top, see if your children can spot any landmarks, such as Denver International Airport's tented roof, which is more than 30 miles away!

The rocks surrounding the summit are covered in lichen, a beautiful and complex life-form created by two separate organisms, a fungus and an alga. An interpretive sign offers more information.

Retrace your steps to the Tilting Mesa Trail. (**Option:** Families with very young children should turn right here and descend on the North Table Loop. This out-and-back option measures in at 1.2 miles.) We'll turn left onto the Tilting Mesa Trail and follow it north across the mesa. Look for herds of deer, and keep an eye out for coyotes.

With urban sprawl, human–coyote encounters are becoming more common, though they are still rare. A coyote that doesn't run away from humans has become accustomed to people. If you see a coyote on the trail, the best thing to do is haze it by yelling and waving your arms, making loud noises with your voice or a noisemaker (whistles are great), and throwing projectiles like sticks and small rocks. Hazing helps maintain a coyote's natural fear of humans. Don't be apprehensive about recreating where coyotes live. Stray golf balls hurt more people each year than coyotes.

FUN FACTOR

WARM UP IN GOLDEN.

First things first: Head to Washington Avenue in downtown Golden, and snap a family photo near the town's famous "Welcome" sign. (You can't miss it!) Next, refuel. The town's cowboy-themed main street has several options for hot cocoa, coffee, and tea, and there's no shortage of yummy baked goods.

It's easy to stay warm all afternoon at the Golden History Museum, featuring interactive, kid-friendly exhibits. Or try the colorful Mines Museum (formerly the Colorado School of Mines Geology Museum), with a large collection of rocks, gems, and minerals. Both attractions are free. If the weather's nice, there's a lovely nature trail laid out along both sides of Clear Creek, where families can take a leisurely stroll, observe public art, and watch daring Goldenites take ice-cold dips in the stream (a popular activity rumored to bolster the immune system).

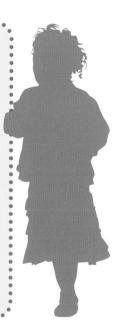

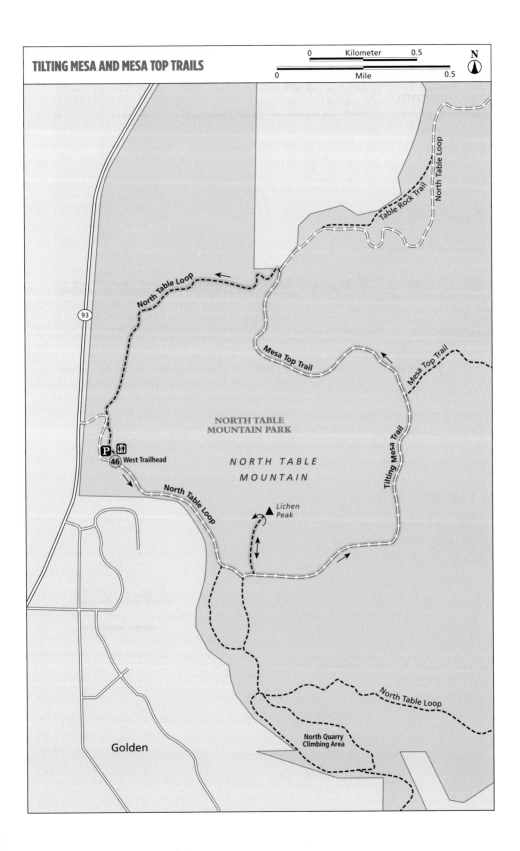

TILTING MESA AND MESA TOP TRAILS

0   Kilometer   0.5

0   Mile   0.5

N

North Table Loop

Table Rock Trail

North Table Loop

93

North Table Loop

Mesa Top Trail

Mesa Top Trail

Tilting Mesa Trail

NORTH TABLE
MOUNTAIN PARK

NORTH TABLE
MOUNTAIN

P   46   West Trailhead

Lichen
Peak

North Table Loop

North Table Loop

North Quarry
Climbing Area

Golden

The Tilting Mesa Trail is wide and flat. Be prepared for large puddles and mud in winter. If your kids laced up in waterproof footwear, let them puddle-hop across the mesa.

After a few bends and curves the Tilting Mesa Trail ends at the Mesa Top Trail. Keep straight at the fork to begin a gradual descent. After weaving between the hilltops, the Mesa Top Trail dips down, reconnecting with the North Table Loop. Turn left to make your way back to the parking lot. The last leg of the journey is a series of wooden ramps and bridges—it's a real treat for kids.

MILES AND DIRECTIONS

- **0.0** Start at the West Trailhead, and begin hiking uphill on the North Table Loop. Elevation: 6,046 feet.

- **0.5** Arrive at the top of the mesa. To the right, the North Quarry Climbing Area is a fun stop-off on a warm day. Explore the area at your leisure (mileage not included here), and return to this intersection. Bear left at the fork. Walk slightly uphill toward a large boulder with a plaque.

- **0.55** Turn left at the junction for the North Table Loop and Tilting Mesa Trail.

- **0.6** The turnoff for the Lichen Peak Trail appears on the left. Follow the out-and-back, hikers-only footpath toward the summit of Lichen Peak (6,552').

- **0.85** Stone steps take you to the top of Lichen Peak. When you're ready, turn around and hike back to the Tilting Mesa Trail.

- **1.1** Turn left onto the Tilting Mesa Trail, and hike across the mesa.

- **1.95** Reach a fork. Keep straight to begin a gradual descent via the Mesa Top Trail.

- **2.75** The Mesa Top Trail ends at the North Table Loop. Turn left.

- **3.5** Come to the north side of the parking lot where you started. Turn left onto a narrow footpath.

- **3.6** Arrive back at the trailhead.

47 **RED ROCK CANYON HISTORY LOOP**

Not far from the quirky town of Manitou Springs, Red Rock Canyon Open Space has everything you need: miles of family-friendly trails, massive rock formations, a stunt park for young bike enthusiasts, picnic sites, and fabulous views of Garden of the Gods. When snow starts falling, the park's sandstone monoliths really burst to life. Many trails inside Red Rock Canyon Open Space are great for snowshoeing, but with traction devices, plain old hiking also works.

Start: Red Rock Canyon Trailhead, on the east side of the big parking lot
Distance: 2.0-mile loop
Hiking time: 1–3 hours
Difficulty: Easy to moderate
Elevation gain: 157 feet
Trail surface: Dirt
Hours: Open daily, dawn to dusk
Best seasons: Year-round
Water: None
Toilets: Portable toilets near the trailhead
Nursing benches: At the large pavilion at 1.65 miles
Stroller-friendly: No
Potential child hazards: Steep ledges near the quarry, a large pond
Other trail users: Equestrians, mountain bikers
Dogs: Two off-leash dog loops have been developed on the mesa. Pets must be leashed on all other trails inside Red Rock Canyon Open Space.
Land status: Colorado Springs Parks, Recreation & Cultural Services
Nearest towns: Colorado Springs and Manitou Springs
Fees and permits: None
Maps: Colorado Springs Parks, Recreation & Cultural Services Red Rock Canyon Trail Access brochure
Trail contact: Colorado Springs Parks, Recreation & Cultural Services, 1401 Recreation Way, Colorado Springs 80905; (719) 385-5940; coloradosprings.gov/parks/page/red-rock-canyon-open-space
Gear suggestions: Sunscreen, layers, waterproof shells or ski jackets, waterproof gloves, fleece or wool hats, waterproof boots, Smartwool socks, micro-spikes, high-energy snacks that won't freeze, herbal tea

FINDING THE TRAILHEAD

From I-25, exit eastbound onto West Cimarron Street. Cimarron Street becomes US 24 (Midland Expressway). After passing the stoplight at 31st Street, turn left (south) onto Ridge Road. The parking lot is located at the end of Ridge Road. To reach it, drive through the roundabout and take the second exit. If the first lot is full, overflow parking is available farther down the road. The trailhead is on the east side of the first lot.

THE HIKE

Red Rock Canyon's sandstone ridges have more to offer than pretty views. In addition to tangible lessons in sedimentary geology, families get a 10,000-year-old slice of human history told through ancient projectile points and ruins.

The hike begins with a steady climb up the Mesa Trail—a soft, wide path bordered by yucca, cacti, and shrubs. From the gate, you'll spy the site's namesake rock formations, which are eye-catching year-round, whether wrapped in grass or dusted with snow.

You'll pass three narrow trails in the first 0.5 mile. Avoid turning right on these off-shoots. At the fourth junction, go left to begin hiking on the Quarry Pass Trail, a short connector trail granting hikers access to a former sandstone quarry. The terrain flattens out, and the path narrows. Take in aerial views of the quarry as you tell your children about the park's fascinating history.

According to an archaeological study from 2004, the earliest evidence of human life in the Red Rock Canyon site comes from projectile points such as arrowheads dating back to 7000 BCE. Given its proximity to Fountain Creek and its abundance of deer, the canyon has probably offered food and shelter to humans for a very long time.

Fast forward to the late 1800s, when the same canyon generated building supplies for the Pike Peak region's first settlement, Colorado City, a gold rush town founded in 1859. The communities of Colorado Springs and Manitou Springs also used gypsum and sandstone mined from the area. In fact, significant quarrying occurred into the early 1900s, when building stone was replaced with concrete and steel, and the quarry closed due to declining demand.

After the trail circles a rim, a series of stone steps drops you directly into the historic quarry. Watch young hikers closely; this segment of the trail is steep.

Prepare to be wowed! Quarry work left behind enormous geometric cuts in the rock face, and you'll get an up-close view while hiking. After crossing a particularly rocky patch, the Quarry Pass Trail picks back up. A hand-placed rock border helps with navigation and guidance.

FUN FACTOR

VISIT GARDEN OF THE GODS.

This iconic Colorado Springs destination attracts an estimated 5.8 million tourists annually—all coming to gawk at the towering red rocks that inspired a surveyor in the 1800s to observe that the area was fit for the gods (hence the name).

From the Garden of the Gods Visitor & Nature Center, it's possible to walk into the Garden of the Gods via the Gateway Trail, a 0.5-mile path linking to the park's most frequented route: Perkins Central Garden Trail. Families can also access the Perkins Central Garden Trail by driving into the park and parking at P2, the first lot you'll encounter.

The Perkins Central Garden Trail is a 1.5-mile, stroller-friendly and wheelchair-accessible sidewalk looping hikers through a scenic area that's packed with a series of steep and narrow sandstone formations.

There are more than 20 miles of trails to explore inside Garden of the Gods; all are considered easy to moderate. For families, the short but steep Siamese Twins Trail is especially fun, passing two conjoined formations over a 0.5-mile course. Reach the trailhead via foot (take the Palmer Trail west from the Perkins Central Garden Trail) or car (continue on Juniper Way Loop, veering right onto Garden Drive until reaching P14). If you drive, pull off at P3 for an incredible place for a family photo.

RED ROCK CANYON HISTORY LOOP

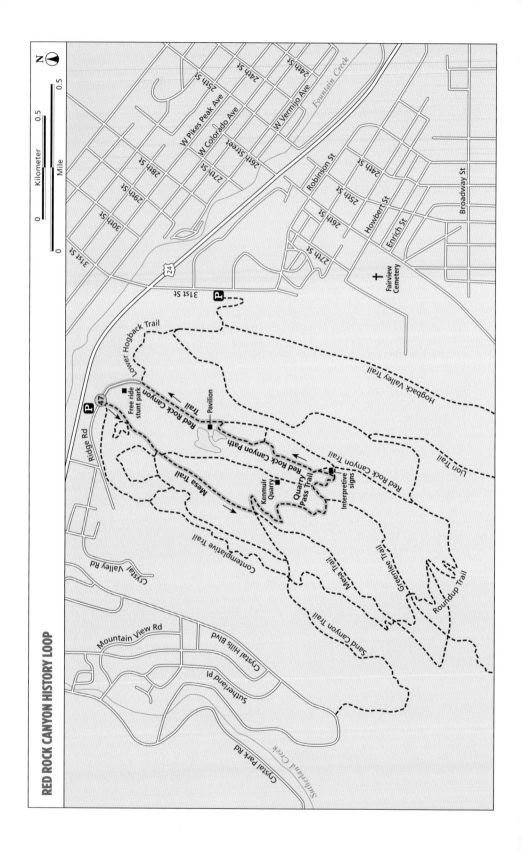

N

Kilometer
0   0.5

Mile
0   0.5

Fountain Creek

W Pikes Peak Ave
W Colorado Ave
W Vermijo Ave

24th St
25th St
26th Street
27th St
28th St
29th St
30th St
31st St

24

31st St

Robinson St
24th St
25th St
26th St
27th St
Howbert St
Enrich St
Broadway St

Fairview Cemetery

Lower Hogback Trail

P

Ridge Rd
47
P

Free ride stunt park

Red Rock Canyon Trail

Pavilion

Red Rock Canyon Path

Mesa Trail

Kenmuir Quarry

Quarry Pass Trail

Interpretive signs

Red Rock Canyon Trail

Crystal Valley Rd

Contemplative Trail

Hogback Valley Trail

Lion Trail

Greenlee Trail

Mesa Trail

Roundup Trail

Sand Canyon Trail

Mountain View Rd

Crystal Hills Blvd

Sutherland Pl

Crystal Park Rd

Sutherland Creek

Exit the quarry, and walk toward two interpretive signs in the clearing ahead. Continue downhill on the Red Rock Canyon Path. The hikers–only trail passes several rock climbing walls. Make sure children heed the "No Scrambling" signs. Rock climbers must have a valid permit to recreate at Red Rock Canyon.

The Red Rock Canyon Trail, which is open to bikers, also departs from the interpretive signs. The two pathways link back up near an open–air pavilion over-looking a pond—a great place to break for drinks or a snack while listening for geese.

Walk straight through the pavilion, and continue downhill on the Red Rock Canyon Trail. Pretty soon a parking lot comes into view. This is not where you started. It's the second, smaller lot at the very end of Ridge Road. As you follow the trail around the parking lot, you'll pass a free-ride stunt park. If your children have mountain bikes or striders, haul them along for a post-hike bike session.

MILES AND DIRECTIONS

0.0 Start from the Red Rock Canyon Trailhead, and make an immediate right at the trail map to begin hiking on the Mesa Trail. Elevation: 6,130 feet.

0.1 Pass the Lower Dog Loop off-leash area.

0.25 Keep straight at a trail junction.

0.45 Arrive at another trail junction. Continue straight; do not turn right onto the Meadowlark Trail.

0.55 Turn left onto the Quarry Pass Trail at the four-way trail intersection.

1.0 Come to a four-way trail intersection for the Quarry Pass and Greenlee Trails. Walk straight through this intersection, and follow the signs to stay on the Quarry Pass Trail.

1.06 Arrive at a ledge. Turn right, and follow the steps downhill. The trail picks back up soon.

1.15 Turn left and walk toward the interpretive signs in the clearing. Then turn left onto the Red Rock Canyon Path.

1.65 Arrive at an open-air pavilion overlooking a pond. Walk through the pavilion then merge onto the Red Rock Canyon Trail.

1.85 Come to a small parking lot. Bear left, and follow the trail past the lot.

1.98 Pass the free-ride stunt park.

2.0 Arrive back at the trailhead.

48 **ARMY TRAIL INTERPRETIVE SITE**

An animal sighting is pretty much guaranteed when you're hiking through Rocky Mountain Arsenal National Wildlife Refuge. The 15,000-acre site was established to protect roosting bald eagles, but birds of prey aren't the only ones flocking to it. Hundreds of thousands of visitors come annually to observe 330 species of wildlife safeguarded by the US Fish & Wildlife Service. Winter is an especially great time for animal lovers to explore the refuge's one-of-a-kind trails.

Start: Legacy Trailhead
Distance: 4.2 miles out and back
Hiking time: 1.5–4 hours
Difficulty: Easy
Elevation gain: 64 feet
Trail surface: Dirt and crushed gravel
Hours: Open daily, sunrise to sunset; closed Thanksgiving, Christmas, and New Year's Day
Best seasons: Year-round
Water: Drinking fountains inside the visitor center
Toilets: Flush toilets inside the visitor center
Nursing benches: Located at 0.7 mile and alongside Lake Mary
Stroller-friendly: Yes
Potential child hazards: Sunburn, rattlesnakes, two lakes
Other trail users: None
Dogs: Service dogs under leash control are welcome; all other pets are prohibited inside the refuge.

Land status: US Fish & Wildlife Service
Nearest town: Commerce City
Fees and permits: None
Maps: US Fish & Wildlife Service, Rocky Mountain Arsenal National Wildlife Refuge Wildlife Drive/Trail Map
Trail contact: US Fish & Wildlife Service, Rocky Mountain Arsenal National Wildlife Refuge, 6550 Gateway Rd., Commerce City 80022; (303) 289-0930; www.fws.gov/refuge/rocky_mountain_arsenal
Gear suggestions: Layers (if the temperature is below 45°F), insulated jackets, waterproof gloves, wool or fleece hats, micro-spikes, waterproof footwear, Smartwool socks, high-energy snacks that won't freeze, warm herbal tea, binoculars

FINDING THE TRAILHEAD

From I-70, take the Quebec Street exit and drive north. In approximately 2.8 miles turn right (east) onto Prairie Parkway at 64th Avenue. Travel 0.6 mile to Gateway Road, and go left (north). Keep driving along Gateway Road until you pass through the refuge's main entrance. After parking in the large lot at the end of Gateway Road, walk north toward the visitor center. Legacy Trailhead is on the east side of the visitor center.

THE HIKE

Most Denverites have no idea that the north Denver suburb of Commerce City claims one of the nation's largest urban wildlife refuges. From farmland to wartime manufacturing site to wildlife sanctuary, Rocky Mountain Arsenal's complex history springs to life during an easy day hike.

Two main ecosystems—prairie and wetland—attract migrating songbirds, wintering ducks, and raptors, and provide permanent habitat for bison, coyotes, deer, and other mammals. But this adventure begins a few hundred feet beyond the Legacy Trailhead, at a black-footed ferret exhibit. Black-footed ferrets roamed North America's plains for more than 10,000 years until they were almost completely wiped out by westward expansion.

In the 1980s, black-footed ferrets were declared extinct. Then, amazingly, in 1987 a small population was discovered in Wyoming. Through a captive breeding program, the US Fish & Wildlife Service reintroduced dozens of the long-necked mammals into the wild at the Rocky Mountain Arsenal, which provides a near-perfect habitat and prey base due to its large prairie dog population.

The refuge's small Ferret House exhibit features an indoor/outdoor habitat with more than 80 feet of tunnels simulating a prairie dog town. After visiting the house, cut back to the main trail to begin hiking through a grassland community. Look for blue grama, a unique plant with comb-shaped seed heads resembling eyelashes.

Winter is an excellent time to discover birds and mammals. When there's fresh snow on the ground, it's easy to spy predators like ferruginous hawks. When you reach the interpretive sign and overlook at 0.2 mile, look straight ahead to see bison roaming in their enclosure. Never approach the enclosure. If you want to see something really cute, come back in the spring, when calves frolic with their mothers.

After passing through two gates, the trail widens significantly. A bench appears at 0.7 mile, then the Legacy Trail curves sharply right. Do not let children explore beyond the barricade.

Cross Havana Street, and head toward Lake Mary, an idyllic pond bordered by towering cottonwoods. Lake Ladora looms large above Lake Mary. Both are open for

catch-and-release fishing the first Saturday in April through November 30. Minus a few exceptions, a Colorado fishing license is required.

After passing two fishing piers and a picnic shelter, turn left at the fork preceding a large trail map. Hike away from Lake Mary, toward a parking lot, then follow the paved road north for about 0.1 mile. When you reach a dirt trailhead, turn right onto the Locust Loop Trail and look for the abandoned farmhouse and windmill.

FUN FACTOR

STAY AND PLAY.

The visitor center at Rocky Mountain Arsenal is an incredible place for families. A large interactive exhibit hall features a series of displays on the site's uncommon history and abundant wildlife. Around the corner, younger children have access to a colorful Discovery Room filled with wildlife activities, seasonal crafts, and hands-on nature displays.

Every year, the US Fish & Wildlife Service puts on a comprehensive series of on-site programs. In addition to guided wildlife tours, there are family-friendly classes on waterfowl identification, antler anatomy, and the winter habits of raptors, to name just a few. Everything's free.

Learn more at the information desk on the far end of the visitor center, where friendly rangers are available to field questions, recommend additional hiking trails, and help families get oriented. Children can borrow free activity backpacks that come fully loaded with nature games and hiking tools such as binoculars, a bug carrying case, and magnifying glasses.

Pick up a scavenger hunt, and have your children complete it during the 11-mile Wildlife Drive, which follows a paved road through the refuge.

ARMY TRAIL INTERPRETIVE SITE

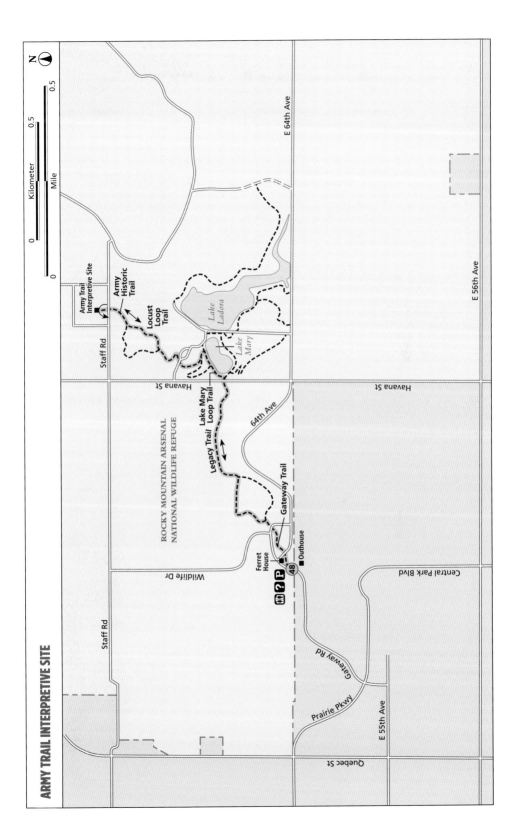

N

Kilometer
0   0.5   0.5

Mile
0   0.5

Staff Rd

Army Trail
Interpretive Site

Army
Historic
Trail

Locust
Loop
Trail

Lake
Ladora

Lake
Mary

Havana St

E 64th Ave

E 56th Ave

ROCKY MOUNTAIN ARSENAL
NATIONAL WILDLIFE REFUGE

Lake Mary
Loop Trail

Legacy Trail

64th Ave

Havana St

Gateway Trail

Wildlife Dr

Ferret
House

48

Outhouse

Central Park Blvd

Staff Rd

Gateway Rd

Prairie Pkwy

E 55th Ave

Quebec St

Don't be surprised if you see deer up close while passing through a short but dense forest. Past the trees, stay right at the fork. A few feet later, stop to read about the refuge's previous use as a chemical weapons manufacturing center during World War II. The US Army operated the facility until 1992, shortly after bald eagles were discovered on the premises. The discovery led Congress to designate the site as a national wildlife refuge in 1992, and a massive cleanup commenced.

For an additional dose of US history, merge onto the Army Historic Trail, cross Staff Road, and head to the flagpole, which is circled by an interesting series of interpretive signs. When you're ready, turn around and retrace your steps to the trailhead while enjoying stellar views of downtown Denver.

If you're hiking with a toddler, cut the mileage substantially by driving to the parking lot at Lake Mary and exploring the Lake Mary Loop Trail. With older hikers, parents can add 1.8 miles to the prescribed route by walking around Lake Ladora too.

MILES AND DIRECTIONS

0.0 Start at the Legacy Trailhead, on the east side of the visitor center. After passing a kiosk and trail map, follow the signs to the Ferret House. Elevation: 5,165 feet.

0.05 Visit the refuge's black-footed ferrets. Then continue hiking toward the massive bison enclosure.

0.2 Stop to read an interpretive sign and view the site's resident bison.

0.35 Reach a fork in the trail, and bear left onto the Legacy Trail.

0.5 Walk through the gates.

0.7 Pass a bench.

0.9 Look for a sharp bend in the trail. The trail tracks right here.

1.0 Carefully cross Havana Street. Walk straight toward the sign for the Lake Mary Loop Trail.

1.1 Turn left at the lake.

1.2 Pass two fishing piers and a shelter with picnic benches.

1.25 Bear left at the fork in the trail, and hike uphill toward a small parking lot.

1.3 To get to the Army Historic Trail, turn left onto the paved road. Follow it toward an old windmill and abandoned farmhouse.

1.4 Look for the Locust Loop Trail sign. Turn right onto the narrow dirt and gravel trail.

1.6 Bear right at a fork in the trail.

1.8 Keep right at the next fork in the trail too, and merge onto the Army Historic Trail.

2.0 Cross Staff Road, and walk toward the buildings ahead of you.

2.1 Arrive at a flagpole and several interpretive signs. Stop to read about the area's historical significance. Then turn around and retrace your steps to the lake.

2.9 Turn right at the trail marker to head back to the visitor center.

4.2 Arrive back at the trailhead.

49 MUD LAKE LOOPS

At Mud Lake Open Space, families discover a glistening lake and broad meadow surrounded by hilly slopes rolling through mixed conifer forests. During the late-summer growing season, the scenery really pops when colorful wildflowers spangle the meadow. Between the wide assortment of animals, scenic trails, and lakeside ecology, this 231-acre property provides a hands-on learning environment for naturalists of all ages.

Start: Mud Lake Trailhead
Distance: 2.2-mile double loop
Hiking time: 1.5–3 hours
Difficulty: Easy
Elevation gain: 200 feet
Trail surface: Dirt
Hours: Open daily, sunrise to sunset
Best seasons: Year-round; snowshoes or spikes required Oct through Apr
Water: None
Toilets: An outhouse in the parking lot (open seasonally)
Nursing benches: Several along the Kinnikinnick Loop and around Mud Lake
Stroller-friendly: No
Potential child hazards: Lake
Other trail users: Equestrians, mountain bikers

Dogs: Must be leashed
Land status: Boulder County Parks & Open Space
Nearest town: Nederland
Fees and permits: None
Maps: Boulder County Open Space Mud Lake Trail Map
Trail contact: Boulder County Parks & Open Space, 5201 St. Vrain Rd., Longmont 80503; (303) 678-6200; www.bouldercounty.org/open-space/parks-and-trails/mud-lake
Gear suggestions: A fleece or windbreaker, waterproof hiking sandals, sunscreen, sunglasses, binoculars, a magnifying glass, a notebook and pencils (to use at the lake)

FINDING THE TRAILHEAD

From downtown Nederland, head north on Bridge Street toward West 1st Street. At the roundabout, take the fourth exit onto West 2nd Street. West 2nd Street quickly becomes Caribou Street then Peak to Peak Highway (CO 72). In 1.7 miles, make a sharp left turn onto CR 126, a bumpy dirt road. After 0.3 mile you'll come to a big sign for Mud Lake Open Space and Caribou Ranch. Turn left onto the first road after the sign, and follow additional signs to the Mud Lake parking lot.

THE HIKE

The route described here begins on the Tungsten Loop, named for the twentieth century tungsten–mining boom that influenced the site's use and appearance. While Mud Lake Open Space includes a number of mines and shafts, such as the Crow No. 4 in the northwest corner, hikers are more likely to notice the site's impressive and diverse plant life.

Right away, the trail dips into a mixed conifer forest. Look for tall lodgepole pines as well as patches of aspen growing in waterlogged areas.

If you're traveling with a toddler, hike straight to Mud Lake by turning left at the intersection 500 feet past the trailhead. You'll see a large fifty-person group shelter in the distance, and then the water comes into view.

With older children, turn right at the trail intersection, and save Mud Lake for the end of your adventure. When you come to another fork at 0.28 mile, go straight through the junction to avoid merging onto Caribou Ranch Link, the 0.7-mile path connecting Mud Lake and Caribou Ranch Open Spaces.

At the next fork, there's an option to turn left to complete the Tungsten Loop. In the directions below, we'll tack on Kinnikinnick Loop by walking straight through the intersection and bearing left at the next fork a few feet later.

This next segment of the trail winds through a dense forest that eventually opens to a scenic meadow. Now's the time to pull out your binoculars and start looking for wildlife. The proximity of water and forest makes Mud Lake ideal for moose, but many species of mammals call the area home, including elk, bobcats, coyotes, snowshoe hares, chipmunks, pocket gophers, montane voles, and the long-tailed weasel.

A bench and overlook preceding the hairpin turn at 1.36 miles is a great place to admire the meadow. Because Mud Lake is located between 8,250 and 8,600 feet, summer wildflowers bloom later here than at lower elevations. By August, open fields should be filled with miner's candle, wild strawberry, mouse-ear chickweed, sunflowers, stonecrop, wild geranium, and scarlet paintbrush.

After an abrupt turn, the trail meanders downhill, back to the beginning of the Kinnikinnick Loop. This time, walk straight past the trail post and return to the Tungsten Loop. To finish hiking the loop where you left off, turn right at the fork. Essentially, you're making a figure eight around the Tungsten and Kinnikinnick Loops.

FUN FACTOR

VISIT MUD LAKE'S NEW NATURE CENTER.

Founded in 1995, the Wild Bear Center for Nature Discovery is Boulder County's only nonprofit nature center. After operating out of a storefront in downtown Nederland for more than a decade, Wild Bear relocated to its current off-the-grid building inside Mud Lake Open Space, where dedicated staff members deliver year-round educational programming.

In addition to hands-on workshops, the center houses an eco-gift shop and a series of interactive exhibits highlighting the local environment. Peruse skulls, pelts, and taxidermy, along with live animal displays and real scat. A modest maker space integrates art with the outdoors. Outside the center, children can explore Wild Bear's nature playscapes at their own pace.

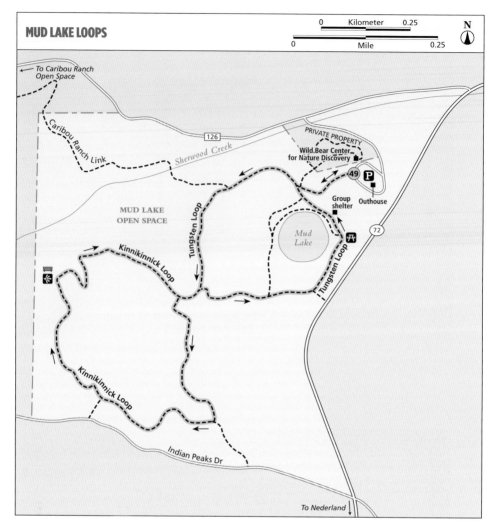

MUD LAKE LOOPS

0   Kilometer   0.25

0   Mile   0.25

N

To Caribou Ranch
Open Space

Caribou Ranch Link

126

Sherwood Creek

PRIVATE PROPERTY

Wild.Bear Center
for Nature Discovery

49   P

Group
shelter   Outhouse

MUD LAKE
OPEN SPACE

Tungsten Loop

Mud
Lake

72

Kinnikinnick Loop

Tungsten Loop

Kinnikinnick Loop

Indian Peaks Dr

To Nederland

Approaching Mud Lake, hikers stroll through a willow carr, or fen. Mud Lake supports
a wetland zone along its shore, which is really its most interesting feature. Diverse vegetation provides increased wildlife habitat, and the area has notable birding.

The lake itself is small, shallow, and muddy, hence the name. While fishing is permitted, the pond isn't stocked. Instead of fishing, look for crayfish, striped chorus frogs, and
tiger salamanders along the shoreline. In 1947 researchers found some tiger salamanders
at Mud Lake to be polydactyl, meaning they grew too many feet or toes during meta-
morphosis. This is considered the first record of mass polydactylism among amphibians.

If that doesn't interest your kids, here's another tidbit: Mud Lake was once called
Muskee Lake, and some scientists believed it was a crater formed by a meteorite. A 2001
study funded by the Colorado Geological Survey concluded that the lake is most likely
of human origin.

MILES AND DIRECTIONS

0.0 Start at the Mud Lake welcome sign and trail map, and begin hiking west toward a trail marker. Follow the arrow toward the Tungsten Loop. Elevation: 8,360 feet.

0.1 Arrive at a fork. Bear right to begin hiking on the Tungsten Loop. You should be moving away from the fifty-person group shelter overlooking Mud Lake.

0.28 Reach another fork. Keep straight to stay on the Tungsten Loop. Do not turn right onto the Caribou Ranch Link.

0.45 Bear slightly right at the next fork in the trail to connect to the Kinnikinnick Loop.

0.5 The Kinnikinnick Loop officially begins. Bear left at the fork to complete the loop clockwise.

0.78 Turn right at the three-way trail intersection.

0.85 Pass a bench and scenic vista.

1.28 Arrive at another bench and overlook.

1.36 Watch for a hairpin turn in the trail.

1.61 Reach a fork in the trail. You've completed the Kinnikinnick Loop. Walk past the trail marker, and return to the Tungsten Loop.

1.67 Back at the Tungsten Loop, turn right at the fork to visit Mud Lake.

1.82 Come to a trail intersection. A left turn takes you to Mud Lake's west shore. We'll go straight, ending on the other side of the lake.

2.0 Arrive at Mud Lake. When you're ready to call it a day, hike past the large group shelter.

2.1 Go right at the trail marker, and follow the arrow toward the parking lot.

2.2 Arrive back at the trailhead.

50 **WILCOX TRAIL**

Northern Colorado is a four-seasons hiking destination. From Loveland to Fort Collins, hikers of all ages enjoy easy access to dozens of trails backing to the Arapaho and Roosevelt National Forests. For an introductory experience, visit Colorado State University's Environmental Learning Center. With two flat trails crossing four distinct ecosystems, the ELC is a marvelous place for young hikers to connect with the natural world—especially in winter, when fresh snowfall makes the 212-acre preserve extra magical.

Start: ELC Trailhead
Distance: 1.2-mile lollipop
Hiking time: 1–2 hours
Difficulty: Easy
Elevation gain: Negligible
Trail surface: Dirt
Hours: Open daily, sunrise to sunset
Best seasons: Year-round; mosquitoes swarm the river in summer.
Water: None
Toilets: Drop toilets near the trailhead
Nursing benches: 2 along the Wilcox Trail
Stroller-friendly: Yes
Potential child hazards: Frozen water, poison ivy, mosquitoes (in summer)
Other trail users: None

Dogs: Not permitted on ELC trails
Land status: Colorado State University
Nearest towns: Fort Collins and Loveland
Fees and permits: None
Maps: City of Fort Collins Recreational Trails System Map
Trail contact: Colorado State University Environmental Learning Center, 2400 South CO Rd. 9, Fort Collins 80503; (970) 491-1661; warnercnr.colostate.edu/elc
Gear suggestions: Layers when the temperature is below 45°F, insulated jackets, gloves, wool or fleece hats, micro-spikes, waterproof footwear, Smartwool socks, high-energy snacks that won't freeze, warm herbal tea, Nuun tablets, binoculars

FINDING THE TRAILHEAD

From I-25, take the Harmony Road exit. Drive west on Harmony Road for 1.5 miles and turn right (north) onto Ziegler Road. Continue driving north through a stoplight and a roundabout. In another 2 miles, turn right onto Environmental Drive. Cross a one-lane bridge. Then make a sharp left turn onto the gravel road. A large ELC sign will come into view. Cross the railroad tracks. The ELC parking lot is at the end of the gravel road; the site's sole trailhead is adjacent to the outhouse.

THE HIKE

Built around a section of Colorado's 126-mile-long Cache la Poudre River, the nature trails at Colorado State University's innovative ELC were developed by students and staff at the Warner College of Natural Resources.

As part of their service-learning curriculum, college students generate environmental programming for kids. Offerings include K–12 after-school programs, eco-courses for tweens and teens, and summer day camps connecting youth ages 7 to 12 to the natural world through learner-led inquiry. All classes and camps are designed to promote stewardship by facilitating high-quality outdoors experiences. The whole idea is to connect

KATY SCHNEIDER

kids with nature in the hope that positive interactions will instill a lifelong desire to protect our planet.

But families don't have to register for programs to enjoy this unique site. The ELC is open year-round, and its flat, riverside trails are easy to reach from I-25. Summer is a busy time, as CSU students run the bulk of their programs between June and August. For a quieter experience, explore the Wilcox Trail in winter, when mosquitoes won't be a problem.

The hike takes off from a really neat bridge just past a bank of pit toilets on the far end of the ELC parking lot. Young children are going to want to race back and forth across the bridge . . . many times. Let them run free. When they're ready, continue on toward a large welcome sign and colorful map wedged between the fork in the trail.

FUN FACTOR

FALL IN LOVE WITH THE SWEETHEART CITY.

The Environmental Learning Center is 14 miles north of Loveland, a community with so much love in its name that it is often referred to as the Sweetheart City.

Both tourists and locals enjoy Loveland's small-town vibe, along with a series of free and low-cost activities for families, including hiking at the Marianna Butte Natural Area, agritourism at Osborn Farm, and tours of the Loveland Museum and Benson Sculpture Garden, a park displaying 154 sculptures across 10 acres.

The town really shines in February. Loveland is famous for its valentine re-mailing program. Since the 1940s, the city and its volunteers have hand-stamped and re-mailed millions of valentine cards from all fifty states and more than 110 countries—all so the cards can be canceled in Loveland.

If you're visiting in February, bring along seasonal letters, or purchase a special Loveland valentine card at the Loveland Visitor Center. Drop items at the Loveland Post Office by February 10 (the deadline for parcels staying within the Colorado-Wyoming region), or place sealed/stamped/addressed cards inside a package, and mail your items to the post office.

The merriment continues at Loveland's free Sweetheart Festival, an annual event held on February 14 and 15 at Foundry Plaza in downtown Loveland, featuring live entertainment, food vendors, local art displays, seasonal craft beer, and a series of street rides and activities for kids.

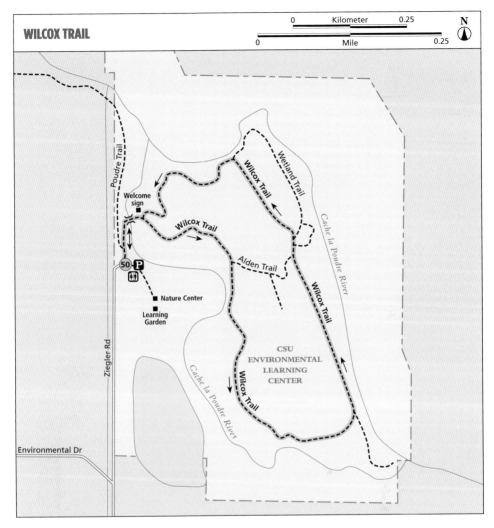

0   Kilometer   0.25

0   Mile   0.25

N

The Wilcox Trail makes a big loop around the ELC. In a short distance, families have a chance to explore four distinct ecosystems, starting with a pleasant stroll through a cottonwood forest. Look for blue spruce, Gambel oak, and box elder as you follow the Wilcox Trail toward the river.

After a bend, the narrow dirt path passes through riparian and wetland ecosystems. Mink, beavers, muskrats, and skunks inhabit the area, but since these creatures are nocturnal, you'll be hard-pressed to spot them during your hike. If there's snow on the ground, try looking for their tracks instead.

When you reach a trail sign at 0.62 mile, bear left to continue on the Wilcox Trail. A right turn puts hikers on a short spur (an option for families looking to up their mileage).

As you continue along the trail, ask children to look left to observe a grassland environment with a variety of plants, including arctic rush, rabbitbrush, and soapweed yucca. Don't cross the wood and metal bridge that appears to the right at 0.86 mile. Instead, follow the main trail as it curves around a bend. A few feet later you'll come to a bench

KATY SCHNEIDER

and trail intersection. If you're following the directions below, continue hiking straight through the junction. Families interested in poking around the area a little more can turn onto the Alden Trail before returning to the bridge and trailhead.

The hike is complete, but there's more to explore. Check out the ELC website (visit the Warner College of Natural Resources homepage), where students publish fantastic earth and life sciences activities for children to complete back home. All activities are sorted by age and have been evaluated by CSU's environmental education staff. To get started, click on "Fun Activities to do at Home."

MILES AND DIRECTIONS

0.0 Start on the dirt trail next to the outhouse, and cross the long bridge to reach a welcome sign and trail map. Elevation: 5,003 feet.

0.22 Steer right at the Wilcox-Alden trail sign to begin on the Wilcox Trail.

0.42 Pass a bench overlooking the Cache la Poudre River.

0.5 Follow the trail as it curves and crosses a small wooden bridge.

0.62 Arrive at another trail sign. Turn left to stay on the main trail.

0.85 Pass a wood and metal bridge.

0.92 Come to a bench. Turn right to stay on the Wilcox Trail. Do not merge onto the Alden Trail unless you'd like to continue exploring the area.

0.98 You're back at the Wilcox-Alden trail sign where the loop began. Turn right to hike back toward the long bridge.

1.2 Arrive back at the trailhead.

51 MEADOW VIEW LOOP

As the name suggests, Elk Meadow Park is one of the most likely places to see herds of elk in the foothills of Jefferson County. From the Lewis Ridge Trailhead, hikers gain access to 14.7 miles of hiking trails weaving through dense forests. The climb to the park's picturesque high point, Bergen Peak (9,701'), is a rigorous one. For families, the Meadow View Trail Loop offers a laid-back option, with interconnected trails circumnavigating a beautiful meadow where elk often graze.

Start: Lewis Ridge Trailhead
Distance: 3.6-mile lollipop
Hiking time: 2–4 hours
Difficulty: Moderate
Elevation gain: 446 feet
Trail surface: Dirt, natural surface, and rock
Hours: Open daily, 1 hour before sunrise to 1 hour after sunset
Best seasons: Year-round
Water: None
Toilets: An outhouse near the Lewis Ridge Trailhead
Nursing benches: At the trailhead and at 0.15 mile, 1.6 miles, and 2.95 miles
Stroller-friendly: No
Potential child hazards: Elk, mountain lions
Other trail users: Equestrians, mountain bikers

Dogs: Must be leashed
Land status: Jefferson County Open Space
Nearest town: Evergreen
Fees and permits: None
Maps: Jefferson County Open Space Elk Meadow Park Map
Trail contact: Jefferson County Open Space, 700 Jefferson County Pkwy., Ste. 100, Golden 80401; (303) 271-5925; www.jeffco.us/1218/Elk-Meadow-Park
Gear suggestions: Layers when the temperature is below 45°F, insulated jackets, gloves, wool or fleece hats, micro-spikes, waterproof footwear, Smartwool socks, high-energy snacks that won't freeze, warm herbal tea, Nuun tablets, binoculars

FINDING THE TRAILHEAD

There are two main trailheads at Elk Meadow Park. To reach the Lewis Ridge Trailhead, where this hike departs, head southwest on I-70. Use the right two lanes to take exit 252 for CO 74 toward Evergreen Parkway. Then use the middle two lanes to turn slightly right onto Evergreen Parkway. Follow the road for about 4.5 miles as it winds through the Bergen Park and Hiwan neighborhoods. At the intersection with Lewis Ridge Road, turn right (west) into the park entrance and follow Bergen Peak Drive to a large parking lot. The Lewis Ridge Trailhead is on the north edge of the lot.

THE HIKE

Getting around the park's namesake meadow isn't particularly complicated, but it does require hikers to hop on several different trails. Don't worry: All the trail intersections are extremely well marked, and the directions below will be easy to follow.

To make a clockwise loop around the meadow, start on the Sleepy S Trail. In less than 200 feet, the first of many forks appears. Walk straight through the intersection. You'll know you're on course when you pass the stone benches a few feet down the natural surface trail.

The first section of the route is fully exposed. After making a broad U-turn, the trail dips into a wooded area before ascending, very gradually, toward Elk Ridge Trail. When you reach the next fork, bear right onto the Elk Ridge Trail to climb straight into a ponderosa pine forest. The terrain becomes increasingly rocky, so keep an eye out for roots and ruts as you go.

In the winter months, when there isn't packed snow, this is where families are most likely to encounter ice. If the trail is slick, use good judgment—and put on traction devices, if available. Always be ready to turn around if conditions are too treacherous.

The Elk Ridge Trail zigzags for another 0.5 mile before flattening out and eventually ending at the Meadow View Trail. A left at the intersection takes hikers south toward the Stagecoach Trailhead, providing access to the Bergen Peak Trail, a tough 3.7-mile (one way) summit hike to the top of the park's 9,701-foot peak. We're turning right onto the Meadow View Trail to begin a scenic stroll through the woods. In 0.3 mile you'll be back in the sun again.

When you reach a bench at 1.6 miles, break for snacks before wrapping around the north rim of the meadow on an elevated ridge. Now's the time to pull out those binoculars and look for elk grazing on the outskirts of the meadow.

Two miles into the journey, the Too Long Trail juts out from the Meadow View Trail. If you'd like to extend the hike, turn left onto the Too Long Trail, and hike 0.7 mile (one way) uphill to a scenic overlook. Additional mileage to the overlook is not included in the detailed directions below.

Back on the Meadow View Trail, the narrow track descends, passing a stone shelter to the left, a great place to unwrap sandwiches. Continue searching for elk, or the rare Abert's squirrel, whose favorite food is ponderosa pinecones. Encourage children to be quiet while viewing nature. Even if you don't see any wildlife, won't it be nice to catch a few quiet moments while listening to the sound of prairie grass rustling in the breeze?

The Meadow View Trail passes the Founders Trail. The shortest way back to the trailhead involves making a right onto the Founders Trail and then another right onto the Painter's Pause Trail. Before reaching the Painter's Pause Trail, stop at the Carol Karlin Overlook. This sunny lookout is the last great place to spot elk.

MILES AND DIRECTIONS

0.0 Start from the kiosk at the Lewis Ridge Trailhead, and begin hiking north on the Sleepy S Trail. In 180 feet, bear left at the three-way intersection to avoid merging onto the Painter's Pause Trail. Elevation: 7,597 feet.

0.52 Come to a fork in the trail. Turn right onto the Elk Ridge Trail.

1.07 At the next fork, turn right onto the Meadow View Trail.

1.6 Pass a bench.

2.1 The Too Long Trail runs into the Meadow View Trail. Bear right at the fork to stay on the Meadow View Trail.

2.55 Arrive at a trail marker and three-way trail intersection. Turn right onto the Founders Trail, a shortcut to the Carol Karlin Overlook.

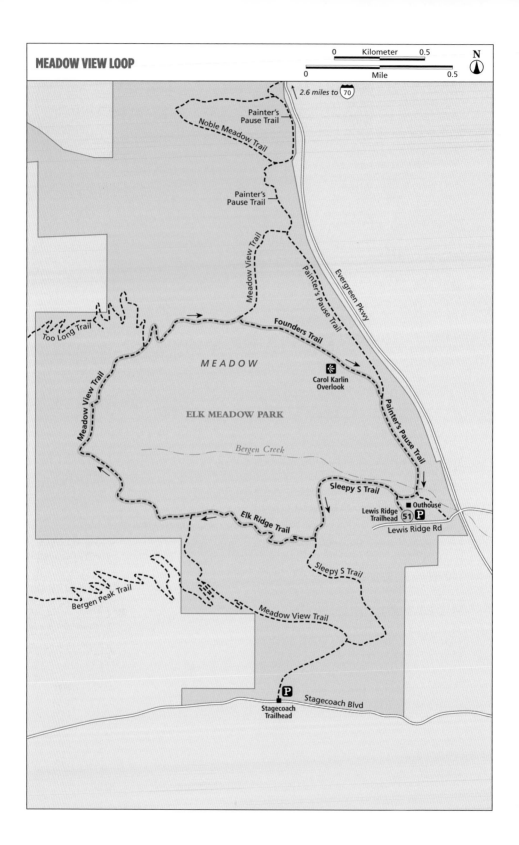

Kilometer 0 0.5

Mile 0 0.5

N

2.6 miles to 70

Painter's Pause Trail

Noble Meadow Trail

Painter's Pause Trail

Meadow View Trail

Evergreen Pkwy

Painter's Pause Trail

Too Long Trail

Founders Trail

MEADOW

Carol Karlin Overlook

Meadow View Trail

ELK MEADOW PARK

Bergen Creek

Painter's Pause Trail

Sleepy S Trail

Outhouse

Lewis Ridge Trailhead 51 P

Lewis Ridge Rd

Elk Ridge Trail

Sleepy S Trail

Bergen Peak Trail

Meadow View Trail

P

Stagecoach Blvd

Stagecoach Trailhead

2.95 Reach the Carol Karlin Overlook.

3.15 The Founders Trail ends at the Painter's Pause Trail. Turn right onto Painter's Pause, and hike back to the Lewis Ridge Trailhead.

3.48 After crossing a raised walkway, take the Sleepy S Trail back to the trailhead.

3.6 Arrive back at the trailhead.

FUN FACTOR

UP YOUR ODDS OF SPOTTING AN ELK.

By some estimates, Colorado is home to 280,000 elk, making the Centennial State the elk capital of North America. There's really nothing like seeing a herd of elk in their natural habitat.

September and October are the best months to view elk. During this short mating season, bull elk can be seen at the forest edge, preparing to battle other males. If you're lucky, you might even hear large bulls bugling. Bugles typically begin with a deep call that becomes a high-pitched squeal before ending in a series of grunts.

Seeing elk in Colorado is a year-round affair. Elk are grazers and browsers, and they eat grass, shrubs, fruits, and trees. A fresh dusting of snow can make it incredibly easy to spot elk on the outskirts of the meadow at Elk Meadow Park, where evergreen forests and deciduous trees provide both shelter and nourishment.

Dawn and dusk are the best times of day to observe the animals. If you head out in the late afternoon, just make sure you don't get caught on the trails after dark. Pack binoculars, snacks, drawing materials, and card games such as Spot It! Jr. Similar to fishing, wildlife viewing takes patience.

Always view elk from a safe distance, using the overlooks along the Meadow View Loop. Never approach an elk. These massive creatures can weight up to 900 pounds, and they're unpredictable.

52 DAVIS PONDS LOOP

Staunton, Colorado's newest state park, opened to the public in 2013 with nearly 30 miles of trails crossing grassy meadows and forested hillsides framed by granite cliffs. One of the park's most popular hikes is the 12-mile round-trip trek to Elk Falls. But families don't have to commit to a massive adventure to enjoy on-site water features. A shorter looped route passes two idyllic fishing ponds with man-made dams.

Start: Davis Ponds Loop Trailhead, near the Ranch Hand Group Picnic Area pavilion
Distance: 2.2-mile loop
Hiking time: 1.5–3 hours
Difficulty: Easy
Elevation gain: 143 feet
Trail surface: Dirt and gravel
Hours: Day use hours, 6 a.m. to 10 p.m.
Best seasons: Year-round
Water: Inside the visitor center
Toilets: Flush toilets inside the visitor center; pit toilets at the trailhead and near the ponds
Nursing benches: At the group picnic shelter and the ponds
Stroller-friendly: Yes, with a good jogging stroller. Thanks to Staunton's Action Trackchair program, visitors with mobility difficulties can explore designated trails on select days.
Potential child hazards: Two large ponds
Other trail users: None on Davis Ponds Loop; equestrians and mountain bikers permitted on other multiuse trails inside the park
Dogs: Must be under owner's physical control and on a 6-foot leash
Land status: Colorado Parks & Wildlife
Nearest towns: Conifer and Pine
Fees and permits: Per vehicle day-use fee or Colorado Parks & Wildlife Pass
Maps: Colorado Parks & Wildlife Staunton State Park Trails Ma
Trail contact: Colorado Parks & Wildlife, Staunton, 12102 South Elk Creek Rd., Pine 80470; (303) 816-0912; cpw.state.co.us/placestogo/parks/Staunton
Gear suggestions: Layers when the temperature is below 45°F, insulated jackets, gloves, wool or fleece hats, micro-spikes, waterproof footwear, Smartwool socks, high-energy snacks that won't freeze, warm herbal tea, a picnic, journaling/coloring materials

FINDING THE TRAILHEAD

From Denver, take US 285 south toward the unincorporated community of Shaffers Crossing, about 6 miles west of Conifer. Turn right (north) onto South Elk Creek Road, and follow the signs for 1.5 miles. Turn right at the large stone sign. Follow the road to the park's entrance station. Drive past the first parking lot. In 0.2 mile, turn left into the Ranch Hand Group Picnic Area parking lot. If it's full, you can park in the upper parking lot, across the street. Two trailheads provide access to the Davis Ponds Loop Trail. We will use the trailhead near the Ranch Hand Group Picnic Area pavilion.

THE HIKE

Staunton is a memorable place chock-full of natural beauty and pioneer history. Several nineteenth-century farms and ranches were combined to form the park, named for its largest parcel, Staunton Ranch, homesteaded by two East Coast doctors who were

FUN FACTOR

TAKE KIDS ON A TREASURE HUNT.

Geocaching (JEE-oh-cash-ing) can turn an otherwise mundane hike into a bona fide adventure.

The term is a mash-up of two words: "geography" and "cache." Instead of searching for treasure with a paper map, geocachers use a mobile device and observational skills to find trinkets hidden above-ground at sites marked by GPS coordinates.

There are millions of caches stashed all over the globe. Staunton State Park's collection is especially great for first-time hunters, since a park manager over-sees the addition of new caches. To play, you'll need a smartphone and an app such as Geocaching or Cachly. Every cache has its own "page," where participants will find useful tips and hints.

When you get to the Davis Ponds Loop, try using the app's map view function to navigate. You'll be able to see how close you are to any given cache, but the map won't tell you the best way to get to your cache. It's your job to figure that out! Tell kids to look for things that seem slightly out of place. Similar to wildlife view-ing, geocaching takes patience and persistence.

When you're getting close to a cache, switch to the app's compass view feature. Sign the logbook when you find the booty. And if you take an item out of the cache's container, be sure to replace it with something of equal or greater value. Always follow the geocach-ing golden rule: Leave no trace during your hunt.

initially headed to California. The Stauntons stopped to rest in Denver—and fell in love with Colorado.

We'll roam around the 1,000-acre Davis Ranch, situated in the park's southeast corner. The Davis Ponds Loop is an interpretive trail. Swing by the visitor center to grab a brochure filled with fun facts to read during your hike.

Once you've made it to the Ranch Hand Group Picnic Area, look for a Davis Ponds Loop welcome sign between the picnic pavilion and outhouse. Begin walking downhill on the dirt and gravel trail. As winter snowpack melts, you might encounter mud. Teach your kids to walk through mud, not around it. This simple tactic prevents trail erosion, and most kids will love having an excuse to get dirty.

A muddy trail is a great place to find animal tracks. Staunton's varied terrain and vegetation create a habitat for many mammals: red fox, coyote, deer, and the rare Abert's squirrel, distinguished by its dark gray back, white belly, and tufted ears. A herd of elk lives in the park, coexisting with predators such as bobcats and black bears.

Ask children to keep an eye on the trail as they hike. Are there any unexpected tracks? At Staunton, an innovative "track chairs" program allows visitors of varying mobility levels to explore three trails with all-terrain wheelchairs known as Action Trackchairs. This explains the vehicle marks on the Davis Ponds Loop.

After bearing right at the first fork, enjoy breathtaking views as the flat trail winds through a grassy meadow overlooking granite cliffs and craggy foothills. For young hikers, Staunton's geological features are thrilling. Most of the park lies on a large granite formation called the Pikes Peak Batholith. Different rates of erosion have created

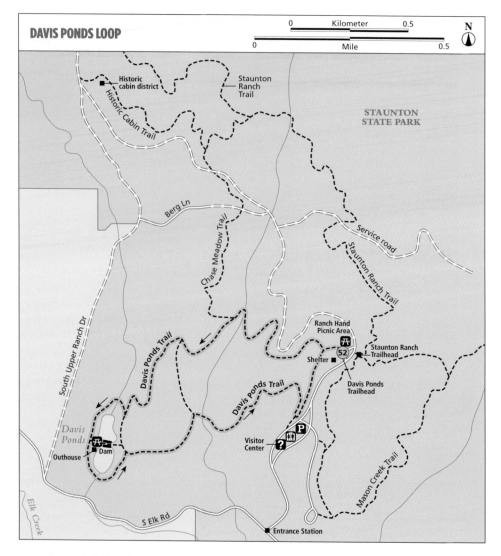

groupings of cliffs and outcrops such as Chimney Rock, Elk Creek Spires, and Lions Head, the latter of which is visible from the Davis Ponds Loop.

When the trail splits at 0.45 mile, keep straight. (**Option:** Families with older kids can turn right onto the Chase Meadows Trail, a 0.7-mile out-and-back path connecting to the Historic Cabin Trail, which ends at Staunton's "Cabin District." This detour adds 2.8 miles round-trip and is not included in the directions below.)

The trail forks two more times before reaching two ponds shaded by ponderosa pines. Turn right to complete a loop around the ponds, which are stocked monthly in summer. If you're planning to fish, a Colorado fishing license is required. Swimming is prohibited, and if you're hiking in winter, always keep an eye on children near frozen or partially frozen water.

Davis Pond is the lower pond. On your way to Davis Pond, you'll pass a man-made dam, picnic pavilion, and outhouse. If the weather's nice, stop for a picnic, and encourage

kids to journal or color in nature. Then return to the trailhead on the southern section of the Davis Ponds Loop.

The trail runs into itself at 1.6 miles. Go right to finish the loop. After crossing a small bridge, the trail splits. To the right is the visitor center parking lot you passed on the drive to the trailhead. Make a sharp left at the fork and hike uphill, away from the visitor center. In another 0.3 mile, bear right at the fork and you're back where you started.

MILES AND DIRECTIONS

0.0   Start from the Davis Ponds Loop welcome sign, and begin walking downhill. In less than 250 feet, turn right at the fork. Elevation: 8,335 feet.

0.45 Keep straight at the next fork to stay on the Davis Ponds Trail.

0.65 Come to a fork. Bear right to take the high road directly to the ponds.

0.95 Arrive at the ponds. Go right to begin a counterclockwise loop around them.

1.15 Continue straight past the dam to walk around Davis Pond.

1.25 Walk over lower dam.

1.37 Reach a four-way trail intersection. Turn right, and begin walking away from the ponds.

1.6   The Davis Ponds Trail runs into itself. Go right at the fork.

1.9   Cross a small bridge.

2.0   Make a sharp left turn at the fork. Hike away from the visitor center parking lot.

2.17 Turn right at the fork to hike uphill toward the Ranch Hand Group Picnic Area.

2.2   Arrive back at the welcome sign.

HIKE INDEX

THE TEN ESSENTIALS OF HIKING

American
Hiking
Society

American Hiking Society recommends you pack the "Ten Essentials" every time you head out for a hike. Whether you plan to be gone for a couple of hours or several months, make sure to pack these items. Become familiar with these items and know how to use them.

1. Appropriate Footwear
Happy feet make for pleasant hiking. Think about traction, support, and protection when selecting well-fitting shoes or boots.

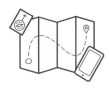

2. Navigation
While phones and GPS units are handy, they aren't always reliable in the backcountry; consider carrying a paper map and compass as a backup and know how to use them.

3. Water (and a way to purify it)
As a guideline, plan for half a liter of water per hour in moderate temperatures/terrain. Carry enough water for your trip and know where and how to treat water while you're out on the trail.

4. Food
Pack calorie-dense foods to help fuel your hike, and carry an extra portion in case you are out longer than expected.

5. Rain Gear & Dry-Fast Layers
The weatherman is not always right. Dress in layers to adjust to changing weather and activity levels. Wear moisture-wicking cloths and carry a warm hat.

6. Safety Items (light, fire, and a whistle)
Have means to start an emergency fire, signal for help, and see the trail and your map in the dark.

7. First Aid Kit
Supplies to treat illness or injury are only as helpful as your knowledge of how to use them. Take a class to gain the skills needed to administer first aid and CPR.

8. Knife or Multi-Tool
With countless uses, a multi-tool can help with gear repair and first aid.

9. Sun Protection
Sunscreen, sunglasses, and sun-protective clothing should be used in every season regardless of temperature or cloud cover.

10. Shelter
Protection from the elements in the event you are injured or stranded is necessary. A lightweight, inexpensive space blanket is a great option.

Find other helpful resources at AmericanHiking.org/hiking-resources

PROTECT THE PLACES YOU LOVE TO HIKE.
Become a member today and take $5 off an annual membership using the code **Falcon5**.

AmericanHiking.org/join

American Hiking Society is the only national nonprofit organization dedicated to empowering all to enjoy, share, and preserve the hiking experience.

American Hiking Society